T0125930

OF SILENCE AND SONG

DAN BEACHY-QUICK

MILKWEED EDITIONS

© 2017, Text by Dan Beachy-Quick
All rights reserved. Except for brief quotations in critical articles or reviews, no part of this book may be reproduced in any manner without prior written permission from the publisher: Milkweed Editions, 1011 Washington Avenue South, Suite 300, Minneapolis, Minnesota 55415. (800) 520-6455
milkweed.org

Published 2017 by Milkweed Editions
Printed in Canada
Cover design by Mary Austin Speaker
Cover artwork by Megan Canning, *All my body calls*, 2008, Hand embroidery on linen with cotton, 16" x 12" x 3"
17 18 19 20 21 5 4 3 2 1
First Edition

Milkweed Editions, an independent nonprofit publisher, gratefully acknowledges sustaining support from the Jerome Foundation; the Lindquist & Vennum Foundation; the McKnight Foundation; the National Endowment for the Arts; the Target Foundation; and other generous contributions from foundations, corporations, and individuals. Also, this activity is made possible by the voters of Minnesota through a Minnesota State Arts Board Operating Support grant, thanks to a legislative appropriation from the arts and cultural heritage fund, and a grant from Wells Fargo. For a full listing of Milkweed Editions supporters, please visit milkweed.org.

Library of Congress Cataloging-in-Publication Data

Names: Beachy-Quick, Dan, 1973- author.
Title: Of silence and song / Dan Beachy-Quick.
Description: Minneapolis : Milkweed Editions, 2017.
Identifiers: LCCN 2017036026 (print) | LCCN 2017036678 (ebook) | ISBN 9781571319432 (ebook) | ISBN 9781571313621 (pbk. : alk. paper)
Classification: LCC PS3602.E24 (ebook) | LCC PS3602.E24 A6 2017 (print) | DDC 811/.6--dc23
LC record available at https://lccn.loc.gov/2017036026

Milkweed Editions is committed to ecological stewardship. We strive to align our book production practices with this principle, and to reduce the impact of our operations in the environment. We are a member of the Green Press Initiative, a nonprofit coalition of publishers, manufacturers, and authors working to protect the world's endangered forests and conserve natural resources. *Of Silence and Song* was printed on acid-free 100% postconsumer-waste paper by Friesens Corporation.

OF SILENCE AND SONG
DAN BEACHY-QUICK

Also by Dan Beachy-Quick

Nonfiction
Wonderful Investigations
A Whaler's Dictionary
A Brighter Word Than Bright: Keats at Work

Fiction
An Impenetrable Screen of Purest Sky

Poetry
North True South Bright
Spell
Mulberry
This Nest, Swift Passerine
Circle's Apprentice
Gentlessness

for Kristy, Hana, Iris, & my mother

—prism, light—

Every spirit makes its house; but afterwards the house confines the spirit.
— RALPH WALDO EMERSON, "FATE"

✦

There is indeed the inexpressible. This shows *itself; it is the mystical.*
— LUDWIG WITTGENSTEIN, *TRACTATUS LOGICO-PHILOSOPHICUS*

✦

Light that makes some things seen, makes some things invisible.
— SIR THOMAS BROWNE, *THE GARDEN OF CYRUS*; OR, *THE QUINCUNX*

✦

What is worse, knowledge is made by oblivion.
— SIR THOMAS BROWNE, *PSEUDODOXIA EPIDEMICA*

✦

Thought kills me that I am not thought.
— WILLIAM SHAKESPEARE, *SONNET 44*

✦

Methinks my own soul must be a bright invisible green.
— HENRY DAVID THOREAU, *A WEEK ON THE CONCORD AND MERRIMACK RIVERS*

OF SILENCE AND SONG
DAN BEACHY-QUICK

1.

On our walk my youngest daughter asked me, "What are the songs you don't know."

"That's a hard question," I said.

"Tell me the songs you don't know."

✦

Silence was the best description.

✦

On the same walk we found a bird lying dead on the ground. It had a long, dark, slightly curved beak. Streaks of white not quite white on the head, a color I might call *dry wheat*. "Not a woodpecker," I said. Iris said, "Nope, not a woodpecker." Not the right markings. The shafts of the feathers had no bright colors. I couldn't identify the bird. A plover? A snipe?

Later I asked Iris if the dead bird scared her.

"No," she said. "It gave me an idea."

2.

I had thought for years how best to begin.

✦

Maybe just a blank page.

✦

Some way of showing the precedent silence. But then I doubted so simple a gesture could make it felt: that silence. I worried the gesture would seem *obvious*. But then I remembered what's most obvious is what I'm most interested in.

What the obvious hides in itself. Not as a secret. Like a breath being held.

Like a child believes in the dark and so doubts God, but every morning reverses the conclusions. Like doubt or faith when they begin in us by acting like one another. Only later do they act opposed.

The trouble is not that what is pure is complicated past our understanding. What's quiet is just too simple to be understood. One method might be to liken that silence to the inner life once you learn to accept that the "inner life" is just another myth.

Socrates asks: *Can a man know and also not know what he knows.*

Know thyself. The imperative acts so simple, but then you try to follow the command for your whole life, as one might follow an echo back to a source, but the source is just a cave, and the shadows living there are quiet. And all along you thought you'd find yourself there. That you lived there. That you'd come home, source somehow of yourself. But it isn't true.

In Greek, ἀλήθεια, the word for truth, might best be translated: "that which makes itself obvious." There are other best ways to define it.

"The stone the builders cast out has become the cornerstone." In Psalm 118:22 I found a comfort and a clue. I'd like to say that I repeated this verse to myself ceaselessly, but that would be a lie. I didn't even know it mattered to me until I happened upon the words as a child happens upon a forgotten toy and remembers suddenly the life that had been in it. Mostly this experience happens to children when they become adults. I just found the words in the box. But the box was my head.

I needed to find the cast-out stone. That's how to begin. I thought of the names of my daughters: Iris. Hana. Before they were born, before I had any inkling of their existence, they each were such a stone. But not now. Too many years have passed. My love for them isn't silent. They do not fill me with silence. And what is silent in them is theirs alone. A rock cast away from me. Something I can't pick up.

I thought of my wife, Kristy. But her silence is the prism that breaks white light into the rainbow.

I thought of a dream I had after I fell in love with Kristy and decided I must become a poet. In the dream I wandered down a dark road through a kept field. The grass all mown. I thought it was a cemetery but there weren't any stones. A tree by a bend in the pitch-black asphalt, so black I knew it had been raining. That's when I saw the rainbow. It kept still in the sky as I neared it. The closer I got the more intensely I could see the colors, and in the spectrum I saw lightning flashing like a sensation between synapses. So I imagined it. Going closer I could see the rainbow had no breadth, no depth; it was thinner than a razor. That's when I saw the letter floating in the colors. Just one letter. It flashed, made of electricity. "It is the letter aleph," I thought to myself. Then the lightning in the letter struck my hand and the pain woke me up. It wasn't until years later, when I finally began to study Hebrew, that I realized I'd recognized the letter before I could have known it.

I gave Hebrew up. It took too much time away from writing poetry.

Fifteen years passed.

Now I'm studying ancient Greek. Every hour I spend in declensions and conjugations deepens my sense of my own ignorance. It's a kind of revelation, I guess. I'm not the student I thought I was.

To mark silence ( ) or * seemed like options for a while.

But the open-close parentheses began to seem like hands closing in prayer, or like hands circling a mouth that is unseen but open and about to yell out.

The asterisk—despite being that mark in Proto-Indo-European linguistics that marks the existence of an ur-word whose primary meaning undergirds and supports every iteration through time of every related word but whose proof etched in mud or in wax or on papyrus has never once been found—just felt like a notation that meant either to look up at the night sky at the grand silence of the stars, or to look at the bottom of the page for a note to help explain what might have been unclear in the text above. Usually, an allusion.

But what I want to point to isn't in any direction because it's in every direction.

Ubiquitous. Obvious.

Unavailable by the means at hand.

All.

3.

I want to ask a question about silence.

✦

The answer is in the disappearance of the question.

Riddles, Labyrinths

Asclepiades of Tragilus, a fourth-century poet, records the Sphinx's riddle: "There is on earth a two-footed and four-footed creature with a single voice, and three-footed, changing its form alone of all creatures that move in earth, sky, or sea. When it walks on the most legs, then the strength of its limbs is weakest." It's likely he took the riddle from other authors who have slipped back into anonymity—by which I mean, I guess, that they fell back into time. I have to remind myself those poets had thumbprints like labyrinths unique to themselves, just as I have my own. But it is the riddle, whose answer for each of us is the same, that gets to have an identity more or less permanent.

The Sphinx seized and devoured young and old, large and small. A scholiast, writing about Euripides, notes: "But also the handsomest and loveliest of all, the dear son of blameless Creon, noble Haemon." How blameless Creon is any reader of ancient tragedy can decide for herself. No one seems very blameless. We sense in the riddle some compulsion to answer, though we know it might be wiser to keep quiet. The words seem to contain a secret just as we ourselves seem to contain one. Mostly we fear what we want—that the answer will let the secret out, and somehow, as if by magic, we'll be released by letting go of the answer we had contained.

The riddle seems immune to mortality, and though to answer wrong is to face death in the form of the Sphinx's punishment, to answer correctly admits to the same fact: a man begins weak and gains strength only to become weak again. The riddle is deathless, even when the answer is death. Nor does answering correctly release you from the Sphinx's crisis. It just presses in the air an invisible button called *pause*.

Words that, for many years, felt to me they admitted intellectual failure, have changed their nature: *I don't know*. Now they seem to me words of spiritual honesty.

When I read *Oedipus Rex* I say to myself a silent prayer that this time Oedipus, brash man of brilliant mind, might reach the gates of Thebes and in answer to the Sphinx's question say, *I don't know*, and walk past the walled city that he does not know is his home.

But the prayer never comes true.

Today a milk-white butterfly landed on the lavender to take her fill of nectar, and the humble-bee scared her away to sip at the same blossom. I guess they heard the same question though it was silent to me, eating honey on toast.

Such strange hopes persist in silence. The grief substitute. The alternate.

✦

Riddles riddle silence. Pierce it. Bewilder it by betraying it. It is as if a question had been asking itself forever without being heard, somewhere behind the mind or deeper than it, somewhere within the intangible reaches of soul, and then so gradually it escapes notice until it can no longer be ignored, the silent thing called out into voice. The riddle says, *Tell me what you know*, and when you do tell, you open your eyes to the fact that you don't know what it is you know.

Wisdom makes the problem worse.

An apocryphal fragment written down by Pseudo-Plato and attributed to Homer speaks to the issue: "He knew a lot of things, but knew them all badly."

We think we're talking about others, but later see we've been speaking the whole time about ourselves. It's disappointing even as it's a revelation. Just another one of Fate's riddles, even if fate is no more than realizing you are yourself and have been, without interruption, yourself your whole life—even as one late night you cried when you left behind your lovely wife holding to her fragrant breast your son because you needed to return to battle, and as she wept the child laughed to see the sun shine on the bronze helmet, but even then, I wasn't Hector.

Nor was Homer, of whom such stories abound that he seems to both exist and not at the same time, as if he is one man of many voices and is also nobody at all. I like to return to the stories of his death. Pseudo-Plutarch writes: "Not long afterwards, when he was sailing to Thebes for the Kronia, which is a musical contest they hold there, he arrived at Ios. There, while sitting on a rock, he observed some fishers sailing up, and he asked them if they got anything. They (having caught nothing but for lack of a catch de-loused themselves) answered, 'All we caught we left behind, all that we missed we carry.' The riddle meant that the lice they had caught they had killed and left behind, but the ones they had not caught they were carrying in their clothing. Unable to work this out, Homer became depressed and died."

Subtle variations abound. Homer, hearing the fisherboys, calls out: "O huntsmen from Arcadia, have we caught anything?" One answers with the same riddle, and in this account by Proclus, Homer, who best understood the mysteries of human hubris set against the myriad realities of the heart, could not find the answer. He became depressed, wandering around preoccupied by the riddle, "and in this condition he slipped and fell on a stone, and died two days later."

Of his blindness, there's much to think but little to say, other than to mention that some authors suggest we make Homer blind to excuse our own blindness, for he saw more clearly than any man to ever live. He is blind because we cannot see.

Even such a man a riddle baffles.

More simply, from someone known only as Anonymous, "They say he died on the island of Ios after finding himself helpless because he was unable to solve a riddle of the fisherboys."

Part of the riddle of Homer's life is that all the biographical material is spurious past factual belief. He is in his way wholly anonymous, just as we are anonymous, or quietly on the way to becoming so. To wander through our days preoccupied by what makes to us no sense means we keep good company. It eases some the sorrow every riddle burdens us with, a weight I call *sight-with-obscurity-included*.

The Muses sang in my ear the rage of Achilles and the rites of Hector, tamer of horses. But a question a child asked has destroyed me.

Sing me the songs you do not know.

One is a song about lice.

✦

But aren't there other ways to think?

Riddle that doesn't lead to death. Riddle that doesn't seduce us into all those facts, damaged by desire, we call knowledge.

But, as Emily Dickinson says of eloquence, that it is when "the heart has not a voice to spare," perhaps there is another kind of riddle one asks and answers oneself, not a work of words so much as a kind of deed doing and undoing itself forever, as night undoes day, and breath undoes breath.

At odd moments in life, waking up in the middle of the night and trying to find some trick to put my mind back to ease and sleep, I find myself thinking about Penelope weaving her shroud each day to keep her suitors at bay, and each night undoing the work.

She makes an image to cover up the face of death, and each night, undoes the image. The suitors must sense it. Death's face all uncovered. It looks like nothing.

I like to think Penelope became so skilled in her art she could weave threads together with one hand while the other hand simultaneously took those threads apart. Her shroud might look like a thin black fragment briefly hovering in the air, thrilled occasionally by the gold thread of a star or the silver thread of water from a spring. But the whole could never be seen. It would be something like the trick of the famous philosopher who reportedly could write a question with one hand and with the other write the answer at the same time. But Penelope's art would be finer, for she'd know the question and the answer are the same thing—one is just the disappearance of the other.

Unlike the Sphinx, this riddle kept men at bay, kept them silent, kept them apart from the "valor of action." Not eliciting desire, her work put desire on delay, and by delaying desire, paused for many years the deaths of those she wanted to stop wanting her.

Such a riddle creates a rift in time. Beginnings and ends cease to oppose but become one. To do is to be undone. But there's a strain of music. It's just the hands working by themselves, sound of thread against thread, like the work of the Fates—if you can call that sound a sound, it's the only sound.

5.

There must be a way to begin that doesn't include paradise.

But maybe not.

Ezra Pound's "Notes for Canto CXX":

I have tried to write Paradise

> Do not move
>> Let the wind speak
>>> that is paradise.

> Let the Gods forgive what I
>> have made
> Let those I love try to forgive
>> what I have made.

I've gone over this poem in my mind many times. I think about the made-thing that is a poem and the making-thing that is a poet. Sometimes I've thought a line of verse is only a placing of words on wind, but then the wind dies down and in my mind I see the wild thrashing of the storm-tossed tree grow horribly still. Other times I've thought the lines of verse that make a poem are nothing more than telegraph wires carrying voices inside them; but those voices matter little, if at all, for their importance isn't in *what* they say but *that* they say. There is no other way to write but to string them like wires taut across some distance so that the wind can blow across and sing its own song. Sometimes I think it can be heard in no other way, that song—the one you cannot sing. And then I think, you can put your ear against anything, any made-thing, and hear that supernal vibration that is paradise, I mean the wind speaking, I mean the actual poem, the un-making one, the un-made one we can only glimpse by the making of our own.

Such thoughts lead to other considerations. Place your ear gently against the page. It's a poem about the ocean, maybe. Maybe I think I hear waves. Obscure waves.

✦

I'm writing these words sitting inside the Houghton Library. The ocean is somewhere not far away. Next to me, propped open, Emerson's journal from July 1847 in which he is thinking about Thoreau. Next to it, in a manila folder not yet opened, Wallace Stevens's typescript for "Notes Toward a Supreme Fiction."

I hope to open it before my time is up.

"HURRY UP PLEASE IT'S TIME."

"As if you could kill time without injuring eternity."

Emerson quotes from Thoreau: "So it remained in a degree of obscurity for me." He's referring to the name of a nameless place.

Emerson writes:

> Henry pitched his tone very low in his love of nature,—
> [handwriting illegible for a few words] tortoises (?), crickets,
> muskrats, [illegible], toads + frogs, it was impossible to go
> lower. Yet it gave him every advantage in conversation: for
> who could tax him with transcendentalism or over-refining
> that found him always skilled in facts, real experiences
> in objects which made their objects + experiences appear
> artificial: and yet his position was in Nature, + he
> commanded all its miracles + infinitudes.

One of the things that has only grown in degrees of obscurity for me is what the fact of the poem might be. Even that grammar feels wrong. Might be? Then it's not a fact.

Or is the possibility of the thing not yet made a fact? A fact beneath the matter of the fact, barest bound against infinitude, that says, *Here in this space something can come*, but the saying of such a fact is silent.

If it can be said at all.

Experience agitates itself. Eventually the fact of it appears artificial.

You keep recalling it and each time, though you cannot notice it, something changes, something alters, until perhaps the memory appeals to nothing experience means. You forget even what you've forgotten.

Turn the page.

Emerson quotes and reminisces for twenty-five pages and then inserts between two blank sheets a newspaper article: "Thoreau and His Writings: His Habits of Thought: Cape Cod." The article is just a single column, but long, and folded in thirds. It opens by saying that Thoreau "addresses Spartans in taste and Spartans in life," that he does not appeal to the sentiments of readers that have made other authors more popular. I don't know what the rest of the article says, or if Emerson himself wrote it. I was scared that unfolding the old paper would destroy it. But what I did take note of is that clipping is followed by twelve blank pages in the journal and the next entry is a torn-out sheet of ruled notebook paper on which, in deep brown ink, Emerson wrote: "His 'nightwarbler' June 19 1853 seen + described." On the backside:

1853
Feb 13. in the driving snowstorm, a dense flock of snowbirds out under the pigweed in the garden.

The torn page nesting in the blank white sheets a kind of songbird lost in the snow.

Then Emerson transcribes Thoreau's poem "Inspiration." The first line is: "If with light head erect I sing." At first I think *light* means dizzy; then I think it means light. Behind my eyes there's a dim glow better than the din of thought. It's dizzying.

Let those I love try to forgive what I have made.

The rest of the journal is blank.

6.

And then I opened Stevens:

> To find of sound the bleakest ancestor,
> To find of light a music issuing

✦

That the desire for truth seems fatal to truth . . .

Appoint me my place in the music . . .

So that my presence alone ceases to hush the thrush . . .

Replace the click-clack of reason with the hum of thought . . .

Let *is* not *be* be my most accurate song . . .

7.

Sensation of staring so long through the bars of the window that the bars appear in front of anything I see. The field is a kind of jail, but the jail is inside me, inside my eye. What is there when I stare at nothing and look at the field? Some grid so fine I don't know it's a grid. Or a sheet of ruled notebook paper like a child learns to write on. Look up at the sky and it's ruled. That's why it's blue. All those lines have run together.

Is it a depth, or a surface, or a distance, or is it so near as to be within?

To say something like: *the difficulty of blankness.*

But so much of it all isn't quite right.

Paul Celan in Paris, walking with his friend, so fond of repeating what Kafka said: "Sometimes God, sometimes nothing."

8.

A stain or strain of music. Stain: tinge with color other than the natural one. Strain: to draw tight.

When I had my first child I felt inside myself what I never had to feel before: my solitude. I felt it strain under the new shape. Those first days when eternity is the caul, the child's timelessness leaks into time, staining it with some tone so pure it creates a rift in what hardly exists—the place within myself, more mine than saying *I* can mean, not where I am by myself, but where solitude lives its own involuted, involuntary life.

I didn't know it existed until it was broken.

Singularity not of the self, but in it. Gravity from which not even sound escapes. Fear of the infant crying, also known as the event horizon.

The letter aleph, which makes no noise, draws silence tight and then a sound can follow.

Heraclitus might say, *As of the bow, the arrow.*

Sometimes I think we carry within ourselves an aleph somewhere behind our heart, or is it within the liver, purging noise as blood is purged of its stain. I guess I don't know. A transplanted spiritual organ given to us on loan. But I don't know the terms of the agreement.

Keep quiet. But I fear I can't.

The letter *bet* is the first sound. Just silence precedes it. It is shaped like a house missing a wall, and mystics say it should be thought of as a house or a tent. When I studied the mystical importance of Hebraic letters I read that we house ourselves within the fear of God and the letter bet informs us of our position. It is a letter that acts as a portrait of the human condition. Or is it that we live within the love of God? I can't remember exactly our condition. Bet says we begin to exist by dwelling. *Buh-buh-buh*, the first sounds a baby makes. Maybe the letter is a kind of shelter from whose safety sometimes we must grope our way back out into the unlettered universe through which aleph blows her silence. Housed in fear or housed in love and silence at the door. Learning to speak.

The words for *beginning*, *head*, and *blessing* also begin with bet.

Where I learned this I forget. *Midrash Rabbah*, or the *Sefer Yetzirah*, I can't remember. I forget how the blessing began in my head.

The source goes astray or it goes missing.

Heliopause

At the edge of the solar system a spacecraft named New Horizons just woke up. It slept for nearly three billion miles and now it's opening its eyes to take photos of Pluto. Astronomers are hopeful to find craters, mountains. Any features clearly seen would please, as the best photos we now have show only a blurry rock.

Maybe they'll find rings, my favorite planetary feature.

Πλοῦτος means wealth. Rings are a form of wealth, and I like to think of Pluto circled by the very thing that typifies the god for which the planet is named. I like to think the rings might ring and that New Horizons has ears and not just eyes and will send us music back from the very edge, the outermost circle, of our sun's influence.

One way to consider a poem's relationship to itself: it tries to discover its own limit so that it can fill the shape with song. There are other ways, but I know them less well.

George Oppen: "If there is another horizon, I haven't seen it." Maybe I'm misquoting.

How likely is it, that in seeking out some utmost edge, the very limit of sound, and using sounds to arrive there, that I will not deceive myself just to feel I've arrived. And how would I even know.

Prufrock twice being told:

> That is not what I meant at all.
> That is not it, at all.

I remember being an undergraduate, writing my honors thesis. As in high school when, I wrote a term paper on existentialism for which

I received a failing grade for having misspelled the word "conscious-ness" throughout, I was reaching past my grasp. The topic: Czeslaw Milosz and Eschatology. I was curious about the end of time, I sup-pose, not because it offered some glimpse into heaven, but, heathen that I was, because it promised return to the world before time began, moment of origin, when the earth was without form, and void; and darkness was upon the face of the deep. Existence before existence occurred. I read an essay by Paul Ricoeur about language and limits, and in it I came upon a sentence that so filled me with the sense of truth that I quickly memorized it. When I saw Kristy on campus I hurried to her to recite it, but I couldn't find the exact order of the words, just some semblance of what they meant, enough to convey a sense, but I wanted it exactly, and grew angry, depressed, felt some rage at my own failure, that a sentence memorized just two hours before had already loosed itself from my hold, and I felt stupid, filled with some drift of loathing that only now I realize was shame. It was an odd reaction to have; it should have taught me something about myself; it didn't. Now I don't remember even the gist of the sentence that meant so much to me I hated myself for failing it. Not even a syl-lable remains. Just some shame as faint now as a scent remembered years later from an earlier day.

I do recall that Ricoeur suggested that certain figures of speech in the Bible, notably paradox and metaphor, functioned to riddle the ratio-nal mind and take a reader to that most uncomfortable of horizons in which one feels the thing that cannot be said.

Then you sort of say it anyway.

It's hard to put your ear against a horizon and listen to what speaks from the other side. The horizon likes to retreat. And there's no bar-rier, no membrane, no page, no film, no pane, no nothing, to mark as other the other side.

Then you sort of wonder if the horizon is the farthest line or the near-est, the edge of what can be seen, or the edge of the eye that does the seeing. Or is it the separation between.

Simone Weil: "Two prisoners whose cells adjoin communicate with each other by knocking on the wall. The wall is the thing which sepa-rates them but it is also their means of communication. It is the same with God. Every separation is a link."

I think I agree.

But you have to go knocking everywhere, just knocking your hand against the air, if the sky is the prison though we cannot see the wall; and then we do not know how to listen because we do not know where to knock, or if we're knocking.

Seen from afar it looks like a ritual gesture of the ancient world, a kind of simple dance: a step, the hand knocks in four directions, a step, the hand knocks in four directions.

It doesn't feel like faith, but it's a method.

A poem considers the situation and tries to offer a wall.

Wittgenstein writes:

> To say nothing except what can be said, *i.e.* something that has
> nothing to do with philosophy: and then always, when someone
> else wished to say something metaphysical, to demonstrate
> to him that he has given no meaning to certain signs in his
> propositions. This method would be unsatisfying to the
> other—he would not have the feeling that we were teaching him
> philosophy—but it would be the only strictly correct method.

Prufrock twice being told:

> That is not it at all,
> That is not what I meant, at all.

How childish it is to see it as I do, a spacecraft like a child opening its eyes. Solar panels rubbing the sand out of the sensors.

It's very lonely out there. That's why the baby in her crib reaches up at night for the rings spinning on the mobile.

Properly seen, every word of these sentences has been used without having given meaning to certain signs.

This past summer *Voyager 1* left the solar system. It is beyond the reach of the sun's gravity, and what light it now gives is no brighter than any other star *Voyager* can see. Like a mystic who has wandered away from his wealth, it has entered into desert places to feel nothing so deeply a new influence might be found. This space is called *the heliopause*. *Voyager* is the only made-thing that has crossed the limit. It can send no word back about its experience. Such a strange, sad poem.

Existing wherein it cannot speak.

Wittgenstein: "Whereof one cannot speak, thereof one must be silent."

It doesn't feel like poetry, but it is the only strictly correct method.

10.

Paul Antschel, Paul Aurel, Paul Ancel, A. Pavel.

So he signed his earliest work before deciding on Paul Celan. In anagram a kind of diaspora. Hope that one permutation will be right and one will arrive in the name that is one's own.

But mostly a name is a form of exile.

"Todesfuge" ends "dein aschenes Haar Sulamith."

(Thy ashen hair Shulamith.)

"Return, return, O Shulamite; return, return that we may look upon thee."

Jewish mystic tradition equates the beloved in the Song of Songs with the Shekinah, the divine presence of God on earth, thought of as a bride. She dwelled in the Temple. Descending as pure grace that lights up the smoke or sits on a cushion.

When the Romans destroyed the Temple the Shekinah stayed on earth. She wanders even now in the dust.

Many prayers call her back home. Prayer that might begin with those words by which the Shekinah is sometimes symbolized: *Moon Queen Apple Orchard Bride.* Empty vessel with no light of her own but the earthshine of this nearness. Mystics say she is married to Beauty. I don't know. To sanctify oneself they recommend waking up at midnight and weeping, weeping.

The hope is to return her name to its proper place, but this name wanders the world; nor does it ease the pain of the problem to think that a name can say itself to itself and so become its own place, a kind of portable altar.

A name is not a home.

The mystics say repentance begins by denying oneself the sleep the body needs and the mind desires. Prayer occurs in the absence of oblivion. So it seems. And I didn't even know that absence and oblivion were different. At night I dream about the bride in my arms even as the bride sleeps dreaming beside me, oblivious of me as I am of her.

I didn't know I had to make my own absence.

O Shulamith of the dust-covered orchard purple hair, exhume the grave they dug in the air. O Sulamith of the ashen hair, end your wandering through the dust in the clouds, and return.

Paul Celan, A. Pavel, Paul Ancel, Paul Aurel, Paul Antschel. All the light comes in under the crack of a door.

Blank page called a day.

God.

Memory & Poppy

Marcel Proust and Montaigne both claim to have bad memories, but *In Search of Lost Time* and the *Essays* are made mostly of memory, and nowhere does it seem to be at fault. But it's hard to find the failure in a mind that isn't your own, and so I try to believe them when they say it to me. I think I have a bad memory, too. Others don't believe me. But when I look through my mind something is always missing or awry, like those dreams of searching for something but you don't know what it is you're looking for—and those dreams too of being sought by something, but you don't know by what.

Memories of dreams. What could be stranger?

Underground in a chamber I'm lying down on a stone table and hooded figures stand around me. I can't see their faces or their mouths but a voice speaks and says that I learned a word I should not know and now I have to die. A kind of sacrifice. Wake up at the point of the knife.

How much life we do not exactly live.

Only now do I understand the dream wasn't about the precocity of mind seeking to learn what it should not know—in kabbalah there are questions one shouldn't ask before the age of forty—but of the need to forget what I do.

If I could have forgotten that word my life would have been saved.

That word? I don't know. I didn't wake up knowing it.

> And suddenly the memory appeared. That taste was the taste
> of the little piece of madeleine which on Sunday mornings
> at Combray (because that day I did not go out before it was
> time for Mass), when I went to say good morning to her in

her bedroom, my aunt Léonie would give me after dipping it in her infusion of tea or lime blossom. . . . But, when nothing subsists of an old past, after the death of people, after the destruction of things, alone, frailer but more enduring, more immaterial, more persistent, more faithful, smell and taste still remain for a long time, like souls, remembering, waiting, hoping, upon the ruins of all the rest, bearing without giving way, on their almost impalpable droplet, the immense edifice of memory.

Memory pretends to be about our own life, having been made, supposedly, by our living it. But each memory has its own life. Like some wandering underworld, we gather into ourselves the shades, and of those souls whose ardent desire is only to exist again, we find ourselves subject to their demands for sacrifice. Just a crumb, just a bite, just a sip of wine; just the scent of a rose enduring past its prime; just light on an oak leaf; just a touch; just a glimpse of another's skin . . . such desire we feel and seek to satisfy not for our own pleasure, but to bring life back to the horde within us who have no bodies but our own.

Such acts used to be known as *sacrifices of aversion*.

We think we're hungry because we do not hear those voices within us begging their offering, threatening us with sickness or death if we do not comply. Mostly we're deaf to their demands even as we obey them. Repast at morning, noon, and evening. Sustenance not simply of the body, but maintenance of the undergloom. Life that feeds the afterlife.

✦

Throughout Homer the battle-weary heroes pray for the boon of sleep. Nightly oblivion comes to wash away the blood and dust the morning will wake them to again. Dreams of wives and children, dreams of home, offer sweet escape. Often, for lesser reasons, I feel the same.

Grateful that the night will remove me from the day. But the night is its own experience, and instead of oblivion we find ourselves occupied by strange visions that, rather than removing us from memory, give us more to remember.

Does the bee dream of its toil or of its dance. Or are those the same dream. The worker bee.

> For nine days' time I was borne by savage winds over the fish-filled sea; but on the tenth we set foot on the land of the Lotus-eaters, who eat a flowery food. There we went on shore and drew water, and without further ado my comrades took their meal by the swift ships. But when we had tasted food and drink, I sent out some of my comrades to go and learn who the men were, who here ate bread upon the earth; two men I chose, sending with them a third as herald. They departed at once and mingled with the Lotus-eaters; nor did the Lotus-eaters think of killing my comrades, but gave them the lotus to eat. And whoever of them ate the honey-sweet fruit of the lotus no longer wished to bring back word or return home, but there they wished to remain among the Lotus-eaters, feeding on the lotus, and to forget their homecoming. I myself brought back these men, weeping, to the ships under compulsion, and dragged them beneath the benches and bound them fast in hollow ships; and I bade the rest of my trusty comrades to embark with speed on the swift ships, for fear that perchance anyone else should eat the lotus and forget his homecoming. So they went on board quickly and sat down upon the benches, and sitting well in order struck the gray sea with their oars.

Odysseus hard to admire, his mind so quickly outstrips his valor. His cruelty is his cunning. I think about those three men he sent into the field to meet the Lotus-eaters. I remember them at strange moments, as if some pollen has carried the memory in the air, and just by breathing in, I forget what I was doing, and wonder. What happened to them when they ate the lotus? Alfred Lord Tennyson has it—

> There is sweet music here that softer falls
> Than petals from blown roses on the grass,
> Or night-dews on still waters between walls
> Of shadowy granite, in a gleaming pass;
> Music that gentlier on the spirit lies,
> Than tir'd eyelids upon tir'd eyes;
> Music that brings sweet sleep down from the blissful skies.
> Here are cool mosses deep,
> And thro' the moss the ivies creep,
> And in the stream the long-leaved flowers weep,
> And from the craggy ledge the poppy hangs in sleep.

—that the lotus lets a music fall upon those men. This is different than listening. The music falls upon them, a melody that lulls the nerves, that brings sleep down from the sky but leaves one still aware—*aware*, if that word can mean the release from every form of driven care, and whispers instead that all things are at home in themselves and in one another, and homecoming is a shallow wish that thinks toil earns the gift that everywhere already exists. This being at home. It's just a music. Not a music that lives in you; a music you live within.

Like the thrush in her song. Like the bee in her dance.

Note how the "poppy hangs in sleep." It' is not for us to eat. It's taken its own medicine. It's succumbed to being.

Maybe the remedy to the problem of self is falling asleep. It must be a different sleep than that which occurs most every night, though each night is a glimpse into what such sleep must be. Mostly, we're insomniac. Don't know, as the poppy knows, how to sleep inside ourselves as the blossom sleeps in the bud. Don't know how to take a dose of our medicine, because our medicine is us.

No wonder those men wept, dragged back to the boat to go *home*. The honey-sweet lotus freed them of their purpose, released them from their desire, and desire sees with eyes that find distances in every direction, distance hidden in distance, time hidden in time; desire shows us who suffer it a gap that must be crossed, an ocean of climbing waves we must ourselves climb only to find the next one towering even higher; and say somehow we hear a music come to us, we think at first it's the music of our own beating hearts; but no, it's not a music within but a music without; say we hear that music, say we breathe it in, and find our wives and children, our home and homeland, all dispersed like pollen in the air, blown into every open thing, the lotus-opened heart and the sleeping poppy.

Who wouldn't weep to be brought back to the ships and tied up with rope and placed in the belly of a boat.

Image of false labor. Forget it. I mean: give yourself forgetting.

The only work is breathing in.

✦

Genius guards us from forgetting what we'd die to neglect: breath, heartbeat, digestion. Genius tends the body so that we can begin to forget more deliberately all that can be forgotten.

Linguist Daniel Heller-Roazen recounts a Middle Eastern tale:

> Abu Nuwas asked Khalaf for permission to compose
> poetry, and Khalaf said: "I refuse to let you make a poem
> until you memorize a thousand pages of ancient poetry,

including chants, odes, and occasional lines." So Abu Nuwas disappeared; and after a good long while, he came back and said, "I've done it."

"Recite them," said Khalaf.

So, Abu Nuwas began, and got through the bulk of the verses over a period of several days. Then he asked again for permission to compose poetry. Said Khalaf, "I refuse, unless you forget all one thousand lines as completely as if you had never learned them."

"That's too difficult," said Abu Nuwas. "I've memorized them quite thoroughly!"

So Abu Nuwas disappeared into a monastery and remained in solitude for a period of time until he forgot the lines. He went back to Khalaf and said, "I've forgotten them so thoroughly it's as if I never memorized anything at all."

Khalaf then said, "Now go compose!"

Betray, betray, Genius demands; betray, betray is the poem's command.

Abu Nuwas's poetic education is the only tale I know in which forgetting is the work that is done. It is harder work than memory is, forgetting. For many years I didn't know what to think about the story. Even so, I shared it with many of my classes. I'd read it to them out loud, and no matter the amount of class time remaining, I'd send them out to begin forgetting it. In my heart I kept a secret wish. That the door to the classroom filled with a mist made of water from the river Lethe so that walking away from the desk was to forget all that had been heard.

Now maybe I glimpse it. Abu Nuwas memorizes the ancient poems, chants, odes, and occasional lines and recites them not to prove to Khalaf he has succeeded in accomplishing such an impossible task, though it must have felt so to him as he recited perfectly those thousands of pages over many days. You don't become a poet by swallowing the library whole. He recites them to put back into the air those words pulled down and made by others into poems. A kind of repair. As if one could breathe back into the sky a cloud that had gone missing, but the cloud is transparent, and not made only of dust and water and air. Abu Nuwas gives back all the words Genius gave others, strange sacrifice to the minor god who keeps life for each of us intact. The only way the sacrifice is pure is if nothing of it remains, and so Khalaf orders Abu Nuwas to forget those lines he'd memorized quite thoroughly. That labor of forgetting repaid a debt inherited from others but nonetheless also his own, for to become a poet means to accept the debt of others as one's own, and to labor to repay it so that the dead can go free from their bonds. The work isn't writing poems so much as it's forgetting them. And if you forget them well, those poems you love, then Genius has some pity on you, and in the absence of what once you knew places in you some words you didn't know you knew, and so you write them down.

(Then a finger pushes a bead across the metal bar on the abacus. The bead is but a dried poppy head. The finger belongs to the accountant we cannot not know. And what is owed begins to accrue.)

12.

Through lidless eyes they stare, the gods.

The animals turn their gaze away.

    Pascal speaks of the *wretchedness* of our condition—
    that we cannot be one nor the other,
    that our ignorance cannot rescue us from what our reason can-
        not grasp.

    We stare at what we want to exist so that it exists,
    or we stare at what threatens us, or what confound us,
    the *object of contemplation*—

And blink.

Some Burial Rites

John Keats writes to Fanny Brawne in February 1820: "I have found other thoughts intrude upon me. 'If I should die,' said I to myself, 'I have left no immortal work behind me, nothing to make my friends proud of my memory, but I have lov'd the principle of beauty in all things, and if I had time I would have made myself remember'd.'"

The work of his greatest brilliance is behind him. The odes are littered with forms of immortal silence:

> *tuneless numbers*

> *secrets*

> *Thou still unravished bride of quietness,*
> *Thou foster-child of silence and slow time*

> *Heard melodies are sweet, but those unheard*
> *Are sweeter*

> *spirit ditties of no tone*

> *Thou, silent form, dost tease us out of thought*
> *As doth eternity*

> *Darkling I listen*

> *Fled is that music*

> *a silent deep-disguised plot*
> *To steal away*

and leave my sense
     Unhaunted quite of all but—nothingness?

     Where are the songs of Spring? Ay, where are they?

Keats feels eternity's silence. Some quality heaven and the gods keep to themselves. How is it we come to value most those qualities we are incapable of grasping? The figures on the urn, and only later, the ashes within it. To speak the words, "Thou still unravished bride of quietness" ravishes the bride away from her quietness, shatters the silence of her eternal life. The awful irony the poet lives in: to write *immortal work* requires the shattering of that silence where immortality might exist.

I want to say you cannot trespass into death, but I guess you can.

Orpheus.

Keats.

But trespass is reciprocal. What you trespass into also trespasses into you. From eternity, a little eternity. From death, a little death.

Keats writes to his friend Charles Brown: "I have an habitual feeling of my real life having past, and that I am leading a posthumous existence." He'll live another seven weeks, but he wouldn't call it living. He's already in eternity. Not heaven. He doesn't believe in heaven. But he can hear that great silence that makes his fevered breath all the louder in his ears, silence that will unthread the Gordian knot of self into nothing, drawn into the silence the odes tried to, but could not, shatter. Drawn into the silence that mocks what's known.

Or I think about it another way. You can't ravish the bride of quietness. You can't break apart her silence with your song. It's the song that gets shattered by the silence it breaks. It's immortality that wrecks the immortal work.

Mostly, it's unthinkable.

✦

Percy Bysshe Shelley dies with Keats's third book open in his breast pocket. The pages of *Lamia* as rippled as a wave, last marker of the sea that drowned him.

> The God, dove-footed, glided silently
> Round bush and tree, soft-brushing, in his speed,
> The taller grasses and full-flowering weed

Shelley's body washes ashore after more than a week in the sea. Some accounts have much of his flesh eaten away or missing and much of what remains putrid with rot.

Louis Édouard Fournier paints the funeral scene. Shelley's body dark on the dark wood just lit so there is no flame to see, only a lifting shroud of gray smoke. Three men stand close: Edward Trelawny, Leigh Hunt, and Lord Byron. A crowd in the background too dark to distinguish. A woman kneels near the edge. Maybe Mary, his wife.

The painting is somber, moving, but it's a lie.

Trelawny brought to the beach some portable furnace, some oil, some wine, some salt. He collected wood. He writes: "The heat from the sun and the fire was so intense that the atmosphere was tremulous and wavy. The corpse fell open and the heart was laid bare. The frontal bone of the skull, where it had been struck with the mattock, fell off; and, as the back of the head rested on the red-hot bottom bars of the furnace, the brains literally seethed, bubbled, and boiled as in a cauldron, for a very long time." Hunt stayed in his carriage. Byron watched from out in the ocean; he'd gone swimming in the sea. Somehow the heart didn't burn, and Mary and Hunt fought over who should keep the miraculous relic. But as the critic Daisy Hay is quick to point out, it was likely not the poet's heart, but his liver.

I don't know why it's on my mind. Byron alive and afloat in the very element that killed his friend. Hunt in the vehicle that, having brought him, will also take him away. Something about the distance each man has from the moment even as it's occurring, and how the painting lies about that distance—or if it doesn't exactly lie, allows us to discover some trick of honesty, which is to say, the painted men hide within themselves the distances to which they fled, and though we can't see it on the canvas itself, contained within Hunt and Byron both is some silent gap undisclosed in which the truth of the event resides, invisible right there in what you see.

14.

A student asks, "What is it to seek beauty? What is it to try and live a life that's good?"

"That's a question," is my answer.

The class is silent.

I think I have a point to make.

Why does the flower seek the sun? It wants to eat the thing that gives it life. The daisies think they can swallow the star. But then a bee lands in their sunlit open mouths and the field lives and honey fills the hive.

We're studying John Keats.

I thought I had a point to make, but now I see I don't know exactly what a point is. What it is to have a point.

A point has no part.

Some purpose belongs to nothingness. Beauty is just one thing among many that obliterate consideration. One might even say consideration also obliterates itself.

Sibboleth

Imagine a flower.

I do.

Its petals bloom by folding inward, like arms reaching into a mouth, not another's mouth, but the mouth that is your own. The petals bend into the dark pollen of their own being and it does not look like bloom-ing until the petals reach so far through themselves they invert and blossom in reverse.

Maybe I'm not speaking in the right dimension.

Maybe the stars are bees whose buzz brightens them in this other di-mension. Maybe the flowers are invisible. Maybe you need to be made of light to see them, like the bees. I mean, like the stars.

Or imagine in the fact of someone's face the dark pupils of her eyes, of just one eye, and magnify that darkness so that it's as large as the sky.

So many ways to imagine flowers and the night.

So many ways to make open and closed the unopenable, uncloseable thing. These images of the mind not mine. This pure intent. This virtue-crime.

✦

A euphemism is to use an auspicious word in place of an inauspi-cious one. For *death* we say *passed away* or *went to sleep*. Often we say these words to children who, being closer to those fears we pre-sume ourselves immune from, hear what we mean in what we don't say. They hear the unspoken word. That's why they're so afraid to go to bed.

The verb in the Greek from which the word derives is εὐφημέω. In the dictionary I keep in the no-space of my smartphone the definition goes: "*Avoid all unlucky words*, during sacred rites: hence, as the surest mode of avoiding them, *keep a religious silence*." The italics aren't mine; I don't know whose they are. In the imperative, it means "*Hush! Be Still!*"

For so long I've felt to speak in euphemisms proved a kind of cowardice, an unwillingness to say those words most difficult to say. But every time I tried to speak the truth when doing so was difficult I resorted to less inauspicious words. I told the truth, but I told it slant.

In class people wonder why I blush so often. You can't see your own face, so I don't know I am blushing. But looking in the faces of others who are looking at your face, though it sounds like a riddle, is to get the smallest glimpse of yourself, even if the realization is no more than *I exist*, a fact we never speak of, it is so common and holy, and then the blush deepens by burning brighter, shame at my own nakedness, even in class, when I'm wearing all my clothes. Just like in those dreams we all have of going to school or coming into work and realizing you've forgotten to dress. The euphemism is "that you look nice today," but what is silent in the words is *I see you're naked, too*.

It's hard to know when the rites are sacred, or when daily habit is just routine. Making the children's lunches. Getting them to school. Feeding them at night. Doing the dishes. Readying both girls for bed. Reading them stories. Turning out the lights. Singing to Iris in the dark, the dark of which she is very afraid, while Hana in her room listens to music in her headphones no one else can hear. I might describe it all this way: "It's tiring; but it's nice." By which I might mean: "My soul is dead; this is the sacred work."

Now I've learned that euphemism isn't cowardice, but a kind of virtue. It is speaking so as to keep silence, lest a word that is unlucky enter into the sacred blank light of day or page and defile it. Maybe this is why so many people make clichés into mantras. But I have no mantra. I just say a lot of words to many different people, and I fill pages with lines and sentences. I don't know why it is I do these things: talk so much, write so much. Maybe there's no other way.

✦

Jacques Derrida, writing about Paul Celan, defines the shibboleth:

> The Ephraimites had been defeated by the army of Jephthah; in order to keep their soldiers from escaping across the river (*shibboleth* also means 'river,' of course, but that is not necessarily the reason it was chosen), each person was required to say *shibboleth*. Now the Ephraimites were known for their inability to pronounce correctly the *shi* of *shibboleth*, which became for them, in consequence, *an unpronounceable name*. They said *sibboleth*, and, at the invisible border between *shi* and *si*, betrayed themselves to the sentinel at the risk of their life. They betrayed their difference by showing themselves indifferent to the diacritical difference between *shi* and *si*; they marked themselves with their inability to re-mark a mark thus coded.

I've seen the shame, and felt it myself, when in a class a student reading aloud comes to a word she doesn't know how to pronounce, pauses and waits for someone to rescue her, and, hearing no help, stumbles through the syllables, knowing it's wrong just as we know it's wrong, assumes she has been excluded from the knowledge she's there to learn, but no one helps because no one else knows how to pronounce the word either, including me, and each one of us is excluded, too.

Teaching Celan's poems, while in springtime it snows. His mother shot to death in a forced march in the snow. We speak of I and You. Of God and I and You. Of a God that sings but does not sing of I and You. O one O none O no one O you. That God. We spend our hour on one poem:

With the voice of the fieldmouse
you squeak up to me,

a sharp
clip,
you bite your way through my shirt to the skin,

a cloth,
you slide across my mouth
midway through the words
I address to you, shadow,
to give you weight.

Whose voice speaks. One that does not say I.

Whose voice is your voice. Is it the fieldmouse's squeak, the bite of the tooth, the cloth across the mouth. You is also no voice at all. When on the street I hear someone say, "You," I turn around with my whole face open and look at them; and when I say, "You," to another, she does the same. Emmanuel Levinas says that is the command of the other we hear in our voice when we say, "You." Her face turns toward us and says in our own words, "Thou shalt not kill."

Such is the "nudity of he who borrows all." This is the way I'm nude; it's the way you're nude, too. All of language floats above us—so I think of it—some cloud in which the letters combine and recombine, eternal and impossible, the alphabet speaking itself forward and backward at the same time, and from this cloud we pull a word, a line, a sentence or two. Writing volumes diminishes it none. It does not cease; it does not decrease. From it we say all in our lives we do say. At the grocery store, at home, to those we love the most, in those unlit chambers made only of ourselves, we clothe our thoughts in what we do not own.

Celan in his nakedness on the page. To feel with him his shame so we can feel our own.

Celan translates from Samuel Beckett: "And yet I am afraid, afraid of what my words will do to me, to my refuge, yet again. . . . If I could speak and yet say nothing, really nothing? Then I might escape being gnawed to death."

In the poem we do not know what the fieldmouse's squeak means. Is it greeting, or warning? Happiness, or fear? Does it bite to wake up the man speaking, or does it bite to escape him, or to hurt him, or to gnaw him to death?

I don't know.

Celan describes a poem as an encounter, as a handshake. The poem is a thing between You and I. It builds, line by line, a ground across which You and I can meet, can see one another, can be in the moral bind of the gaze.

An elegy is a poem to a You gone missing. When the poem sings, You appears.

But what if there were a world in which, on a forced march, a guard calls out not a name, but yells out only "You," and a young man, a prisoner, steps out from the line in which he trudges forward through the cold forward, and, realizing he wasn't the one being spoken to, blushes as if embarrassed at his mistake, and then the guard shoots him. What if there were a world in which children were packed into train cars and shipped to camps, and those that were too young to know their names had them written on scraps of cardboard hung on strings around their necks, but with no food, no water, and the train ride so long, the children ate their names for they had no other food, and when they arrive, no one knows what to call them, those children called only "You." But what if there were a world in which a crippled boy in a camp speaks over and over a variant of one word but no one knows what that word means, and he limps from person to person saying *mass-klo* or *matisklo*, and others in the camp think it is the child's name, and some think it means "bread," or "meat," but no one knows with any certainty this one word the boy speaks, his only word, and now nothing of him remains, because in the camp he died. What if there were a world in which that word remains speaking forever in the air. What if there were a world . . . O one, O none, O no one, O you . . . in which that word were the only word of witness.

Celan writes, "You of the same mind, moor-wandering near one." To be near and far at once. Same and wholly other. To invoke the You you must also avoid, this You so deep inside you it wanders far away on the moors.

A shadow or a shade is the ancient way of considering the person in the afterlife, you still yourself, but without substance, though in another way your nature stays complete. Your character that built a life remains without a life around it. If it were not so, the poet's You could not drag up from underneath the daylit world the one he is addressing.

In Greek the verb λαμβάνω means "to grasp, take, receive; to seize with the senses; to understand. The compound form ὑπολαμβάνω means "to pull up so as to see," "to grasp and pull up" as one might a plant to examine its roots. For Paul Celan—for whom poetry was the grasp of the hand, a reaching across because a reaching toward, a reaching out over abyss that may be infinite even as one's own body falls back in retreat away from the approaching other—poetry seeks a "reality it is also stricken by," and the verb that speaks of the poem's action is one that grasps to know, that pulls up from underneath to understand.

But what if there were a world in which the words one wrote become those traces by which others harmed your safety, your refuge, as the plow cuts in two the fieldmouse's burrow? And the shadow, that You the poem addresses, that dear one called up from her far-wandering in the moor of the mind, memory-field buried in springtime snow—what if the words of the poem let her also be found, let others find the You you love so deeply that you write the poem that must be written which is the same poem as the one that must never exist. Then does You

> slide across my mouth
> midway through the words
> I address to you, shadow,
> to give you weight.

Does You herself bind the mouth that speaks her back into existence. Cut off the words whose utterance alone gives her weight again if not complete being. For then you can be found. You can be called out on the march. You can be in the snow bank by the river killed.

Again, now, and again.

✦

"River" is one definition of *shibboleth*.

Only those who pronounce it right can cross the river to refuge.

To speak it is to show who you are.

Euphemism might be a means of survival.

Remind me: Is there another word for "river"?

✦

In ancient Greek vase painting, the Gorgon alone looks out with both her eyes. All other figures, heroes and gods and goddesses, are painted in profile. Her gaze is the gaze of the one so real she is unreal, for this is what to see her with your own eyes does to you—not merely to become stone, but to be alive as a stone would be alive, insensate, merest appetite, dead to all but the merest hunger, merest sense, to see without looking, to hear without listening, a human that is left by her gaze not human.

It is shameless. She looks out at us as one from another world whose gaze breaks the boundary that keeps monstrous forces at bay. Sometimes our survival depends on this sense of shame by which we know to look away.

✦

In class, the difficulty of Celan's poems, discussing.

Sometimes the transitive verb speaks more truly when forced into becoming intransitive.

Only then do we feel the grasping within it, when it cannot reach the object it pursues, when sense is an approach but not an arrival.

Only then do we sense the shibboleth of our own speaking, when we feel we might be doing it wrong, this thing we do all the time, talking, thinking, writing grocery lists, writing poems. Or is it we learn to speak, to write, so that no one who reads the poem knows exactly how to say the words in it, and so that You brought up from shade into substance can live there in that field with the fieldmouse and be safe from the approach of any other but the one who says, *I*. Or is even that too much, and even I can't know how to say the words of the poem, even those of the poem I wrote. Aren't I the one who is the danger, plowing the blank field with my head, searching for the home I wreck by finding it. Or am I just one of the dangers, among many. Or is my refuge only found in that You whose only refuge is the poem.

I guess I don't know.

All these questions that end in periods.

What we say to others we also say to ourselves. We hear the words we say; it can be no other way.

Pure shibboleth of the crippled boy saying over and again *mass-klo, matisklo mass-klo matisklo*. Maybe the word meant nothing at all, had no referent, not signification, he just wanted someone to tell him if he was saying it right, if he could be let in, deep inside the word, if he could cross the river of its utterance, where alone he might be safe from death. *Mass-klo. Matisklo.*

Every day I say thousands of words. So do you. O Gorgon, turn your head aside. Each one of them goes:

Sibboleth sibboleth shibboleth

Gorgon Poetics

Years ago I went to a museum. In it I learned that the Assyrians etched prayers onto the bricks with which they built their temples, and the façade in the museum proved it. I also learned that, not knowing from which direction the gods looked, they carved the same prayer on every face of the brick, including those cemented together, including that faced another wall.

In another room I looked at Sumerian and Egyptian seals. Carved from bone or ivory or stone, rolled across wet mud or dipped in ink and drawn across vellum, the images repeat as if forever. My favorite: a girl braiding her hair. First it's loose, and then in plaits, and then a single braid; then, it's loose again.

Vision of the daily as the afterlife.

So like but unlike the Gorgon's art.

Celan quotes Georg Büchner: "Yesterday as I was walking along above the valley, I saw two girls sitting on a rock: one was putting up her hair, the other helping her; and the golden hair was hanging free, and the pale, solemn face, and yet so young, and the black peasant dress, and the other one so absorbed in her task. The finest, most heartfelt paintings of the Old German School scarcely convey an inkling of this. At times one wishes one were a Medusa's head."

Celan writes: "Poetry can mean a breathturn. Perhaps it travels the route—also the route of art—for the sake of such a breathturn? Perhaps it will succeed, as the strange, I mean the abyss and the Medusa's head, the abyss and the automatons, seem to lie in this direction—perhaps it will succeed here to differentiate between strange and strange—perhaps it is exactly here that the Medusa's head shrinks, perhaps it is exactly here that the automatons break down—for this single short moment?"

Medusa must hear the hissing of the snakes about her ears as white noise so constant it's merely the drone of the world. No wonder she has to look at things to notice them fully. She gazes at what catches her eye and then it can catch her eye forever, exactly the same, every nuance of expression, posture of body, angle of fingers stretching out through her sister's hair and also, every hair thinner than a thread, all stone the breeze blows through but does not move.

Or Gorgon-like to find those words that capture beauty and still it into image, to appreciate beauty, to make of it a thing others can find, removed from the world, infinitely available to be turned to again and again, breathless, perfect, monument of—.

Fateful Gorgonism of poet and poem.

I like to imagine it another way. The hiss around my ears just the wind through leaves or the wind through grass. Just a kind of noise, or a kind noise. To learn to walk through the world looking only at one's feet, and though in the eye's periphery the swift might swiftly pass, or the hem of a dress brush the cotton off the grass, or a dragonfly catch fire in the sun, or a child running with thin branch in hand whip off the heads of the flowers, you learn not to look up and at anything, lest seeing it, lest by catching it in the eye, you kill it into its beauty and make of the living body the deathless stone.

But to learn to walk without looking up, to learn to look at nothing directly, not even those you love as they talk with you in the morning about their dreams . . . I don't know . . . it's difficult.

Breath takes a route. Outermost air becomes innermost. Countless times a day, from birth to death, there is a point in us that pivots, when the breath taken in becomes the breath given out, when the words articulate in the air alone—that silent speaking—turn around in the cavern of the lungs and carry your own words out on it, moment that belongs to none, to no one, instant when othermost and selfmost are one. There the Medusa's head shrinks, unable to see across the distance that keeps separate I from you because there is no distance.

A point is that which has no part.

A pivot is a principle given a heart.

I want to say *our heart* though I know the grammar is absurd.

This is why I walk like I do. Looking down. Talking to myself. Breathing in the pollen and the air. Much can be seen on the ground that belongs in the air. See: the shadow of the shadow-dark crow? I think I must train my eyes to see at their edges until I learn to see as poetry requires—with my breath—

>   thin shadows   of the broad-leaf
>   grass the thin   dark shadows of
>   these bent green   leaves of grass

ΟΥ ΤΙΣ

Nobody speaks. Even being nobody doesn't save you from yourself—nobody might survive, but you cannot survive yourself. Even nobody can be swallowed whole.

✦

Every night, Iris walks into our room saying *Mommy* or *Daddy* and sounding wide awake. I stand up. Kristy moves to my side of the bed. And Iris climbs in the warm empty spot where nobody is.

I take my pillows to Iris's room and sleep in her small bed.

A lion. An elephant. A dog. A lamb. An alligator, or crocodile. A dragon with shiny wings. A bear so large it sits on the floor, forlorn, its paws resting in its lap. Sometimes a zebra. Bestiary of the bed. Or a stable, and I sleep among the animals.

Caedmon left the mead-hall when asked by others to sing because he said he could not do so. He felt shame and he left. He went to sleep with the animals in the stable and there he dreamed a dream.

There is a certain color in the cheeks that cannot be hidden when you feel the shame in having no song but only silence.

> When he there at a suitable time set his limbs at rest and
> fell asleep, then some man stood by him in his dream and
> hailed and greeted him and addressed him by his name:
> 'Caedmon, sing me something.' Then he answered and said:
> 'I do not know how to sing and for that reason I went out
> from this feast and went hither, because I did not know how
> to sing at all.' Again he said, he who was speaking with him:

'Nevertheless, you must sing.' Then he said: 'What must I sing?' Said he: 'Sing to me of the first Creation.'

"Now we must praise," Caedmon woke up singing.

But what I think about far more than the man in the dream, that angel or daemon who bestows the gift of song where none is known, more than the song itself which knows the imperative hidden inside song is praise, is the warmth of the animals, their bodies, and the scent of their fur in the straw. I think about their breathing which is its own praise, and needs no song to sing it, and as I drop the animals crowding the bed onto the floor so I can fall asleep, I wonder what song I've been asked to sing, I wonder why in the dark night I've left my own bed to go to the stable lit by the dimmest light, I wonder what dreams will come, and who in them will appear asking me to sing despite my protest that I have no song, none at all, that I'm nobody who has a song. I wonder what in the morning I'll say.

Who's making lunches? Who's dropping off the kids? Who's picking them up?

Is that a song. Is that a song of creation.

✦

In the late fourth century a chasm opened in the flat plane between the Palatine and the Capitoline in Rome. "For a long time the chasm remained thus, refusing to close at all or even to be filled, although the Romans brought and cast into it masses of earth and stones and all sorts of other material."

Some forms of emptiness can only be filled by emptiness, but how to do this work is a mystery.

Emily Dickinson:

> To fill a Gap
> Insert the Thing that caused it—
> Block it up
> With Other—and 'twill yawn the more—
> You cannot solder an Abyss
> With Air

Air can mean the element we breathe; it can also mean a feeling or sense, a song, or absence of anything, or nothing. Most of these meanings are archaic. They are buried inside the word.

When the gap opens by itself it's hard to know what caused it. Nothing seems to have been removed. Masses of earth and stones and all sorts of material only deepen the abyss.

Abyss, from the Greek, ἄβυσσος: "with no bottom, bottomless."

In this sense a sheet of paper is an abyss.

Also: "unfathomed, boundless, the great deep, the infinite void."

"In the midst of their uncertainty an oracle was given them to the effect that the aperture could in no wise be closed unless they threw into the chasm their best possession and that which was the chief source of their strength; in this way the prodigy would cease." The obscurity of the oracle proved paralyzing until a young patrician, Marcus Curtius, came forward, saying,

> Why, Romans, do we blame the obscurity of the oracle
> rather than our own ignorance? We are this thing sought and
> debated. For nothing lifeless is to be accounted better than

that which has life, nor shall that which is uncomprehending, speechless, and senseless be preferred to that which has comprehension and sense and the adornment of speech. . . . For, if I may speak somewhat boldly, man is naught else but a god with a mortal body, and a god naught else than a man without a body and therefore immortal; and we are not far removed from divine power.

So saying, he put on his armor, mounted his horse, and rode into the chasm which closed behind him, neither hero nor gap ever to be seen again.

Iris is scared of the dark. She has dreams in the dark and she's scared of the dark and of those dreams, who in the dark might arrive and tell her to sing. The carpet beneath her bed is a dark green and in the night looks black and deep.

One by one I drop the animals into the gap, but none of them is living, and the gap won't close. I know the sacrifice isn't right. But every time I step into the abyss my foot meets solid ground, and I walk out of the room, down the stairs, to the kitchen where the coffee has turned itself on, and where I spend an hour, before the family wakes, Iris in my own bed, reading Dio Cassius's *Roman History*.

I guess I mean to say that the oracle is dark to me. The hole won't let me in. The command is loud, but hard to obey.

The song must begin in ignorance. Nobody knows the song.

18.

Socrates on the day he is to die running his hand through Phaedo's golden hair.

How to imagine it so fully as to feel it. The boy's hair in my hand; or, the man's hand worrying though my hair. What do I want to feel.

He's talking about the immortality of the soul.

He says that all his life he's had a repeating dream. In it a voice speaks and tells him to *make music*. Thinking philosophy the best of all music, he spoke to men and listened to their answers, making of ignorance found a truer melody, one maybe only the gods could hear.

But now, in these days leading up to his death, that oblivion now only hours away, he wonders if he has obeyed the command given to him night after night. Has he made the right music? Has he sung the song?

Maybe all the words have ended up being silence. He doesn't know. Maybe all the words fell into the ignorance they emerged from. Maybe *I guess I don't know* isn't a song.

And so, every day in his prison cell, he has composed poems about animals for children to hear, and hearing, to learn to sing along.

✦

One poem is about running your hand through the fur of a sleeping lion.

One poem is about a lion feeling a hand worry through its mane.

Some Scholiasts believe these two poems are one and the same. Others claim they were never written.

Phaedo, who alone might know, never told.

Omens

"To Carthage then I came, where there sang all around me in my ears a cauldron of unholy loves," writes Saint Augustine before he was a saint.

A strange and lovely phrase: *there sang all around me in my ears.*

A kind of omen, or so I've come to think it—a kind of description of an omen.

In Greek the word is ἡπατοσκοπία. It means *inspecting the liver.* What is most inner becomes most outer and then the future might be known. The blood flows through the body, whispering the secrets the liver cleanses it of, secrets that, like Augustine's song heard in Carthage, come first from the air itself, molecules adhering to the blood cells coursing past the lungs, turning red the blood that circulates the rumor through the body entire. Some augur comes to cut the abdomen open and read there in the entrails what is to be read. I might call it the creation of the mind. It has to learn to see itself outside of itself. It can't be kept a secret. It must spill out. Like a poem.

Of course, the augurs don't perform this action on themselves. Not like poets do.

✦

Maybe, more than teach us *what* to fear, they teach us *how* to do so. Maybe hope follows, or not. Nothing they warn of do they speak of plainly, those omens. They elicit the interpretation that in their obscurity they frustrate. In the silence we feel when we witness the omen, we learn something about quietness: that we cannot speak into the omen's speaking. So seldom is it charged with peace, that quiet. Often we call it *mystery*, by which we mean *helplessness*. We want a teacher, but none exists—or the ones who call themselves teachers we don't know how to wholly trust. Instead of a teacher we get an empty space. It floats in the head or above it. *Fill me up*, it says. But we don't know how to fill it. Or it's just a banner with a headline scrolling past on the nightly news. The Dow Jones Industrial Report. Or the Sphinx with a riddle made just for you.

✦

Throughout their history the Romans took note of the omens that worried them. It begins at the beginning:

> . . . landed near Laurentum, called also Troy, near the river
> Numicius, along with his son by Creusa—Ascanius or Ilus.
> There his followers ate their tables, which were of parsley or
> of the harder portions of bread loaves; for they had no real
> tables. Furthermore, a white sow leaped from his boat and
> running to the Alban mount, named after her, gave birth to
> a litter of thirty, which indicated that in the thirtieth year
> his children should get fuller possession of both land and
> sovereignty. Since he had heard of these portents beforehand
> from an oracle he ceased his wandering, sacrificed the sow,
> and prepared to found a city.

I guess some oracles predict omens, and if this happens to you, as it happened to Aeneas, then you're always on the lookout lest, in missing the sign, Rome never gets founded.

Not that he knew.

Alba is the city he founds. It is the mother of Rome. Rome is founded by Romulus. His mother was a wolf.

Another, of Lucius Tarquinius:

"When Tullius had at length reached boyhood he went to sleep on a chair once in the daytime and a quantity of fire seemed to leap forth from his head. Tarquinius, seeing it, took a lively interest in the boy."

And of Tarquin, Lucius's son or grandson, whose tyranny ended the reign of kings in Rome:

Once the Sibyl came to Tarquin carrying many books "gifted with divine inspiration" and offering to sell them at a high price. When Tarquin refused she burned some of them and offered what remained at the same price. When he declined to purchase them again she burned more and offered what remained for the same price as before. Impressed by her audacity, he bought the few books that remained for the cost of what it would have been to buy them all in the first place. Though no one could understand the contents of the pages, many men came to read them to glimpse the truth of what they held. One man copied out some pages for his own use, and when this deed was found out, Tarquin thrust the man between "two hides sewn together and drowned, in order that neither earth nor water nor sun might be defiled by his death." They killed the man who copied from the ominous books by making him into a book, binding him between covers. The death between those covers wouldn't contaminate the world. Afterward, this punishment became standard for those who committed parricide. The copied word is the child of the original, τόκος to λόγος, a token of the first power, and it steals the force that doesn't belong to it. Just as a child does when he kills his own father. He pretends his pages are the first ones.

Sometimes it seems safer to write down nothing at all. I wonder, writing about omens, if the quotes around all these words that are not mine, words copied from other books, will exculpate me from my guilt in copying them down.

And more of Tarquin:

"Out of his garden vultures drove the young of eagles, and in the men's hall, where he was having a banquet with his friends, a huge serpent appeared and drove him and his companions from the table. . . . But as Apollo declared that he should be driven from his domain only when a dog should use human speech, he was inspired with confident hope, thinking the oracle could never be fulfilled."

Omens abound when Rome by her enemies is threatened:

"On the Capitol blood is reported to have issued for three days from the altar of Jupiter, also honey on one day and milk on another—if anybody can believe it; and in the Forum a bronze statue of Victory set upon a stone pedestal was found standing on the ground below, without anyone's having moved it; and, as it happened, it was facing in that direction from which the Gauls were already approaching."

"Meanwhile portents had occurred which threw the people of Rome into great fear. A river in Picenum ran the colour of blood, in Etruria a good part of the heavens seemed to be on fire, at Ariminum a light like the day blazed out at night, in many portions of Italy three moons became visible in the night time, and in the Forum a vulture perched for several days."

Even in the midst of battle, eyes stay lively for omens:

"Meanwhile a wolf in pursuit of a hind entered the space between the two armies, and darting toward the Romans, passed through their ranks. This encouraged them, for they looked upon him as belonging to themselves, since, according to tradition, a she-wolf had reared Romulus."

But my favorite omens emanate from the Punic Wars. The truer the threat, and Hannibal—who, not taking advantage of a battle won in which he could have overrun Rome, spends the rest of his life lamenting the error, chanting to himself, *O Cannae, Cannae!*—seemed a god of threat himself, the wilder the form an omen takes:

> Now Heaven had indicated beforehand what was to come
> to pass. For in Rome an ox talked with a human voice, and
> another at the Ludi Romani hurled himself out of a house
> into the Tiber and perished, many thunderbolts fell, and
> blood in one case was seen issuing from sacred statues,
> whereas in another it dripped from the shield of a soldier, and
> the sword of another soldier was carried off by a wolf from
> the very midst of the camp. And in the case of Hannibal,
> many unknown wild beasts went before him leading the way,
> as he was crossing the Iberus, and a vision appeared to him in
> a dream. He thought once that the gods, sitting in assembly,
> sent for him and bade him march with all speed to Italy and
> receive from them a guide for the way, and that by this guide
> he was commanded to follow without turning around. He
> did turn, however, and saw a great tempest moving along and
> an immense serpent following in its wake.

Other examples:

"A hermaphrodite lamb was born, and a swarm of . . . was seen, two serpents glided under the doors of the temple of Capitoline Jupiter, the doors as well as the altar in the temple of Neptune ran with copious sweat, in Antium bloody ears were seen by some reapers, elsewhere a woman with horns appeared and many thunderbolts . . . into temples . . ."

Plutarch records "that shields sweated blood, that ears of corn were cut at Antium with blood upon them, that blazing, fiery stones fell from on high, and that the people of Falerii saw the heavens open and many tablets fall down and scatter themselves abroad, and that on one of these was written in letters plain to see, 'Mars now brandisheth his weapons.'"

Lastly, and oddly, a favorite, after the death of Scipio Africanus:

"And this in particular seems to me to have been the meaning of the mass of stones that had poured down from heaven, falling upon some of the temples and killing men, and of the tears of Apollo. For the god had wept for three days, so that the Romans on the advice of the soothsayers voted to hew the statue in pieces to sink it in the sea."

✦

The ocean that is made of tears and in its grieving wears the stone away.

The god of prophecy crying while the stonecutters cut him limb from limb to throw the severed stones into the sea.

Some fear far above the clouds. That there is a weight there waiting to fall. That the gods etch in clouds as on stones the messages that might rain down. That a tempest rains down a library. That a book cracks open a head.

Is it omen when the world begins to speak for itself, long weary of being spoken of or for. The passive voice refuses its position. The accusative wants to accuse. That old contract by which the names name the things of the world rests on a secret agreement that those things keep silent. But then a shield begins to bleed, a statue cry, a vulture presides over Law, and language doesn't work the right way anymore. It doesn't describe what it names. It does different work. It beseeches. Then the words that come out our mouths beg the things we name to tell us what they mean.

A child in the moonlight looking up at the moon cups her hands around her ears.

O Cannae, Cannae!

There sings all around me in my ears the song I cannot listen to hear.

20.

Iris once told me that we have to close our eyes at night when we go to sleep so that the darkness doesn't get in our heads.

I said, "But when we close our eyes it's dark."

"That's a different kind of dark, Daddy. Everyone knows that."

✦

Hana when she was only two, putting her to bed for the night, rocking her to sleep, says with her eyes closed, already in dream: "A cricket in the desert, a cricket in the desert."

Now she puts her headphones on and closes her eyes; no one else can hear the cricket's song.

Some Animal Poems for Children to Learn and Sing

The Golden Age

Then the animals could talk in words.
    The sparrow to the farmer sang
and the farmer sang along,
    the pine and the laurel counseled

the honey in its tomb to sing a tune,
    and the bees agreed with the deities
that the flowers perfumed the muse
    and made prophecy the deeper root.

✦

The Lion and the Bow

The fox pulled the arrow out
    from the lion's belly,
and told him to feel no fear.
    "If this messenger stung you,
Fox, as it stung me, you'd see
    courage snares the heart,
binds the foot, blinds the eye.
    Better to live in the lonely glen
than be a brave fool and die."

✦

The Net and the Fish

The big ones stay in
    and the little ones swim,

what's glory in a frying-pan
    compared to the living fin?

✦

The Horse and the Ass

The burden you refuse
    becomes the weight you bear,
the horse that scorned the ass
    wears the whole pack
he refused to share.

✦

The Fox on Fire

To punish the thief of the vines,
    the farmer dipped in tallow the tail
and lit it on fire. But the fox in his fear
    ran straight through the fields.
Now the threshing floor has no piled grain,
    and the crop is cinder and ash.

✦

The Nightingale and the Swallow

By singing in the dark the same song
    They recognized each other—
The nightingale and the swallow.
    "Come live with me under the eaves
and lessen with song the load of men
    who till the earth to live." "My song

is a torment I sing alone, the desert rock
    echoes it, and the morning dew that cures
thirst is now my humble home."

✦

Some poems of Sappho's found in the winding cloth around the body
found in the sarcophagus. A poem of Catallus's printed on thick vellum found, claret-stained, plugging the bunghole of a tun of wine.
Ancient manuscripts discovered in bookshelves kept in tombs, reading
for the afterlife, there with the jars of sealed honey and the mirrors of
polished bronze.

Bees used to be thought psychopomps, traveling between the living
and dead, gathering pollen, dancing their dances, and if you put a
poem up next to your ear and wait patiently, sometimes you can hear
in it the whole hive still buzzing.

Maybe, maybe not. Maybe that's a lie.

These poems were found in a cell with a bench carved from the same
stone that formed the walls. You can imagine the cell as a single chamber of a honeycomb, hexagonal, scented by honey that left, like tears,
traces where down the wall it dripped. Outside the cell was Law—
where Law used to be. There they sentenced a man to death for creating new gods and corrupting the youth. He wrote poems to pass the
time, and these poems are those, here for the first time printed. All the
casual reader won't be able to appreciate is the paper itself the poems
were written on. Dark gray and the ink barely darker. And, held up to
the light, a faint watermark drawn by hand of a bee in flight.

Grave Work

Ignorance not enough, but to be aware of ignorance without ending it. To know that you do not know. Can it be more than a riddle? To know and also not know what you know. To live within it as one would live within a plot. I don't mean a narrative. I mean a small space just big enough for your body, a square of grass, a grave.

As a child I helped my grandfather tend the graves. The pinecones fell from the trees he'd planted with his grandfather, and though half lamed by polio, he and I would walk the outer edge of the cemetery picking up the cones and throwing them in the dented metal pail. The oldest stone belongs to General John Cantine, who kept his eye on the Iroquois nation during the Revolutionary War. The land was deeded to him as a governmental thanks. Almost effaced from the stone, the date remains legible: 1806. Behind the stones of all the veterans I placed small American flags for Memorial Day and the Day of Independence. It's how I got to know some of the dead. Others I knew because one day I would join them. The Quick plot, a column carved on each of its four sides, including poor Lettie, who died falling from a train as it went into a tunnel on the way to New York City. She wanted to see the inauguration of the Statue of Liberty. No one knows if she jumped or if she was pushed. She just "fell."

Fell into a different liberty than she might have imagined. Liberty beneath the ground.

> *Fell from an*
> *Excursion train to NY*
> * & was killed at*
> *Musconetcong tunnel*
>
> *Oct. 25, 1886*

I'd look at the stone and think, *Here I am, here's my land.*

Robert Pogue Harrison writes: "Let me put forward a premise here to the effect that humanity is not a species (*Homo sapiens* is a species); it is a way of being mortal and relating to the dead. To be human means above all to bury." He goes on to quote from Vico's *New Science*: "*Humanitas* in Latin comes first and properly from *humando*, burying." We become human by maintaining our relation not to death, but to the dead whose fortune it is to be located in death. Maybe that's not right. Death doesn't have a place, and so we must make one for it. All you need is a shovel, and some dirt. Some fire, and a box. Anything hollow can be an urn. Even your cupped hands for a little while will do. Until they have to learn to bury themselves.

Thoreau writes: "My instinct tells me that my head is an organ for burrowing, as some creatures use their snout and fore-paws, and with it I would mine and burrow my way through these hills." Let his instinct suggest that the head is a tool for digging, and that one of the more unexpected results of thinking hard is that you've dug a grave on the page that may or may not be your own.

We don't know exactly who it is we're digging the grave for. There's just the command singing in the air: *dig.*

Celan: "There was earth in them and they dug."

Imagine the blank page is the world entire, a kind of wilderness, none of it legible. The poem makes a place by digging a grave in that nothingness, and the words keep buried within them the breathing silence and the names of things to which they are also memorial. Or is the poem a kind of cenotaph naming the names of those beings and things that drift back out past the border of the spoken world and get lost again in the depthless depth of the margin. We say the words because we don't know where the lost are lost. We don't know how to be lost with them.

The ocean? But the ocean is just a page thick.

Witnesslessness is a word I've made up to describe a certain kind of human condition. Though English has none, it must be heard with the quality of the *middle voice*. It is a condition that is active and passive at once.

That's why I feel so hollow sometimes, digging with my fingers in the blankness.

"The dead body will not bear witness to that," replies Antigone, to Creon's claim that in burying the brother, Polynices, who had just killed her other brother, Etiocles, she has committed an act of impiety. In Sophocles, Creon's language is vague, but direct, trying to tease out quickly the nature of the error: "You bestow a grace that is impious." I didn't know grace worked that way. Sometimes ethics seems concerned with doing what is right in difficult situations. At other times it feels more basic: How do I stay human?

Keep burying.

The dead body is no witness to impiety. It is no witness at all. It can't see, so we must see for it. We must put it in the ground and remember the place. Must make the ground a place by putting the body in it. It is the dead that bury the dead. By being within our mortality we do this digging. By becoming one who dies we tend the dead. By seeing that we are dying. By seeing ourselves as they would see us, the dead.

Some say the first houses were built upon graves, and the first cities upon those houses. Some say in the Neolithic Age the earliest Europeans looked at the oaken markers built above the bodies of their ancestors and said, *Here I am, here is my land.*

The philosopher Thales of Miletus, who believed water the source of all being, asked, at the end of his life, to be buried in "an obscure and neglected corner of the city's territory." But he had predicted that one day that plot of weird land would be the marketplace of Miletus, place of every economy—discourse of exchange philosophic, poetic, commercial—from οἰκία and νόμος, the "habits of home."

After the destruction of Troy, Aeneas travels with those who survive, bringing with them the ancestral gods, in search of new homeland. He carries the living with him; he carries also the dead who keep the living human. To say they are searching for a new home is also to say they are looking for a new place to bury themselves. So begins Rome. In the tumult of their voyage, Palinurus, a navigator well known for his expertise in a storm, is blown overboard not by mischance, but by the will of the gods who are seeking a sacrifice of one to save the many. Aeneas thought Palinurus simply failed, until he finds him in the underworld. Then he learns the whole story. Fulfilling Apollo's prophecy, Palinurus did not die by drowning but survived in the ocean and washed ashore. There the natives ran him through with a sword, and now his body lies in the strand, buffeted onto the land by the strength of the same waves that, in withdrawing, pull him back into the sea. His is an unquiet grave. He's homeless, and even the dead want a home. He begs Aeneas, the ghost of him begs for the hero's hand to guide him across the Stygian marsh: "Let me at least in death find quiet haven." But the Sybil refuses the transport. "Would you though still unburied see the Styx / And the grim river of the Eumenides, / or even the river bank, without a summons?" To hear that call even the dead must be at home. She tells him to be patient. Be patient, ghost. Many will come to appease your bones, "building a tomb and making offerings there / on a cape forever named for Palinurus." Eventually his body will be buried and the wild in which now the sea roils his broken body will be named after him. No longer will his name point to a person, but a place, a land, a location. Then the blessings asked for can be granted, when the person succumbs to that larger fate, not to have had a life one lived, but to become a place where others do their living.

These blessings aren't exactly one's own.

But it is his plea to Aeneas I hear echo most often in my head: "Throw earth on me."

According to Daniel Heller-Roazen, "the earliest surviving alphabetic texts of classical Antiquity consist not of literary works or economic inscriptions . . . but of graffiti and funeral inscriptions commemorating and recalling the dead." For example he notes that "on a Theban object from the eighth century B.C., for instance, one finds an inscription that reads, 'I am the kylix of Korakos'; and on memorials from the same period, one encounters such phrases as 'Eumares built me as a monument,' or, more striking still, 'I am the commemoration (μνῆμα) of Glaukos.'"

The history of saying *I* might be far different than typically we assume. So easy to think the first-person pronoun refers to the livingness of the life of which it speaks, but maybe not. Saying *I*, more properly heard, isn't heard at all. It's found carved on a stone, or on the pedestal of the image that points in its odd way at the life that has gone missing below the ground. Μνῆμα meaning "a memorial, remembrance, memory" and "a mound or building in honor of the dead" relates to μνήμα, difference being only in the stress the first vowel carries, meaning "memory as a power of the mind." Memory must bear within it the fact of what yet hasn't happened, it remembers while living that it has already died, and so works as an oracle works—by looking behind, it predicts the future. In saying *I* we speak from within the grave; or is it the grave speaks for us, because we cannot speak for ourselves, even as the words are coming out of our mouths, somehow it is not we who are saying them.

Heller-Roazen goes on to mention the etymology for *I* proposed by Karl Brugmann: "the Greek term *ego*, as well as its Indo-European relations, derives from a neuter noun (**eg[h]om*), meaning simply 'here-ness.'" No claim of an inner life in saying *I*, the word functions originally in claiming not a place *for* the self, but in claiming the self *as* a place.

Who am I? I am who is here.

The grave can speak it just as well as I can. The stone says *I am the memory of myself.* But the memory lives so much longer than the life. It points at what is departing, a kind of elsewhere that I am, an elsewhere that is me. I live it so I cannot see it.

Witnesslessness.

For a long time as a child I thought of the Quick Cemetery without reflecting on it. Later it seemed a kind of joke—cemetery filled not with the dead, but the living. But now I see there is no truer name for a cemetery. It is there where whatever living is goes on past the lives that lived it. There in the ground where memory builds her house, and the letter *I* points down at the ground and at the same time gives this gentle advice to look up at the passing clouds.

23.

In the Paleolithic Age humans begin the work of representation. What they hunt and what hunts them, bird-headed shamans, mastodons, bulls, horses, all appear, and often with great subtlety of form, on the walls of the caves. I like to think they painted the images in the mind that only later we'd find to be our own. There is little evidence that the men and women who made these images lived in the caves where they painted. Life seemed to happen elsewhere. The images lived in the cave alone.

More than the animals, more than the occasional geometric pattern, what fascinates me most are the portraits of humans themselves. The portraits aren't of faces.

Lovely when the anonymous reveals itself as the intimate, when identity isn't a marker of unique self, but the self that here occurred. Not the recognition of a face, but the fact of a hand.

More moving still, these hands weren't painted onto the rock. Mixing ochre or soot with water and putting it in the mouth, the artist put his hand on the stone and spat out the ink that would mark his presence not by painting it in, but by leaving it absent.

The hand that made this silhouette has gone missing, and only its absence remains. It exists by showing forth its own being forgotten, ghost-figure pointing back at the body that made it, its own absence most profound predictor of each human's common fate, that against all time for most of it we have been missing.

Might it be true to say that the hand is a truer portrait of humanity than the face could ever be? That I grope my way toward being long before I open my eyes to the light in it? That the face can only stare out at the one approaching and through the nakedness of its own gaze say, *Thou Shalt Not Kill,* knowing all the while that being killed is what happens to a face, by other hands, or by one's own, or by the hand of time.

Or it's simpler, less violent, less dark. To be human is to be a made-thing, and the hand is the tool of our making.

I mean to say I cannot see my own face.

But I can see my hand.

Maybe that's the first thought.

This hand I'm holding in front of me is me. Impossible to tell by looking at the images of the hands in the caves if they were held palm out or palm against the rock.

I'd like to say palm out.

Then the palm is the first mirror. It goes missing when you make a fist or when you die. To paint it is to make it go missing before you go missing yourself. I can't tell if it offers a welcome or a warning, greeting of the upheld hand or command to stop, if it says stay back, back from this rock wall; or if it says the opposite, come, come, walk into the stone and find out how there to make your next home.

✦

William Wordsworth, in another effort at portraiture of the human, questions: "I ask what is meant by the word Poet? What is a Poet?" In ancient Greek, *poet* comes from the verb "to make, to do." Word of the hand more than the mouth. The poet is a hand that acts like a face: it speaks, it thinks. He goes on:

He has added a disposition to be affected more than other men by absent things as if they were present; an ability of conjuring up in himself passions, which are indeed far from being the same as those produced by real events, yet (especially in those parts of the general sympathy which are pleasing and delightful) do more nearly resemble the passions produced by real events, than anything which, from the motions of their own minds merely, other men are accustomed to feel in themselves:—whence, and from practice, he has acquired a greater readiness and power in expressing what he thinks and feels, and especially those thoughts and feelings which, by his own choice, or from the structure of his own mind, arise in him without immediate external excitement.

Deep in the riddle the poet lives, where absence is present and presence grows absent.

Maybe it's like holding water or sand in cupped hands; maybe it's like holding ink in the mouth, wondering whether to swallow or to spit it out.

24.

Wondering why my mind keeps turning back to ancient history when all I want to do is dwell here in my life. I guess I don't know what my life is, don't know what the horizon is. In every direction that border-line retreats with every step I take. But *step* isn't a true word. I'm not moving at all. Just quiet in a chair, thinking silently to myself. Is that life.

I might say life is what persists through time. It has a duration, and to become an adult is to feel that duration as something both growing longer and diminishing, growing heavier and turning daily into almost nothing. It's like a word in a sentence grown aware of itself, hearing faintly the echo of those words already said and dimly perceiving that more words are to come, single part of the meaning no single word can hold, just as a day is made possible only by all the days already lived, and this day will drift away into those to come which would not exist without this one, and these moments that seem to be the ones in which we live abandon themselves before we realize we too have been left almost behind.

But I might say other things. Or life might speak better for itself.

It's hard to keep up; memory keeps looking backward. Love, or is it fear, or is it hope keeps peering ahead. Or maybe I have it wrong, and love looks both ways at once, into the past and into the future; or maybe I'm wrong again, and love like the bashful youth looks down at her feet in the grass; or is it love looks you in the eye. I don't know.

Poor words.

✦

Numa was the second king of Rome, born on the same day the city he would rule had been founded. They came into the world together.

It is said he knew Pythagoras and so followed the inner laws of silence.

After his mortal wife passed away he wandered the fields and in the quiet grasses a goddess consorted with him. Some deny this is true. They don't believe a deity would make love to a human being. But almost every day he wandered into the meadows.

Maybe the calm was erotic. Maybe the grasses bending over in the wind.

He put at peace the warlike ways of the Romans. He instituted many religious observances.

Numa commended all to devote themselves to the Muses, giving special honors to one, a tenth Muse seldom mentioned, Tacita, the Muse of silence or speechlessness.

A temple in Rome kept open its doors as long as the country fought in war. During peace the doors were shut. Never had they been closed until Numa ruled. No step stepped into that temple for forty-three years.

Then the shrine was silent, or silence was its prayer.

Tacita might be the Muse of such peace.

Before he died he had two stone coffins made. Into one his body was placed, and into the other, the books on which he'd written his laws. He didn't want those words to go on speaking without him, and if anyone wanted to recall what he'd said, they'd have to remember, and speak it for themselves.

Books are also bodies to bury.

Like you could bury your breath after having finally breathed out all of it.

＋

So my mornings pass. Iris in bed with Kristy and both still asleep. A blue jay sings its metal song outside the window and the song stops. Hana is flying right now over the Pacific Ocean, and there's a house finch on the needles of the pine.

I want to learn to pay attention without paying any mind.

Perform the rituals to honor the Muse of speechlessness.

Close the doors of this temple. Shut my eyes on this peace.

25.

"otototototoi" "feu feu" "ouai ouai" "otototototoi"

Such are some of the words used in ancient Greek to express mourning. Mostly, we don't know how to hear them. The awful music of their ululation. Most translate them as "Alas! Woe is me!"

Words no one says when grief-struck. No one says, "Alas! Woe is me!"

"otototototoi" "feu feu" "ouai ouai" "otototototoi"

✦

Dylann Roof walks into the Emanuel AME Church in Charleston, South Carolina, and kills nine members of the prayer group.

That the word of his last name is a token of safety and shelter. His middle name is Storm.

He said he was "awakened" by typing into Google "black on White crime." I don't know what answer the oracle gave him or how he heard it. He wrote, "I have no choice."

That he is a storm underneath a roof.

That others took him in to pray with them.

That they opened their doors.

Don't speak the unspeakable things.

Let us pray the prayer to Tacita who keeps the doors of violence closed. Please don't open the doors.

26.

Solon—poet, philosopher, general, statesman, archon in sixth-century-BC Athens—so feared the nature of grief that he made laws to regulate mourning. "Laceration of the flesh by mourners, and the use of set lamentations, and the bewailing of any one at the funeral ceremonies of another, he forbade. The sacrifice of an ox at the grave was not permitted, nor the burial with the dead of more than three changes of raiment, nor the visiting of other tombs than those of their own family, except at the time of internment."

"Alas! Woe is me!" becomes the standard expression of grief in Greek tragedy because the words themselves move beyond speech and no translation is possible. Like when a body moves beyond life. One might say it has translated itself by living into what life can no longer be; and so of the words that try to describe the dilemma, they move through themselves and end up beyond the limits of their own utterance.

Some say laws restricted mourning to stop the living from doing all they could to join the dead who have left them. That commitment to life continuing which society depends upon seems under threat when the mourner wants only to live inside the ground with the dead.

Or maybe it is that lamentation lets out that silence deep in words so that the words mean nothing; as if the blankness between words on a page, or the abyss between letters by which the word alone can be read overwhelms what's been written, and the manageable absence by which all that makes sense can be seen as sense becomes wild, flouts grammar, mocks definition, erodes orthography, and even the civil space of the page is undone into sympathy with death. Or like a blank page could insert itself in the continuity of a book and refuse to take part in anything that has been said. A reminder that the mind has its limits.

~~Ox at the grave.~~

I don't mean to break the law.

~~Otototototoi.~~

✦

Emerson writes,

> People grieve and bemoan themselves, but it is not half so
> bad with them as they say. There are moods in which we
> court suffering, in the hope that here, at least, we shall find
> reality, sharp peaks and edges of truth. But it turns out to
> be scene-painting and counterfeit. The only thing grief has
> taught me, is to know how shallow it is. That, like all the
> rest, plays about the surface, and never introduces me into
> the reality, for contact with which, we would even pay the
> costly price of sons and lovers. Was it Boscovich who found
> out that bodies never come in contact? Well, souls never
> touch their objects. An innavigable sea washes with silent
> waves between us and the things we aim at and converse
> with. Grief too will make us idealists. In the death of my
> son, now more than two years ago, I seem to have lost a
> beautiful estate,—no more. I cannot get it nearer to me.
> If tomorrow I should be informed of the bankruptcy of
> my principal debtors, the loss of my property would be a
> great inconvenience to me, perhaps, for many years; but it
> would leave me as it found me,—neither better nor worse.
> So is it with this calamity: it does not touch me: some thing
> which I fancied was a part of me, which could not be torn
> away without tearing me, nor enlarged without enriching
> me, falls off from me, and leaves no scar. It was caducous.

> I grieve that grief can teach me nothing, nor carry me one
> step into real nature.

He was a man, it must be remembered, who, when younger, bereaved by the death of his first wife, Ellen, and visited by dreams in which she still breathed, became so convinced that somehow she still lived that he ran to the cemetery carrying a shovel and dug her grave up. But she had died and was still dead. That fact was real. And he carried the shovel home.

Older, of grief he says, "It does not touch me." What he grieves is that he cannot feel grief, that it brings him no closer to the reality of the world, and what he hears, instead of the ritual lamentation tearing sense into meaningless dark rags, are those silent waves that wash between us and all the things we love. *Feu feu feu*, he doesn't say; he doesn't say "Alas!"

Herman Melville had a word for those of us who feel this thing we have is a life: *Isolatos*.

What's strange is that we discover so late that our life might be real; it's not happy. We feel the silence around us and suspect everyone with whom we converse exists in the same quiet.

Their silence is as real to them as mine is to me.

I guess what Emerson dug up when he exhumed Ellen's body was her silence, and he kept it with him as one might keep a lock of hair in a box or a locket. Some say the hair of corpses keeps on growing in the grave, but I think that's a rumor. But silence does. He didn't even know he had kept it with him, that silence between the living and the dead that, once your life is real to you, means you are mortal too, and within life itself lurk those silent waters—of old called the river Styx—that keep separate life from death. You cannot shout from one shore to another, even if the river is not wide, even if it's thin as a thread or a vein, you cannot shout across it. The far strand is a distance contained within, and what is inside us, we cannot traverse.

I mean to say, I cannot get across myself.

Ellen's last words: "I have not forgot the peace and joy."

Digestion

They call out demanding back the blood that once ran through their veins, those heroes, our ancestors. Some who heard those laments would dig a hole and pour in the blood. Others made the simplest oaten cakes, no yeast by which to rise, and buried them for the dead to eat. I guess you die and keep wanting all you always wanted, but can get none of it for yourself, like a child in a crib calling out in the night to her parents, save it's the parents who are in the crib, and the crib is underground, and something more than water is wanted, and it's worse.

Poor Tantalus who deserved exactly what he got, bending down to drink from the river but the river goes away, reaching up to the fruit-heavy bough but the branch rises up past grasp. Only when Orpheus descends into the underworld playing his lyre and singing, searching for his lost wife just wed, can Tantalus eat for the fruit stays at hand, can drink for the water doesn't move, but so taken is he by the music played by a living hand, by the words sung out from a living mouth, that he doesn't realize that fate has for a brief moment been suspended, that he can put to an end the hunger and thirst that are his eternal torment—except that, after just a little while, when the music went away, he'd hunger and thirst again.

It's hard to know what kind of reprieve music is. It makes us forget our needs; it doesn't remove us from them. The baby's mobile plays a tune in the dark.

It worked out for Orpheus, but it didn't work out well, desire and song.

To pour blood in a hole in the ground or to put there a cake made from the gathered acorns were *sacrifices of aversion.*

Properly performed, the dead for a while would leave us alone—until they want again what all they want. The world, for example. Theirs is a silent call we cannot not hear, singing in our blood and not our ears, for our blood was first their own, and they keep reminding us that we owe them the life they gave up to give us our own. They want to eat it.

✦

According to Vico, quoted at length by Robert Pogue Harrison, the Latin word for law, *lex,*

> first . . . meant a collection of acorns. Thence we believe is derived *ilex,* as it were *illex,* the [holm] oak (as certainly *aquilex* means collector of waters); for the oak produces acorns by which the swine are drawn together. *Lex* was next a collection of vegetables, from which the latter were called *legumina.* Later on, at a time when vulgar letters had not yet been invented for writing down the laws, *lex* by a necessity of civil nature must have meant a collection of citizens, or the public parliament; so that the presence of the people was the *lex,* or 'law.' . . . Finally, collecting letters, and making, as it were, a sheaf of them for each word, was called *legere,* reading.

A book is but a gathering of acorns, and we fatten ourselves as do the swine, but reading is what sweetens the meat of the mind.

Eve takes a first bite from the same fruit she offers Adam, and by swallowing a mouthful of food they gain knowledge of their own nakedness, realize within a shame seen from without, they digest desire into knowledge, and what is wanted, once known, means the toil to come is in the dirt, far east of Eden, and paradise becomes just this empty lot. I guess they suddenly knew what they saw and the garden just withered away. In the off-hours to come, they'd try to describe it themselves, what they lost.

Harrison goes back further to the Greek λόγος. He tries to begin at the beginning. The word before the world. He says that certain linguists suggest that the word derives from the Proto-Indo-European root *leg*, "which meant 'to gather, to collect, to bind together'" as one might gather a sheaf of grain or pages.

John Keats, during the refulgent months of spring to fall in 1819, writes the six odes that make him immortal. I don't use the word lightly. He finishes "To Autumn" in September and then begins that other human business of dying. Digging your own grave inside your life is hard work, like working in an hourglass trying to dig a hole in the sand as it sifts away, and though a wiser person might remind you that the sand is falling down below and gathering there, you know you cannot believe it, for the bottom becomes so suddenly the top, and the unseen hand that governs all mocks the work it demands.

But maybe the hourglass is a granary, and the sand is grain. Keats's second stanza:

> Who hath not seen thee oft amid thy store?
>> Sometimes whoever seeks abroad may find
> Thee sitting careless on a granary floor,
>> Thy hair soft-lifted by the winnowing wind;
> Or on a half-reap'd furrow sound asleep,
>> Drows'd with the fume of poppies, while thy hook
>> Spares the next swath and all its twined flowers:
> And sometimes like a gleaner thou dost keep
>> Steady thy laden head across a brook;
>> Or by a cyder-press, with patient look,
>> Thou watchest the last oozings hours by hours.

She runs her hand through her own hair, the goddess, though her hand is but the winnowing wind, letting the chaff fly away, letting the seeds drop so carelessly one might think, seeing her, that of abundance there is no end. Or the goddess falls asleep, caught by the poppy-scent of the flowers she harvests, dreaming deep in the half-reaped row. So easy to think that death comes because there is no more of life, but Keats knows it's not true. It's still all there to put in our mouths, the grain, the fruit, the honey in the comb, and how is it we disappear in the midst of world overbrimming, and become ourselves the little nothing in the center of the seed. The midges blown apart by the wind fly back together into their cloudy shape, and the swallows twitter their song of departure, their migration song, which some below can hear though they cannot follow.

We forget how to gather what it is we want to eat, forget the laws we know, and become ourselves poor Ruth amid the alien corn, gleaning behind the reapers.

Morning as homonym to mourning.

And I've sown these pages with words just to make silence more heard, but I don't know how to gather the gatherless grain, if it's even there, blank inside the blank, so much of whiteness, if it even exists, that silent grain.

✦

In 1917 Marcel Duchamp chooses a urinal, turns it upside down, signs it R. Mutt, and turns it into an art exposition whose policy is to accept every work submitted. They reject his *Fountain* and he resigns from the board.

People think of *Fountain* as if it were a kind of joke, but I don't think so. I think it's a work of Law.

Sometimes the thing has to stare you in the face for you to know it's as concerned with knowing what you are as you are with knowing it. That's how I learned I'm the fountain, and so are you.

I drink a glass of water, some coffee, a beer, and sometime later, I'm a fountain.

I gather into myself the things that feed me; only some of them are food. I read book after book, poem after poem, and sometime later, I write a book, I write a poem. But it's never quite right, those books, those poems, those fountainings.

It's as if you glimpse a land of such abundance the bees themselves think summer will never cease and then you fall asleep while gathering the blossoms and leave the grain to winnow itself, which it will, as also it will winnow those who slumber through the harvest. You see that land as if through a window in the air and think: now I can describe it. But what comes to the page is but a vestige of that supernal vision, and what inspired has fed the imaginative vein pulsing in the head and heart, but hasn't found a way out through the hand, and so the work must begin again. I thought I had the essence to sing; but all I made was this receptacle, turned upside down and signed R. Mutt, called a poem.

The thing we want to make stays silent within us, like the mouthful of fruit becoming the end of paradise, and we feel strange forms of shame in discussing what comes out.

Arthur Rimbaud: "La poesie c'est de la merde."

✦

Keats, one of the last poems he wrote before dying on February 23, 1821, at the age of twenty-five:

> This living hand, now warm and capable
> Of earnest grasping, would, if it were cold
> And in the icy silence of the tomb,
> So haunt thy days and chill thy dreaming nights
> That thou would wish thine own heart dry of blood
> So in my veins red life might stream again,
> And thou be conscience-calm'd—see here it is—
> I hold it towards you.

Do you hear, as I hear, the demand to pay our debt?

His hand wants the blood that flows in our veins, and should we give it, then our debt would be cancelled, if only briefly. The cost of his immortality burdens our conscience. I have to find a way to dig a hole in this page and fill the pitkin with blood.

But all I have are the gathered acorns of these sentences.

And I'm not sure if I've even dug a hole in the page. I can't quite see in the blankness if I've dug down in it far enough to pay my debt.

Tacita, hear my prayer: Keep the meat in the shell, the word in the poem, the marrow in the bone. Bury all this silence in the ground. The dead want to eat it.

Monadisms

G. W. Leibniz writes: "*The monad* which we shall discuss is nothing other than a simple substance that enters into composites. Simple means without parts." To think of the word as a monad.

The line of the poem is a composite of many monads in a row. That we read in one direction is an accident of our nature and no fault of the poem. Through different eyes—say, the compound eyes of the butterfly—the poem could be read in every direction, each word could be the beginning of the poem, no matter where it occurred, as it's a part of the whole, and just like the head feels the pleasure when your lover caresses your most hidden skin, so the word *singing* in the first line of the poem on page sixty-seven thrills through the whole song.

The monads look in every direction except within. They cannot see inside themselves. Everything there is dark. Each monad has a face that reflects all it sees, but its complexity is all within—there but unavailable.

Kind of like another monad I know.

The poem, like the world, is a plenum. That's only to say it is filled, like the world, exactly with itself.

To read a poem in a worldly sense we would need to be able to see how words in vastly different realms of the poem influence each other. We would read not for meaning, but for the harmony that holds the poem together in the same way harmony holds the universe together.

Meaning likes to look in only one direction. It is as base and baseless to ask of a poem what does it mean as it is to ask the same question of life.

Not what's the meaning, but where's the music?

But like the monad's complexity, the music is all within, hidden in the darkness, and the words show back to us on their mirrored surfaces an image we seem to know, of a face bending closer, and closer, to smell the flower or to read the poem.

Leibniz writes: "It is even necessary that every monad be different from every other. For there are never in nature two beings that are perfectly alike and in which it would not be possible to find difference that is internal or founded on an intrinsic denomination."

Leaves. Snowflakes. Petals. The pollen-combs on legs of bees. Hexagons of the hive.

Difference is spreading.

✦

So it may be, according to Jorge Luis Borges, that Pierre Menard—whose curious publishing history includes monographs on ideal words whose vocabulary only informs poetry, a monograph on Leibniz, and poetry most beautiful in its use of punctuation—wrote his most significant work. "This work, perhaps the most significant of our time, consists of the ninth and thirty-eighth chapters of the first part of *Don Quixote* and a fragment of chapter twenty-two." His effort wasn't to mimic Cervantes, nor merely to know seventeenth-century Spanish idiom so fluently as to write as if the other author himself. He wanted to write *Don Quixote* as Pierre Menard, and believed in the impossible vision that his own experience could lead him to the very same sentences. For example, Borges offers us a comparison from both books:

> It is a revelation to compare Menard's *Don Quixote* with
> Cervantes'. The latter, for example, wrote (part one, chapter
> nine): ". . . truth, whose mother is history, rival of time,

depository of deeds, witness of the past, exemplar and adviser to the present, and the future's counselor." Written in the seventeenth century, written by the "lay genius" Cervantes, this enumeration is a mere rhetorical praise of history. Menard, on the other hand, writes: ". . . truth, whose mother is history, rival of time, depository of deeds, witness of the past, exemplar and adviser to the present, and the future's counselor."

But might it not be that the very same words fill the plenum of a life in a very different manner. The same words, in the same order, but comprising a different world. So it may be that day passes into day, and though I wake up and feel I am the same man, and see my family and feel they are the same people to whom I said good night but some eight hours ago, I also admit to suspecting each of us slightly different than we had been, and this day yet to come, that will be like all that have passed, will fill itself with words that only pretend to mean what they have always meant, and I'll believe them, for it's easier than seeking out the truer vocabulary, in which each same word speaks itself differently.

Then Pierre Menard can write the *Quixote* word for word as Cervantes himself did, and yet, for all the obvious similarity, they are different. May I go on to suggest that the two *Quixote*s are different only to the degree to which they can be read as exactly the same? Only then do we train our ears to hear within sameness those subtlest strains of difference that make of living a life.

Mostly they're all the same, lives. And to praise as worthy only those men and women written down in the old books as unique proves a violence somehow, like tearing out of a poem a single word and saying, *See, this is the word, the only one needed*, and those small words, the pronouns and the articles, the *it* and *a* and *the* that alone in their inability to name things but merely point at words that name things offer us who read them, and regard their small syllables with something like love, our most accurate human portrait.

Now I'll share with you a poem I've been working on for some time. I haven't yet finished it, nor do I know how it begins, but like the grass of the field, it grows quickest from the middle out:

> . . . aelda barnum
> heben til hrofe   haleg scepen.
> tha middungeard   moncynnæs uard
> eci dryctin . . .

✦

And so too of memory, which in trying to recall clearly days long past so quietly alters them that we hardly notice the difference. We speak a memory as if in calling to mind the past the experience is retrieved intact, shareable to others just as it is repeatable to ourselves. But I guess it's not the case at all. Each time we tell a memory we change it by the telling, and from whatever humic chamber in the mind it is stored, we alter it by the effort of digging it up, and what is meant to be a testament to the ongoingness of experience in human life becomes instead the helpless fact that nothing repeats at all.

Gertrude Stein says, "There is no such thing as repetition. Only insistence." Mostly I agree.

But when I remember the quote it ends, *Only instances.*

Heraclitus: "Change alone is unchanging."

But when will it be that we, like those surveyors of arctic white seeking within sameness some sign of where the ice is weakest, or purveyors of blankness, or those peddlers on the Silk Road who by the color of white of the grains of salt know from what sea it came, or those Chinese scholars riding horseback across their vast country writing a monograph on how water tastes from various springs, wells, or ponds, find difference in what appears the same. For if Leibniz is right about words, perhaps the same insight applies everywhere, and between things of which we have no ability to sense alteration, profound differences exist: as in, say, the difference between the silence before a poem and after it, the white of the four margins, the emptiness in the center of the eye and the opened palm, the silence I keep and the silence I choke on, and all the other dizzying varieties of sameness, unspeakable as they are.

Pythagorean Silence

For Pythagoras, as for Leibniz, the primary unit is the monad. From it the dyad. Then numbers. Then points. Then lines, planes, figures. Then sensible bodies. Then fire, water, earth, and air each turning completely into the other. Then the intelligent sphere concerned with its own center.

It used to be that to have a thought you must first explain the world in which the thought occurs.

When I picture it I see a dandelion gone to seed before a breeze or a child's breath has broken apart the wish into a field.

Dawn is when the air is freshest; at night the atmosphere decays. The stars are gods; and the moon, so like and unlike a star, is a god also. Fire is the principle of life, and thought is no more than a starlike heat that happens in the head. The sun's rays penetrate to the depths of all things—the eye, the ocean, the leaf, the stone.

Pythagoras is said to call "the eyes the portals of the sun." He considers hearing and the other senses the same. We feel the sun on our skin; we eat the sun. The body is filled with the light by which we see.

At first the soul is bound by veins and sinews; later reason is its bond. The soul feeds on blood. It sits between the heart and the mind, casting through the body the winds of its pleasures.

When the body dies the soul wanders through the air; so the whole sky is filled with souls called *geniuses* or *heroes*. These are they that send us our dreams, but send them also to the cattle in the pasture, the horse in the field, and the rabbit or the poet in his burrow.

His father engraved gems, but Pythagoras counseled not to "put God's image on the circle of a ring."

He would eat no meat, for all living things have souls. He refused to let his followers eat the crumbs that from the table fell, for those morsels feed the heroes who live beneath the floorboards. He ate no beans, some say because they create flatulence which shames the virtuous harmony of the body, but others claim he abstained "because they are like genitals, or because they are like the gates of Hades . . . as being alone unjointed, or because they are injurious, or because they are like the form of the universe."

Lifetimes ago, given by Hermes the choice of any gift save that of immortality, he asked to "retain through life and through death a memory of his experiences." No detail of his life escaped him, and when life itself escaped, the memories of it kept living in him. Or is it truer to say that, like the nightingale in her song, he lived within his memories, memories which grew larger than his life. Once he was Euphorbus, and once Aethalides. Then his soul wandered into and out of plants and animals, wandered through the underworld. He became Hermotimus, Pyrrhus, and when Pyrrhus died—that fisherman who lived on the holy island of Delos—he became Pythagoras. Life not eternal, but the having lived it became so, life added to life and not a memory of any forgotten, from the details of the shield of Menelaus (beside whom he once fought), to the feel of sunlight pouring down on a leaf (when once he was a plant); and Hermes must have admired the trick, being a god himself who, no more than a day old, stole Apollo's sacred cattle and, sacrificing one, included his own name among the gods to whom he prayed. These tricks to become what you most want to be.

Coming home to Italy, he once dug himself a hole in the ground and lived in it, asking his mother to drop in notes describing all that passed in the days he went missing, and when he emerged, he looked like a skeleton, which makes sense, given he had been in Hades, reading to the shades the letters his mother sent him, so the dead could have again their portion of the day.

They say he died chased by a man not allowed the philosopher's company, a man who had set the house Pythagoras dined in on fire, and when the old philosopher ran out the door he came to a field of beans and refused to cross it. To step on it would have been to trespass into the universe, to trample on the world, to break some harmony. Or maybe to step through the gate of Hades. It's hard to say. The man caught him and cut his throat.

Maybe the field reminded him somehow that there is no escape from what chases you. Or maybe he remembered all that he remembered, all the lives, and so it was easy to let go of this one he had.

He counseled his followers: "Do not eat your own heart." Then the soul has no place to sit.

Walking with his students he saw a man about to beat a dog in the street, and he stepped quickly over, embraced it, and said, "I know this animal. I know his voice. I met him lifetimes ago when we were both men. We are friends. Don't hit him."

Those who wanted to learn his philosophy had to take vows of silence for five years. Nor could they see the man who taught them. He spoke from behind a curtain or a cloud, a wall or a mist, and the voice emerged from nowhere, as if the air itself were speaking, and the souls that in it dwell. If the students passed the examination after their vow of silence ended, they could study with the philosopher. It probably took some time for sounds to come again from their mouths.

I like to think of it as the silence between the letters of words, that novitiate vow. But in the poem you can observe your duty only by writing the words that make the silence present. You have to devote yourself to basic oppositions: black ink, white page.

Pythagoras was the first to say that the morning star and the evening star were the same.

It's easiest to do this work in silence—to see in difference what's the same.

Heraclitean Thirst

All things begin in fire and in fire end. All things have souls.

Dark exhalations of the earth, and bright from the sea, rise up into the sky where bowls with their concavities turned toward us collect them, and those bowls are stars, gathering the light and heat they pour back down upon us.

The moon too is a little bowl traveling across a path less pure. So its light is dimmer; so its light varies.

The sun is no larger than it appears. What is is what is. There is no more.

You can lean back in the long grass and cover up the sun with your toe.

✦

For fire to return to fire brings the cycle of a life to its close. It isn't a line, but a circle. Perhaps it is the work of every life, as Emily Dickinson says of her own, that our business "is Circumference." The circle ends where it begins, and makes of all that was said, all that was lived, some null set called zero in which silence regains its old supremacy, not as denial of life, but some reminder underneath the living of it, that it must end to begin, so that we arrive back at nothing.

✦

Heraclitus claims wisdom is not in listening to what he says, but in hearing the words that speak through him. He speaks to get out of the way of those words, and so speaks best when we hear that he speaks silence.

Mostly we forget what we do when awake, even as those who sleep forget their dreams. It's hard to find someone wholly awake. Some might say our whole lives we never shake the sleep from our eyes, our whole lives we never quite wake up.

"The stupid when they have heard are like the deaf; of them does the proverb bear witness that when present they are absent."

Who hasn't walked into a room with purpose set only to arrive and wonder why you find yourself standing, empty-handed, exactly there?

These small rehearsals of what life might be.

When you go somewhere to collect absence or forgetting.

It hides from us because we want so much to know it. Maybe ourselves; I mean, our own lives. But also the world. "Nature loves to hide."

It is as important to know that day and night are one as it is to know you are you and other than yourself.

✦

Heraclitus writes: "For it is death to souls to become water."

He writes, "It is delight to souls to become moist."

✦

Of his death, variations of a single story abound.

So despondent at the lack of virtue in the men he met, he began to hate the company of anyone and could bear only his own solitude, so he went far from the city "and wandered on the mountains, and there he continued to live, making his diet of grass and herbs."

But this diet gave him dropsy, one ancient cure for which was to cover the body in manure so as to draw the moisture out. Marcus Aurelius, considering how death overtakes healers and prophets, philosophers and poets, writes: "Heraclitus, after endless speculations on the destruction of the world by fire, came to be filled internally with water, and died beplastered with cowdung." That this man for whom all life was a principle of fire, who feared water killed the soul and yet souls delighted in moisture, died by his body filling with water it could not rid itself of, so swollen that the print of a thumb might stay on arm or ankle long after the hand let go its grasp, reminds yet again—as if one needed reminder—that for the gods irony is a form of sacrifice more than a form of wit; it is the marker of our helpless, fateful devotions.

31.

Emerson once had a dream in which an angel came to him and pointed out the world floating like a child's bauble in space, took it in hand where it rolled in the angel's palm, no larger than a grape, and said to the dreamer: "Thou must eat."

Emerson did. He swallowed the world whole.

Then nothing remained; everything was inside, irretrievable as the dreamer inside his dream.

Thou must eat. A command so basic it need not be written on stone and carried down from a mountain.

The angel says you have no choice.

You must swallow what it is you want to know.

✦

It's easy to make fun of Pythagoras refusing to eat beans.

But he thought of the universe as one indivisible thing, somewhat kidney shaped, past articulation—word whose original meaning is anatomical, "to cut along the joints of the body"—containing when it is opened no parts, as the source of the many is the one.

When you know you are not dreaming, perhaps it's harder to swallow the world.

Or, even being chased by a man who wants to kill you, to run across the field that is both a field of beans and the starry archipelagoes, a plot to feed hungry mouths and the root ground of the gods, to risk such trespass isn't worth the risk.

+

And who hasn't had dreams in which you're being pursued by someone who wants to harm you, though every time you turn around no one's there. Who hasn't had the dream where the angel arrives. Who hasn't chased a wise man to the edge of the holy acre. Who hasn't been the angel with a world.

But it's hard to know when you're dreaming.

Even when you suspect you live your whole life in a world another person swallowed, or are only a figure in some other dreamer's dream, it's hard to know when you're dreaming, hard to know how to wake up, if that's even what it is you want to do, to wake up, to wake up, which is when by opening your eyes you swallow down a world back into that dark form of digestion called memory.

32.

Iris likes to a play a game where I'm one year old.

✦

"Do you hear that noise, friend?"

"Yes."

"Do you know what it is?"

"No."

"It's thunder, friend. Does it scare you?"

"Yes. It's loud and the whole sky rumbles."

"Don't be scared, friend." She reaches up to touch my face. "It can't hurt you. The noise stays up in the air."

"Okay."

"But the lightning can hurt you."

"What's lightning?"

"I don't know, friend. But it can hurt you. It falls from the sky to the ground." She holds my hand. "Do you know why it rains, friend?"

"No."

"Because sometimes the sun and the moon want to be friends again, and they have a meeting and start talking behind the clouds, and when they're not looking, it rains."

"Is that true?"

"Yes, friend. It is. But don't be scared. It will be all right, friend. The meeting will be over soon."

33.

The poet told us to moan, and we moaned.

✦

She gave us a poem by another poet. The poem had only one word: *Bird*. The word kept repeating and it made a shape. The shape was the cage of a bird.

That's how we learned we become our own limit. Emerson writes, "Every thought is also a prison; every heaven is also a prison." That's how we ended up being this cage with no bird inside it.

All wire, no song.

✦

The poet told us to moan louder.

34.

For many years now my sister-in-law has volunteered at a nature museum in a large Midwestern city bordered to the east by one of the Great Lakes. In a small room with glass shelves instead of walls, and with a work space open to the public, she preserves birds for the museum's collection. It is a painstaking process, and when working on a particularly difficult or rare bird, she'll send me photographs of the process.

On the shelves that are her walls are examples of her craft, some made by her own hand. It's very difficult to make the dead bird act lifelike. The tilt of the neck is important, or the wing reaching out to gain balance on the thin branch that will never drop its yellow blossom from the sudden weight lifting off it back into the air. But one can imagine it—not only that it had once been so, but that it could be so again.

The glass bead has to catch the light just as would an eye.

Most of the specimens she collects come from the museum itself. A wall-size window on one side of the building lets visitors look out at the ponds and paths they could choose to wander themselves, but often don't. The warblers and woodpeckers and raptors, the chickadees and nuthatches, the vireos and flycatchers, see the glass as open space into which they can fly, which is to say they do not see it at all, and lose their lives by crashing into this screen of purest sky.

The museum which preserves the birds in lifelike scenarios is also the instrument of their death.

Strange to think how much emptier the museum would be if the museum did not exist. I guess that's obvious; that's an obvious thing to say. It makes a home for those deaths that haven't yet occurred; but home is what does the killing. Like building a grave in which to give birth. Like building a crypt with a vacancy sign.

Often a child from the suburbs will walk up to my sister-in-law as she works and look confused. The question they want to ask isn't about the intricate process of taxidermy. They've never seen anything that has died. They ask her questions; many of the questions repeat: "Is it real?" "Is it dead?" "Did you kill it?" "Are you hurting it?" "Did it die?" "Are you stuffing it?" "Did it lose its eyes?" "Is that the heart?" "Can I touch it?"

She has to answer, over and again, many times a day, "Yes."

Atlantis

Once upon a time a great philosopher thought the city should be structured as is the soul: reason governing spirit governing appetite. I always imagined it like a pyramid of three parts, each section rotating at its own speed according to its own potency, all aligned on an axis that now I'd call virtue, but when first I began thinking these thoughts, a center for which I had no name at all. Back then the center was missing. Sometimes this philosopher loved poets, and thought their mantic souls inspired by the gods who gave them some vision like prophecy; at other times he distrusts poets, worries their mimetic nature encourages others to act out themselves the extremities the dramas portray—as of Ajax in his hurt pride flogging to death his fellow soldiers, tying them to the post of his tent and whipping them to death, so injured was he by the prize of Achilles's armor being given to another, and waking after the massacre, the madness wiped clean from his eyes, not to find the Greek army dead and vengeance accomplished, but a herd of sheep slaughtered instead. So he walked to the beach, buried the hilt of his sword in the sand, and leapt on the blade.

Hubris. The word in Greek sounds the same: ὕβρις. Along with "excessive pride," it means "wanton violence." I guess one leads to the other, or they are simply the same. Is it that poems urge us, while warning us away, toward the violence they portray? That your hand clenches tight around the handle of the whip even when nothing is what is in your palm? That your heart thrills with power not your own, and your heart mimics Ajax's, whose spirit infuses you, plays like a marching tune through you, and when you go home, and your children hide away and ask you to find them, when they play their favorite game, you enter the house as does a hero of old, a threat to all you love most?

Wittgenstein suggests our moral life could begin truly if only I could feel the toothache in another's mouth as my own. What is the device by which our urge to be in another's suffering could be accomplished.

What is it to feel but not to act.

What is it that makes sense. These are questions, but I don't want to ask them.

I want to make sense. I want to write a poem that makes sense. I don't mean it can be understood. I mean you can read it and learn to touch what it touches, what can be touched in no other way.

When the Athenians lost control of the island of Salamis, Solon feigned madness, wandering past his wits into the agora where all heard him recite a poem sent to him by the gods. So they thought: the poet spoke for the gods. So they went back to war, killed whom they killed, and took back the island.

Then Solon became sane again. He had planned his madness out.

When I picture that pyramid-soul now, its point like a diamond-point points not up to the reasonable sun, but down into the dark earth, drilling down through the sand, a grave for kings making its own grave.

✦

Something is trying to disappear.

One of the stylistic habits inherited from the Sophists is never to name the subject of your discourse. One should just know, I suppose. Mostly, I dislike the Sophists. But sometimes it makes sense to me to write down no names, save those who might deserve the danger being named opens them to. Like a philosopher I love whose name I've mentioned many times already, but today find myself hesitating to say it. Sometimes it feels better, more true, for the name to stay underwater, there with the other made-things, the statues and the buildings, the temples in ruins, the armor and treasuries, weapons and coins, seed-vessels and wine-vessels, the burial grounds, the vases to collect tears, the pillar inscribed with the laws, all the drowned facts beneath the waters, this Atlantis of what all is lost, this Atlantis we share.

Solon wrote an epic poem about Atlantis, its ancient battle with Athens, but not a single line of the poem has survived. There's just a rumor in other pages that once it existed. Those sentences, like fingers aghast at a shipwreck, point at the empty space where what had been no longer is, where the life of it all went down.

This philosopher I love—who loves and hates poets, but who ends his life writing poems—talks about what of Atlantis is remembered. He does so twice.

Long ago Solon visited Egypt, and there met a priest of Saïs who mocked the Athenian, and all the Greeks, for being so new a culture. He said there are cycles of destruction, some by flood and some by fire, some by lesser calamities, but Egypt, whose Nile floods during fire, whose desert dries during flood, has survived these cycles of death and birth, and so knows the fact of those tales we tell ourselves as flights of imagination. Some nine thousand years ago, off to the west, past the pillars of Heracles, where the ocean grows so wild none can sail there, existed a continent with a great city upon it, devoted to Poseidon, and far advanced beyond any other people in the world. Superior in might and knowledge, the confederation of kings that ruled Atlantis, controlling already many islands, ruling over Libya, Europe, all the way to Tuscany, decided to enslave the world entire. "And then it was, Solon, that the manhood of your State showed itself conspicuous for valor and might in the sight of all the world." For the Athenians defeated the armies of Atlantis, and sent them home in shame. But the glory was short-lived. For later in time, that strange medium, "there occurred portentous earthquakes and floods, and one grievous day and night befell them, when the whole body of your warriors was swallowed up by the earth, and the island of Atlantis in like manner was swallowed up by the sea and vanished;

wherefore also the ocean at that spot has now become blocked up by the shoal mud which the island created as it settled down."

The men and women most worthy in Athens all died by the same shaking of the earth that sunk Atlantis beneath the waves, and those "that survived on each occasion was a remnant of unlettered mountaineers which had heard the names only of the rulers, and but little besides of their works." What laws sprang from the minds of the ancients as wheat from the field, what virtues arose as if native to the soil itself, the inscriptions in temples and statues of the gods, fell in upon themselves, leaving no trace, save the names of those who made them. These names the survivors remembered, whispered among themselves, gave to their own children, who bore as guardians over their lives names uprooted from the soil of their deeds. Not once, but repeatedly, these cataclysms occurred. Each time the people altering their ignorance back into virtue, and each time—by fire or flood, by lightning or blight, by the fickleness of a god, by a leviathan's might—every made-thing came to ruin. Only the names survived. And, like having the torn-out title page of a book and nothing else, every other page having gone missing, one has to hope, absurd as it may be, that the whole story exists within the name alone, caught in the inner circuits of those syllables, and to simply say the name, to repeat it over the ages, is still to tell the whole story, even if not another word of it is known.

In another book, the same group of men continue their discussion, returning not to the nature of the universe and how the world was made—words which require us who supposedly serve the gods to make those gods ourselves—but to Atlantis, whose geography, agriculture, government, cities, division of populace, military structure, and much more, are all described. Most of it I forget, which isn't to say I didn't find it interesting. Something shook in my head, maybe in a dream, maybe from walking about running errands, leaving only the names of the subjects and not their content.

One memory remains. The ten princes who ruled the island of Atlantis, when someone had transgressed, and judgment must be made, would go among the free-roaming bulls sacred to Poseidon and using nothing more than staves and nooses would capture one pleasing to them, take it back to the temple where, placing its throat over the holy pillar, they cut it so that the blood rained down and filled the words inscribed on the stone. As the heroes in the underworld demand the blood in others' veins to fill again their own, so even words wish blood to run through them to make them living, whole. Those heroes who otherwise live on crumbs.

The book in which this description of Atlantis occurred—not a book properly seen, but a conversation—has no end. I mean, it was abandoned. In my edition, an ellipsis . . .

As of Solon's epic poem of which only rumor remains, so of this philosopher's desire to compare that Athens even more ancient than ancient Athens to Atlantis—like the cities of its concerns, it has itself fallen back into the blankness from which it briefly emerged. It is to me as if those men stood up and walked away from their words, but the words stayed behind, some of them, in the room left empty, uttering themselves for lack of any other mouth to do so. Or that some Gorgon came in among them, staring each in the eye one by one, turning them into stone, and they are there even now, in that room, mouths open with the last word said, and some electric itch of response, buried like a crack in the center of a rock, waits to shatter the head into rubble.

✦

Strabo, the ancient geographer, commenting on the work of Poseidonius, "master of demonstration and philosopher," says: "On the other hand, he correctly sets down in his work the fact that the earth sometimes rises and undergoes changes that result from earthquakes and other similar agencies, all of which I too have enumerated above. And on this point he does well to cite the statement of Plato that it is possible that the story about the island of Atlantis is not a fiction."

In 1882, Ignatius Donnelly, a politician in Minnesota, writes a long essay to prove the existence of Atlantis, whose history he considers not only factual, but whose advanced civilization was seed from which all the world's ancient cultures sprung. He writes, in prologue, that it "became, in the course of ages, a populous and mighty nation, from whose overflowings the shores of the Gulf of Mexico, the Mississippi River, the Amazon, the Pacific coast of South America, the Mediterranean, the west coast of Europe and Africa, the Baltic, the Black Sea, and the Caspian were populated by civilized nations." Further, the island of Atlantis, in the antediluvian world, was the very place of every paradise: "the Garden of Eden; the Gardens of the Hesperides; the Elysian Fields; the Gardens of Alcinous; the Mesomphalos; the Olympos"; and the gods the people worshipped, from Thor and Loki to Zeus and Hermes, were but the kings and queens of this ancient land whose names survived the disappearance of their paradise.

No doubt, he says, any mean measure of geological upheaval proves that such a devastation could take place, that even a land mass large as a continent could be sunk into the sea by deluge or earthquake, just as, long before, the same forces heaved it up into the air. He believes the Azores Islands are the peaks of Atlantean mountains, and writes of the Canary Islands:

> [They] were probably a part of the original empire of Atlantis.
> On the 1st of September, 1730, the earth split open near
> Yaiza, in the island of Lancerota. In one night a considerable
> hill of ejected matter was thrown up; in a few days another
> vent opened and gave out a lava stream which overran
> several villages. It flowed at first rapidly, like water, but
> became afterward heavy and slow, like honey. On the 11th of
> September more lava flowed out, covering up a village, and

precipitating itself with a horrible roar into the sea. Dead fish floated on the waters in indescribable multitudes, or were thrown dying on the shore; the cattle throughout the country dropped lifeless to the ground, suffocated by putrid vapors, which condensed and fell down in drops. These manifestations were accompanied by a storm such as the people of the country had never known before. These dreadful commotions lasted for five years. The lavas thrown out covered one-third of the whole island of Lancerota.

Atlantis, according to priests of Saïs, devoted itself to Poseidon, god of the sea, pictured most often, oddly enough, behind a chariot pulled by horses. But to Donnelly, this oddity makes perfect sense, for the horse was first tamed on Atlantis, and on its fertile plains the old god rode. Many animals found in variations on many continents derive from Atlantis, proof that millennia ago passage from land to land was possible: the Norwegian elk and the American moose, the cave bear of Europe and the Rocky Mountain grizzly, and the sheep and cattle whose domestication allows us to live came from Atlantis, a gift from the missing ancestors whose verdant fields are now located, according to Donnelly, in the Atlantic Ocean, where "deep-sea soundings have been made by ships of different nations; the United States ship *Dolphin*, the German frigate *Gazelle*, and the British ships *Hydra*, *Porcupine*, and *Challenger* have mapped out the bottom of the Atlantic, and the result is the revelation of a great elevation, reaching from a point on the coast of the British Islands southwardly to the coast of South America, at Cape Orange, thence south-eastwardly to the coast of Africa, and thence southwardly to Tristan d'Acunha." And that the plant which produces a fleece softer and finer than any llama or lamb is found in India and Mexico and Peru is but another proof that the commerce of the ancient ones sowed into the furrows of the world entire the means by which we continue to live our lives.

He considers the biblical deluge a fact, as he does the reasons for its occurrence, the sinfulness of all men and women then, and the giants, too, that took the most fair for their wives, and spawned vicious children. The Chaldeans too have a parallel myth, eerie in its similarity, down to sending out birds to see if land had yet re-emerged, and when they didn't come back, Xisuthros knew land existed again; but it doesn't say if these birds are doves or crows, just "birds." Here the doves give a startling cry when lifting off the ground to fly, and again when they land in a tree; it sounds fearful, to me, as if the ring-necked dove—so new to these parts—would rather always be on the ground or forever in the air, as moving from one to the other contains some terror. And so of Babylon, of Iran, and perhaps most remarkably, of the Aztecs, who "claimed to have come originally from Aztlan. Their very name," he writes, "Aztecs, was derived from Aztlan. They were Atlanteans."

He quotes Sir Francis Bacon: "The mythology of the Greeks, which their oldest writers do not pretend to have invented, was no more than a light air, which had passed from a more ancient people into the flutes of the Greeks." And while not flutes, Donnelly notes the similarity between the great numbers of pipes found in the "raths and tumuli of Ireland" to those Paleolithic pipes found in what now is New Jersey, implying not only that Sir Walter Raleigh did not bring over tobacco to the Old World, but also that the tools by which we smoke it we inherited from Atlantis.

I could go on, but the point would be the same, whatever the point might be. Donnelly's is obvious: Atlantis is real and is the source of all that civilization holds most dear, from the alphabet of the Phoenicians which serves as the seed of our own, to the seeds we plant in the earth that feed and clothe us.

I'm less sure of my own point, of these days spent thumbing through Donnelly's work plucking out phrases here and there as one might pluck the still-ripe grapes from an otherwise wilted bunch; or why I search images of Atlantis that range from a gaudy casino in Dubai complete with a replica of an Aztec temple which, where the steps of the ziggurat should be, has instead a waterslide, to this image taken by satellite for Google Earth which many take to be proof of the lost world to which I find myself returning again and again while procrastinating my years-long study of ancient Greek.

Mostly, what I've learned is that we all long for the destruction we fear, and are as afraid that the deluge won't come as we are that it will, as the Romans felt when, opening the city to surrender to the barbarians, they found no one at their gate. Some answer had gone away. When we watch the birds row away through the sky something in us knows we might be drowning and says, *Finally, it is here*, and there is no more waiting. One learns, slowly over time, that we are ourselves the Atlanteans gone missing, survivors of a tragedy too old to be remembered save by the priests of Saïs, and that pang of nostalgia we feel even as we sit in the comfort of our own homes, this sense that even here, by the hearth, I don't belong, is but the old wound working memory again deep within us, far below the mind, where the heart says, *Atlantis*, though the blood to which it speaks is half-deaf. We find we have upon our foreheads not exactly the mark of Cain, but some similar mark, not a scar, not a smudge of cinder, but an asterisk there where the third eye should be, that mark the old linguists use to note that the earliest form of the word is still missing, and names what meaning we've come to as motherless.

36.

The old story says we watch shadows on the wall. Far behind us a fire burns like a minor sun. Before it, a walkway, across which puppets are carried whose motions mimic all the motions of life, so that the shadows they cast mesmerize as does the world, and to those of us watching on the rock wall this life's parade, we think the shadow-play we see is what is most real. It's only when we feel the binding chain that doubt begins. I like to think a shadow walks by that seems to one of us different, filled with soul, and out of desire to touch it you might reach up your hand, to grasp and be grasped. Sometimes realizing you are shackled is the key that unlocks the fetter. Doubt is the key turning in that lock. Then you get up, and walk past the rut the puppets tread, past the fire somehow dim, and up to the mouth of the cave that is a mouth filled with light.

✦

In the summer of 2012, James Eagan Holmes walked from the midnight alley through the propped-open door of the movie theater into which he threw gas canisters and, wearing a black assault vest, his hair dyed an acid orange, he followed, opening fire on the people gathered there to watch the newest Batman movie. Holmes killed twelve and injured seventy. He put up little resistance upon his arrest; he seemed most interested in watching the aftermath of his own doing, of watching the horror play out. Victims describe Holmes entering the movie theater, the smoke billowing up in clouds, the echoing gunfire, the muzzle flash, as if it all were part of the movie itself. It takes some time to know that what is happening is real, especially in the cave, to which we return to see only what is lifelike, and to escape for a little while life itself.

✦

Mostly I want to weep. That's the protest I'd like to organize. For an hour a day, I'd like everyone to walk outside and at an appointed time, for just a minute or two, to gather back from the air the sadness floating there in the clouds, and weep, all of us who can still weep, weep. Then we can go back to our business, whatever our business may be.

✦

The business of Heracles was his labors. Mostly that meant killing. When he finished all twelve, returning from the underworld, after he'd killed Eurystheus, the ruler of the land where his wife and children lived and who had threatened them with exile, as he was preparing the ritual sacrifice to purify himself and his house, Hera sent Iris to convince Lyssa—snake-haired goddess of madness—to inflict the hero with insanity. It came upon him suddenly. His children wondered at the change. "Here he stripped himself of his garments, wrestled without an opponent, had himself proclaimed victor with himself as herald, and called for silence from a nonexistent throng." His children ran inside. Heracles pushed his father away when the old man tried to restrain him:

> and prepared arrows and bow against his own children,
> believing that he was killing Eurystheus's children. These in
> fear rushed in different directions, one to his poor mother's
> skirts, another to the shelter of a column, another cowering
> like a bird under the protection of the altar. Their mother
> cried out, 'Ah, what are you doing? You are their father: will
> you kill the children?' Old Amphitryon and the throng of
> servants shouted too.
> But he, circling a grim turn around the column, stood
> facing the boy and shot him through the heart. The boy
> fell on his back, and as he breathed out his life he drenched
> the stone pillars with his blood. . . . He aimed his bow at
> a second, who was cowering near the base of the altar,

thinking he escaped notice. But before Heracles could shoot, the poor boy fell at his father's knees and thrust his hands at his chin and his neck; 'Dearest father,' he said, 'do not kill me. I am yours! It is *your* son, not Eurytheus' child you are going to slay!' But he merely turned his fierce Gorgon gaze upon him and, since the boy stood too close for the deadly bow shot, lifted his club above his head and—just like a smith forging iron—brought it down on the boy's blond head and smashed his skull. Having killed his second son, he went off to sacrifice a third victim on top of the other two. But before he could do so the boy's mother snatched him up, took him inside the chamber, and barred the door. Heracles, just as if he were besieging Mycenae, dug under the door, pried it up, pulled out the doorposts, and with a single arrow felled both wife and child.

He falls unconscious. Others drag him to bed and tie him to it. When he wakes his madness is gone. He says, "Ah, what does this mean? I am alive, and I see what I ought to see, the bright air, the earth, and shafts of sunlight. But I am fallen as if into a wave and into dread confusion of mind, and my breath comes hot and in shallow panting, not steadily from my lungs."

Heraclitus says, or once said, or maybe I've made it up, that the string of the lyre and the string of the bow are the same string. Sunlight and arrows both come in shafts.

His father asks him if he knows what he's done. "I have no memory . . ." Then his father tells him what he has done. Then Heracles veils his head in his garments.

He is trying to hide from the arrow that is the sun.

✦

James Eagan Holmes pled innocence due to insanity. He's schizophrenic. I don't know if he heard voices. If Lyssa came to him and spoke.

I think a lot, but it's not what I do. It does me, somehow, thinking. It does away with me—kind of.

I think about James Holmes choosing a movie theater, choosing to seem himself like a character stepping out of the screen into the world, about the heartbreaking ferocity with which we want to return to the cave, or go deeper into it, and those maddened ones for whom the line between puppet and person is no line at all, and who use our imaginations against us, who kill us where we go to escape.

The projector's beam cuts through the dark like an arrow made of light.

Mostly we want to go back to the cave.

37.

You can turn *no* into time by adding *w* to the end, but you haven't won anything. You can't live in *now*. The *o* that looks so like a home, the mouth of a burrow, or circle of safety, is the zero that describes the void into which the future pours so it can sift back out as the past. No, no—don't try. *Now* says *no* inside itself. When the *w* on its wings gathers with those others twittering in the sky, then time returns to its own absence, long ago predicted, sometimes feared, sometimes loved, westward drift far past the red shift, where now the sun says once again begin or be gone.

Circles

In July 1862—in the midst of her most productive year as a poet—
Emily Dickinson writes a letter to her "mentor" Thomas Wentworth
Higginson in which she says, "My Business is Circumference." A short
time later, perhaps in the very same month, dated only with "Friday,"
she writes in a letter to Dr. and Mrs. J. G. Holland:

> *My* Business is to love. I found a bird, this morning, down—
> down—on a little bush at the foot of the garden, and
> wherefore sing, I said, since nobody *hears*?
> One sob in the throat, one flutter of bosom—"*My* Business
> is to sing"—and away she rose!

My Business is Circumference.

My Business is to love.

My Business is to sing.

I remember the first time I wrote these sentences on a chalkboard in
front of a class, the white dust falling down from the letters, number-
ing them: 1, 2, 3. I remember I drew a circle on the board and we all
stared at it. It stared right back.

A poem begins by making a shape. It draws a circumference. All that
is in it is the poem. What is outside of it is not. There is a silence on the
inside and a silence on the outside but they are different silences. It's
hard to hear the difference. Like drawing with a stick a circle in the snow
while the blizzard keeps storming and stepping out the next morning
to see where the shape is now that it's buried or gone. Like that, but
harder. I like to think of the poet as a bird on the edge of the nest she's
built with nothing yet inside it. I call it the empty space of love. That
poet wanders the perimeter, this self-built line between nothingness

and emptiness, between all that silently extends beyond love's care, and what exists within it, or will, once what will exist, exists. Like an egg or a name. Then in that business of love comes the indweller with all its own life, reader or bird, figment of a child or fragment of a mind, and there it learns from love its own business, and sings its song, which—like the baby whose babble disappears just before she learns to speak the words—ends just before the fledgling takes flight.

I remember at the end of class erasing the board. The eraser had a name. "Ghost Duster."

I guess that's a joke.

✦

I remember speaking in class from memory, "Our life is an apprenticeship to the truth, that around every circle another can be drawn; that there is no end in nature, but every end is a beginning; that there is always another dawn risen on mid-noon; and under every deep a lower deep opens." But I spoke it differently, not remembering the exact sentence.

I guess around every memory some lethargy gathers, putting syntax to sleep, lulling the facts, and what comes out of the mouth is most like reciting a dream.

I remember in class saying, "The way of life is wonderful: it is by abandonment; I am a god in nature; I am a weed by a wall." That's mostly right, but the clauses are each their own sentence, separated by many others in between. How much I forgot by remembering them.

All the wild disarray I've poured into others' minds by sowing error in their ears, as "oblivion blindely scattereth her poppy." But I'm in the same disarray.

Maybe we could describe a poem as that form of life which seeks its own limit and, finding it, wants to know how best to break itself apart. That sounds like other definitions of life I might be acquainted with, like maybe my own, that life that wants to learn how to forget itself. Then the broken poem must be left behind, abandoned, left to its own hurt devices, until the next poem is written, whose circle enfolds and cares for the other as does the bird brooding in the nest, not upon an egg, but on the bones of its mother. Sometimes a word dropped on a page causes a ripple to circle out through the blankness it broke as does a stone thrown in a pond. Sometimes there's no other way to know how large the blankness is but to measure its circumference from within, and though they move as do neutrinos spiraling through hardest matter as if it were no thicker than air, such circles in silence pass through us in uncountable numbers minute by minute as the hours count down another day, a whisper through the atoms.

Emerson writes, "The simplest words,—we do not know what they mean, except when we love and aspire."

I remember I've never written those words on a board, never spoken them in class.

I remember, I remember. I keep putting the pieces back together, and each time they fit, but fit differently, this puzzle-life. He says, "The one thing which we seek with insatiable desire is to forget ourselves."

Okay, star. *Star* is a word. Now start.

✦

In the news last week scientists confirmed that they know now when the universe will end. It's producing less and less energy from its two hundred thousand galaxies, and in just a few trillion years will drift past its final circle into shapelessness, all the stars lit inside gone out, like those lamps to which the Greeks dedicated so many love poems, that see the lover in all her nakedness, lamps that are witness to erotic toils, but which have no tongues to tell. "O stars, and moon, that lightest well Love's friends on their way, and Night, and thou, my little mandoline, companion of my serenades, shall I see her, the wanton one, yet lying awake and crying much to her lamp?"

A larger lamp is the sun.

Sometimes my friend's young daughter fears the world exploding so much she won't leave her room. When this happened at a party I went and knocked at her door. "May I come in?" I asked. "Okay." I told her stars don't explode, but implode, and then the shockwaves from the collapse ripple out through space and widen the star by making it singular. That one day, the earth itself will be inside the star that gives us life, though then life will be long over. I told her if she started counting as fast as she could the second she was born and counted all her life to the last breath she breathed she wouldn't come close to the number of years left the earth has to live. And I told her that when a star collapses, if it's large enough—if it has loved and aspired honestly—it creates in its collapse a spark that reignites it, and is reborn. I mentioned that some explosions bring life, and that before all memory, in absolute nothingness hung a point so small no eye could see it, but asleep within the singularity—like the little figures of the gods within a clay Silenus—waited all that would become the universe, and when the dot exploded, the world began. "Do you feel better?" I asked. "Yes." I'm not sure it was true, that she did feel better; but she walked with me out of her room.

Our beginning in fire, and so our end, says Heraclitus, reducing us back into the elements from which we sprung.

Sir Thomas Browne reminds us that, but a few feet under the ground, across the whole of the earth, one can dig down not deep and pull up the bones or ashes of our ancestors. Recently, in a field in England they found 50 urns filled with the ashes of Romans—but recently was 400 years ago. His treatise on urn burial not only sifts through the ashes of those urns but also ponders the recorded history of burial rites, from inhumation to cremation, and though he keeps a sober, medical eye, and never speaks his preference, some readers might suspect he favors the fire that returns one to ash and bone, freeing us finally from the corruptions of the body, and denying those final indignities the body harbors, as of worms in graves, or snakes that house in the spinal marrow; or worse, some enemy that, finding our grave, digs us up and makes of our skull his drinking cup. Beyond such imaginings is what is unimaginable. Though a pyre can be built as a monument to the magnificence of one's life—and so Heracles lay atop a forest, and Patroclus's bier ran one hundred feet along Troy's wall, and a Persian king might burn a city to consume his ashes—that our pride "should sink into so few pounds of bones and ashes" should come as no surprise. Such little fuel suffices: "a peece of an old boat burnt *Pompey*; And if the burthen of *Isaac* were sufficient for an Holocaust, a man may carry his owne pyre."

But so little escapes time, even when life is over and time should end with it. As a mountain of fire will eventually burn out, so too the monuments that mark the graves of the illustrious, and the tombs and sepulchers the stones and cenotaphs, and the circle of the urn itself, time will prove as mortal as the bodies they contain; time, considered properly, "maketh Pyramids pillars of snow." Mostly we bury those we loved in ourselves. "Our Fathers finde their graves in our short memories, and sadly tell us how we may be buried in our Survivors." Or we give our child the name of a grandparent, and each time she's addressed—from a teacher calling attendance at school to saying at night good night—rehearses the funeral to come by repeating the one that's passed. Not even such living memorials will keep oblivion at bay. "Oblivion is not to be hired: The greater part must be content to be as though they had not been." Most all of us find ourselves there, nowhere. "Large are the treasures of oblivion, and heapes of things in a state next to nothing almost numberlesse; much more is buried in silence than is recorded, and the largest volumes are butt epitomes of what hath been. The account of time beganne with night, and dark-nesse still attendeth it. Some things never come to light; many have been delivered; butt more hath been swallowed in obscurity & the caverns of oblivion."

Maybe none of this comforts the child, these circling thoughts, this flame that leads to flame, and compared to those men and women of greatest antiquity, those people who long before the flood lived seven or eight centuries, who is not a child? And who hasn't realized, when walking out of the room with your friend's half-comforted daughter, speaking as if anything was known at all about beginnings and ends, about stars on the very edge of the universe that keeps tangling itself in the infinite shroud no one and nothing has woven around it, that all along, you have been talking to yourself.

Mostly one wants to say, as Sir Thomas Browne writes, "Life is a pure flame, and we live by an invisible Sun within us."

✦

So we learn that even as one can carry one's pyre on one's own back, it is already lit, burning on inside us.

It is a realization that makes of calm breath a panting, leaves a heart sorrowful and cloy'd, and of our high human passions, breaks our peace into a burning forehead, and a parching tongue.

Keats discovered it, holding the Grecian urn. Talking to it so it would talk to him. Turning it in a circle, stanza by stanza, until the circle grew larger by growing complete, turning back to the first stanza on the brede, where the gods frolic among the terrified maidens, and behind the ornament, within the urn itself, oblivion waits to gather its seeds and treasure.

Keats knows he's holding the vessel that will hold him.

A circle.

Circumference loves to sing.

The ashes hold the urn until the urn holds the ashes.

Waves

Homer was buried by the sea. On his grave, written by Antipater of Sidon,

> O stranger, the sea-beat earth covers Homer, the herald of the heroes' valor, the spokesman of the gods, a second sun to the life of the Greeks, the light of the Muses, the mouth that groweth not old of the whole world.

But the grave might be as imaginary as is the epitaph on its stone. Many poets wrote sepulchral epigrams for the great poet, none carved into marble, all written in ink on paper, so that one can begin to suspect the real grave is within the book, and the waves that beat against the shore are no more than the crest of the page as it turns. Some call him the "mouth of the Muses." Some claim the Nereids of the sea "buried him dead under the rock on the shore" because he sang of "Thetis and her son and the battle-din." What most agree upon is that Homer's grave is beside the sea, where the ocean beats the earth, swallowing back into water, wave by wave, the solid rock. And the epitaphs meant to memorialize him were only exercises for poets to hone their craft or show their mastery, each using the same elements, with the best being recited for centuries by schoolboys, where hanging on the wall the mask of Dionysus laughs or yawns.

Nor is there a single grave. Or birthplace. Many cities claim the honor. Salamis on Cyprus has a gold statue; Chios says the same; and so does Egyptian Thebes, about which, in another epitaph on the same subject, Antipater of Sidon writes, "Here is divine Homer, who sang of all Hellas, born in Thebes of the hundred gates." Now the grave speaks of birth which, to the wayfarer seeking to celebrate the life or grieve its passing, is like finding a sign pointing in the direction you'd come from, and you discover you have, once again, confused endings with beginnings.

Like finding an epitaph that says, "Now turn around."

Mostly, weary traveler, you realize—going from island to island paying your respects to the dead—that you've been tricked, and the body is elsewhere, not here among the ruins. And that's when you might hear the waves that circle the island, crashing as if forever against the shore, etching themselves into the rocks there, rippling the sands; that is no poetic exercise, but the epitaph that writes itself by eating the page away from its author.

✦

The ocean, source of life, relentlessly takes life apart. Makes of origins, ends; confounds the extremes of birth and death into one deathlike, lifelike thing, neither ever wholly itself, neither ever untainted by the other.

Keats writes his own epitaph: *Here lies one whose name was writ in water.* It wasn't an exercise.

But the words aren't only his own. Mark Antony, in Shakespeare, commenting on his life by mentioning the protean mutability of the clouds:

> Antony:
>
> Sometimes we see a cloud that's dragonish;
> A vapour sometime like a bear or lion,
> A tower'd citadel, a pendent rock,
> A forked mountain, or blue promontory
> With trees upon't, that nod unto the world,
> And mock our eyes with air: thou hast seen these signs;
> They are black vesper's pageants.

Eros:

Ay, my lord,

Antony:

That which is now a horse, even with a thought
The rack dislimns, and makes it indistinct,
As water is in water.

I don't know how common a name Eros was in the Roman Empire; not very, I suspect. In the midst of history, allegory appears. Desire listens to the man struck by desire.

Catullus, too, pre-echoes the line, when he claims the words a lover speaks "should be written in the wind and the running water."

We borrow from others the words we want most dearly to speak ourselves.

Like waves borrowing brightness from the sun.

I've never written my name in water. But I guess no one does. In water the name is writ. Strangely passive construction that means the hand that writes your name is not your own. But I like to think the name stays there, invisible, unspeakable, a shape of water within the water; though no one can read it, it's there. A kind of knowledge made of emptiness, the emptiness inside a name.

Last night, before bed, Iris said to me: "No one knows you better than you know yourself." *But you know yourself less and less until you don't know yourself at all* is what I didn't say, not able to point at the clouds, because the sun had gone down.

✦

Some grief is no grief at all. Standing before a grave wondering if it's empty, wondering if you should cry, and if so, how to make yourself do it.

Say to a class, "Don't imagine a Pegasus," and everyone sees in their minds the winged horse. But tell them, "Don't cry," and no one starts weeping. Not that I've tried.

Iris, after her first day of kindergarten, said: "I got sad once, but I cried inside my body, so no one could see."

Maybe you learn to weep intellectual tears. Is there such a thing? I had an idea once; I called it crying.

Little ocean, drop.

Drop by drop we drown in Emerson's innavigable sea. But the drowning isn't any different than breathing. The ocean isn't any deeper than the day.

Sometimes I sense it. An ocean in an asymptote. Those silent waves washing between me and those I love most, when the infinitesimal gap reveals itself as infinite space, and how, even for those whose life you've given them through your own, they exist to you as you to them, as an island you can see but that is on no map, and as you sail toward it, it gets further away; and you don't know what to believe, the blank ocean on the page, or the mote in the eye.

Like Homer in his grave. Who, dying for a riddle, became a riddle himself.

Second sun whose mouth when it sings swallows the whole world.

Mostly we forget the answers, and the questions dim. Just the sense that something is awry remains, like looking down at the ground and wondering who has stepped exactly in this place before where right now I'm standing, feeling I'm filling in someone else's body with my own, and that in turn, someone will come and replace mine.

Like there's a grave in the air, just standing there, waiting.

Never standing still is to the problem a kind of answer.

On my run I listened to a podcast. What I learned crashes against the rocks I call my mind. The atomic bomb tests of the middle of the last century cast into the atmosphere an abundance of carbon-14, a carbon that can be produced only under the intense pressures of a collapsing star, and unique for bearing two extra molecules. It is harmless, which is good, as embedded in every cell of our body are trace amounts of the element. It decays at a regular rate, and has allowed scientists to answer a question that long riddled them: How old am I? Now an inner clock ticks away within each cell telling us when it was born. The cells that make up the part of the brain that hold our memories have a life span of thirty years. As I ran I thought about it: all the memories I have in my mind about my childhood, those memories of first writing poems, of falling in love with Kristy, are stored in cellular chambers whose neurons didn't exist when the experiences were lived.

I felt a silent wave wash through me then. Just an innavigable sea between me and myself. Just a door ajar—the door that oceans are.

I kept trying to come up with images to explain it. It's like a new library built next to the old and the sub-sub-librarians carry the books from the old shelf to the empty new. But then I thought it's like copying all the words from a book whose pages are too frail to be handled into a new book, like a medieval scribe, illuminating, page by page, the Book. But the book is the scribe. It's like a child putting tracing paper over the page and drawing for herself the picture she admires, and doing so over and over again, ceaselessly, realizing she could herself make a version of the books she loves, and with invisible tape she binds them together, and then the original goes missing somehow, lost in flood or burnt up in fire, or the library sells it for $1.45 in the yearly sale, and all that's left of the middle-aged man lost in the dark wood is a crayon outline of the trees, and a peach circle with pencil eyes for a face.

Some lament for the original won't bear being sung. You read the cover of the book as you do the stone above the grave. The words point at something. I remember a mask hanging in the hallway to the cellar in my grandmother's house, how scared I was of it, as it never stopped laughing at a joke I couldn't even hear.

Now I think the joke is that there is no face behind the mask, and it's laughing at itself.

Now I wonder, once again, behind my own face, what's gone missing.

✦

In the months leading up to September 2008, as the day came closer when the Large Hadron Collider would finally be turned on, media filled itself with fear. Many worried that a little black hole might form as the atoms collided into one another at near the speed of light, and, instead of reproducing for scientific study the first instants of creation, we'd unwittingly destroy the world. Others thought a chain reaction would occur, a wave whose center rippled out from CERN to the very edge of the universe, changing every particle it touched into some dull gray mud. Fear of the beginning disclosing itself as the end. Though not widely known, the architectural model upon which the Large Hadron Collider was constructed is the Ouroburos: the snake with its tail in its mouth.

Others had hope instead of fear. They thought the long-predicted Higgs boson, otherwise known as the "God particle," might finally—in the miles of circuits and sensors in the most complex machine ever made by human hands—be detected and theory turned into a fact. The Higgs boson, and by extension, the Higgs field—that, some say, extends throughout the universe entire—is what gives mass to the particles that, massless, enter it. It is the field before the field to which no permission allows you return. Nothing waves through the field, and then the field is the waving full fronds of uncut grass.

Sir Thomas Browne liked to spend his leisure hours contemplating mysteries. He loved to quote to himself Tertullian: "It is true because it is impossible." He was so glad not to be alive in the days of miracles, it being so easy then to believe, having seen.

One of the old paradoxes is, *if God created everything, then who created God.* I guess that's a question.

Most of the universe is dark matter. I spend a lot of time thinking about it, and the hours disappear.

In June of this year the Large Hadron Collider started speeding atoms along its miles once again. Now that God exists they're hoping to find proof of darkness.

Sir Thomas Browne writes:

> I could never content my contemplation with those generall
> pieces of wonders, the flux and reflux of the sea, the encrease
> of Nile, the conversion of the Needle to the North; and
> therefore have studied to match and parallel those in the
> more obvious and neglected pieces of Nature, which without
> further travell I can doe in the Cosmography of my selfe;
> wee carry with us the wonders, wee seeke without us: There
> is all *Africa,* and her prodigies in us; we are that bold and
> adventurous piece of nature, which he that studies, wisely
> learnes in a *compendium,* what others labour at in a divided
> piece and endlesse volume.

We carry within us the wonder we seek without us.

My heart keeps beating this wave of blood in the circle that I am. The scientists aren't interested in the nothing I've found, the gravity proof, the god proof. This little bit of dark matter I'm holding now in my hands.

See it? In my hands? My hands.

40.

As the old masters who, to learn proportion and figure, drew studies of the masters before them, so poets in antiquity used to return to themes explored by those before them, truing their song by the measure of others' singing. Sepulchral poems are among my favorites. Many themes repeat: the bride and groom just married who die before the bliss of their first night together, from sudden illness, or calamity, such as the house in which they revel falling down; mothers who, birthing twins, die in the process, and, leaving one child to care after the bereaved husband, takes the other to comfort her in Hades; those in grief who find, by the extraordinary likeness of the statue memorializing the dead, that their sorrow cannot cease; the common prayer that the earth weigh lightly on the little child lost to light; the man who, climbing a thin rope to get at the honey he desired, falls to his death reaching up after that sweetness; the man who leapt from a high wall to Hades, having read one treatise of Plato's, that on the doctrine of the soul.

My favorite poems are those written for sailors and fisherman lost to life by doing nothing more than their work. Often the grave is empty, and the poem on the stone points to the sea in which the poor man drowned, and many of the stones lament what those who loved the man lament: that there is no body, no earth to call home, and what tears fall on the grave will be from strangers who, in reading of the death of another, cannot help but imagine their own. Strange and subtle irony, that the salt in tears is of the same composition as the salt in the sea, so that we mourn for the dead in the element of their destruction, and the wilder the grief, the louder the wailing, the fuller the tears, the more the living mimic the tossing, frenzied seas. "Every sea is sea," writes Antipater of Thessalonica, wondering why poets strive to name "the Cyclades, the Hellespont, or the Sharp Isles" when one can die slipping off the plank in the harbor?

Best among the type—some written as poetic exercises, some found on actual stones—are those few, repeated across centuries, where the fisherman lives out his days to old age, occupied by the tools of his labor, which bear him above the depths. "Hierocles' boat grew old with him, always travelled with him, and accompanied him in life and death. It was his faithful fishing partner, and no juster boat ever sailed the waves. It laboured to keep him until his old age, and then it buried him when he was dead, and travelled with him to Hades." As I write this short essay, a chickadee hangs upside down on the sickly ponderosa, eating the nuts from the cones. To be so at home in your labor the thought of the world subsides, and the danger of heights, the threat of depths, diminishes to a mote of worry, no more, when hunger is so winged with wonder and skill. Hierocles lived a good life, and I think about it often, what little I know of it. The boat that loved him, that aged with him, that he was buried in, or burned upon, and in which—much to Charon's surprise—he sailed across the Acheron himself, steady across the troubled waters, keeping his coin in his mouth, fishing the waters of oblivion.

, *Even*

Thou still unravish'd bride of quietness.

✦

Who is not at some time a dream of oneself and nothing more?

✦

The litany in hell is weeping, saith Dante, Dante saith, as he travels through hell.

Again is again. The copulative verb as the hellish equation.

Reciprocity such a curious law. Sometimes a τέλος, an end proper to the cause that preceded it—as in one's eternal punishment for choices made in time. Sometimes a motion that cannot but be met by a similar motion. As above, so below. And sometimes a motion becomes a notion, and a thought transforms into image, or an image into thought, as Dryope turns into a tree, and her child plays in the shadow of thought beneath her.

Sometimes the mind can't help itself.

"Love, that exempts no one beloved from loving," is how Francesca describes the mortal predicament that in hell has left her buffeted by winds in an "infernal hurricane that never rests," whose howling gale is overblown by the wailing laments of the damned. Like swallows that, once taken to wing, will never touch the ground again, the souls damned for carnal lusts stay up in the air, blown through abyss, afloat in nothing, driven by intolerable winds that are no more than the hellish magnifications of their once blissful sighs.

Come dove, and speak to me. Come thrush. Come nightingale. Come swallow. Come and speak.

Keats writes in a letter:

> The fifth canto of Dante pleases me more and more. It is that one in which he meets with Paulo and Francesca. I had passed many days in rather a low state of mind and in the midst of them I dreamt of being in that region of Hell. The dream was one of the most delightful enjoyments I ever had in my life. I floated about the whirling atmosphere as it is described with a beautiful figure to whose lips mine were joined as it seem'd for an age, and in the midst of all this cold and darkness I was warm. Even flowery tree tops sprung up and we rested on them sometimes with the lightness of a cloud till the wind blew us away again.

"Thou art a dreaming thing, / a fever of thyself," says the goddess, to the man awake only in his dream.

Francesca explains to Dante how she came to commit her sin with the brother of her husband. She and Paulo were reading for their delight of Lancelot, and love so overcame him, reading about love, that he closed his eyes and kissed her on the mouth. Keats reads of Francesca reading of Lancelot and closes his eyes and dreams of a kiss that makes of hell a heaven where the flower-trees make a brief nest for the lovers who from their loving cannot cease.

Sometimes the notion becomes a motion. Sometimes the mind asks the sparrow to sing for me. Sing for me.

Sometimes I can't help myself.

Keats begins his afterlife while still living this one. "I have an habitual feeling of my real life having past, and that I am leading a posthumous existence." He is dying in Rome. He did not bring his beloved Dante with him. Both are exiles, I guess. He will not open the letters the woman he loves sends him. Later they will be wrapped in the shroud in which he will be buried, never to be read, but forever near, next his skin, if not upon his lips. Again is again. He wakes from a troubled, fevered sleep, and speaks out to Joseph Severn, the friend caring for him: "How long is this posthumous life of mine to last?"

Francesca says to Dante:

> There is no greater sorrow
>   Than to be mindful of the happy time
>   In misery.

Henry Wadsworth Longfellow, from whose translation I quote, repeated these lines often, remembering his wife who died in the fire that burned to ash much of his house while the poet worked on translating hell. "There is no greater sorrow . . ."

On which point, I think, John Keats would agree. Having woken up so often, feverish, remembering.

✦

Not every hell is a dismal hole. You can visit other versions more easily. Just walk up the museum steps. You need no Virgil, just the gallery map. Go past the shepherds in the green fields. Past each Christ on the walls. Past the babies tumbling down a grotto like a river made of birth itself. Past Achilles's shield made of crayon and oil and pencil marks. There you will find my favorite hell, made of glass, so shyly reflective you look through yourself as you look through it, a bride hovering in the air, and below her, the bachelors who after her lust, hovering in nothing, too.

A "delay in glass," Duchamp calls it. Kind of like one line of poetry taken out from the whole poem, if only you could see the whole poem through the single line. Like if only it didn't take time to read from first word to last. Like only if grammar were an instant revelation, like light, in the eye.

Sometimes the mind can't be helped.

Marcel Duchamp spent eight years working on *The Bride Stripped Bare by Her Bachelors, Even.* He never finished it. Composed with lead wire and foil between two large panes of glass, Duchamp let time itself color the work, leaving it in an attic where the dust gathered on it over many months. Man Ray's photograph looks like a document made of a lost civilization, of Atlantis perhaps, if, rather than by ocean, that world had been drowned in dust.

The same collaborator keeps drawing on our faces lines we have not asked to be etched, lines which we can see if, ignoring the museum guards, you get close enough to the glass to see in the glare of the pane your own face looking. Then you see yourself seeing in ways in which you never hear yourself hear. Sure, there are echoes in the art-cave. But the syllables keep going away, slipping past the delay that sends the words back our way.

The top half of the glass is the realm of the bride, free from perspective, a creature part machine and part insect, running on love gasoline, sparking her own motor, dreaming of the orgasm she can only bring to blossom herself, dropping her dress from the power of her own imagination, her desire a kind of gearing that "binds the bouquet." Her desire is "ignorant," is "blank," with "a touch of malice" in it; and when she rejects the amorous overtures of the bachelors, she does so warmly, not chastely.

It is ancient trope, the reclining nude, the bride before consummation, the virgin feeling the blush in her cheek. Sometimes the bride breaks in her beauty our expectation of what beauty should be.

A dream blossoms from her head: the "cinematic blossoming," the "halo of the bride," the "milky way." Between the largest part of her body, which contains not only her "steam engine" and "pendu femelle," just above the "arbor type," there is a "letter box." You cannot see it. But those erotic sparks igniting the love gasoline into the blossoming bound only by desire itself carry electrically letters that fill the three nets in the dream cloud, a kind of dream of the self dreaming herself, an alphabet bringing no other being into being but the dreamer in her desire dreaming. An essence made of accident.

Duchamp writes a series of notes he keeps in a green box, and on these notes are his thoughts regarding the bride and her bachelors. Some scholars claim the art piece standing in the museum is but an illustration of the ideas and concepts written in those notes; others disagree, and claim the notes are just a tangential thinking to the ideas inherent in the masterpiece. Mostly I agree.

Duchamp writes: "The search for *'prime words'* ('divisible' only by themselves and unity)." He writes: "These signs must be thought of as the letters of the new alphabet." He writes, "This alphabet very probably is only suitable for the description of this picture."

So hard to read the notes in these words I know so well, to stand before the bride and years later write these pages, using none of the words to describe her she uses to understand herself. The filmmaker and artist Jean Cocteau, so I once was told, could bring himself to orgasm without touching himself or being touched. In the museum, waiting for the bride to drop her dress, I kept worrying I might find myself in an embarrassing situation. I think it might have happened had I been able to hear the words she dreamed, those prime words divisible only by themselves, where death and desire are one, and any who hears them is spoken by them, and desire becomes your only bound. As it was, I looked down. Not in embarrassment, maybe in disappointment. I kept touching the tip of my penis when I put my hand in my pocket, but nothing could wake it up.

Duchamp made a series of suitcases into which he built miniature versions of all the art he'd ever made. Some were special editions that contained a unique piece of art. In one of them, a black silk cloth onto which he'd ejaculated. Earlier in his career he turned a urinal upside down and signed it R. Mutt. The poet William Blake reminds us that our procreative and excratory organs are one and the same. Blake and his wife used to sit naked in separate armchairs before the fire and read out loud John Milton's *Paradise Lost*. Later in his life Duchamp asked his wife to sit on wet clay and then bronzed the result.

Sometimes the nude is the absence of the body. Or is it what waits the body to come fill it. Or is what comes out of the body and like a miniature Milky Way spills across the black cloth, an arm of our own galaxy, but the galaxy reaches inside us. Sometimes you name the edges of the labia after the leaf that covers Eve's shame. Sometimes we're clothed in nudity.

I guess when I looked down I looked down in shame.

Just like the other bachelors, wanting so terribly the bride.

I felt like a set of clothes without a body, an emptiness dressed up. Maybe that's the male condition. To want to be a person, and end up being the mold waiting the clay, waiting the breath, waiting the drop or two of seawater. The patient mold waiting for the illuminating gas.

The litany in hell is weeping, weeping; but there are other litanies. The nine bachelors, the "malic molds," move back and forth on a glider, filling with an illuminating glass that never lights a thing but their own infinite longing, singing endlessly one song on eternal repeat: "Slow life, Vicious circle, Onanism, Horizontal, Buffer of life, Junk of life, Cheap construction, Tin, cords, iron wire, Eccentric wooden pulleys, Monotonous fly wheel, Beer professor." Duchamp writes this list once, crosses it out, and then writes it again. Such is the useless song of the whole "celibate machine." Unable to consummate the marriage each one so desires, the illuminating gas floats up into spindles, which makes dizzy the upward direction each by its nature should go, is caught then by the sieves, and drawn down into the chocolate grinder where, rather than the bliss of the bride, the bachelors only "grind their own chocolate" forever.

Dante didn't see such men in hell, not because they aren't there, but because Virgil didn't want to show him—they are such a version of most of us all—saying endlessly the same words, trying to get Beatrice floating above us to drop down her dress and come naked to our chamber. Recent research places the bachelors on the edge of the second round of the seventh circle, where in an infertile plain the damned walk beneath the sparks raining down on them, but the essay in which I found the hypothesis I've lost, and cannot provide the citation.

But Duchamp writes a little about this hell, though he had no Virgil, only himself. "But *they* will never be able *to pass beyond the Mask* = They would have been as if enveloped, alongside their regrets, by a mirror reflecting back to them their own complexity to the point of their being hallucinated rather onanistically." Then he calls them a "cemetery," which—according to the infernal grammars—is in hell the collective noun for such bachelors.

I thought of this passage, which I'd not realized I'd memorized, when I last went back to the museum to see the bride. I had in myself such complexities of thought, such ardors of passion, but I could see none of it in my own face, looking at myself looking in the mirror of the glass, somewhat older than before, where the bride sang to herself her own song, and I recited my litany beside her, each one of us silent, but mine a different silence, so absorbed by the profundity of my own thought that I almost got an erection, to be so full of ideas like a child filled with too much chocolate; but of her words I could hear nothing. Even if she spoke them to me—her dream, her stars, her milky way—I wasn't able to understand.

I keep wondering if my hands are filled with the invisible bouquet, but I can't see a thing, and the scent in my palms is what? Maybe just my own skin. Maybe fear. Maybe truth. Maybe beauty. Maybe the happy boughs of the trees sprung up in heaven. Maybe the petals the floating lovers knocked down.

42.

CANTO I

Midway in my journey through life I got lost
    In the vertiginous asymptote
Of blank spaces between letters, a forest
In reverse, not made of light, but bright; not
    Darkened by leaves, but the inner heart's
White page released. Inside is where I got
Lost. Some Möbius turn of mind whose short-
    Circuit makes the infinitesimal grow
Infinite. Nearness is another sort
Of distance, more immense the closer you go,
    So that, bewildered by proximity,
I no longer know how to say what it is I know.
Of oblivion—every page—is a variety:
    Blank breath, blank light, an alchemist's
Delight, if instead of gold, silence quietly
Creeping in among the leaden noise, insists
    On absence in the broken toy of each
Name as the fundamental gift, as in a list
For the grocery store, or the owl's screech,
    Or the nightingale ode, or the urn
That in the poet's hands turns, even the black leech
By which the doctor bleeds the head of its burn
    Has between mouth and skin a space
For another universe a moment can erase. Stern
Forms of wonder endure past the place
    Where wonder occurred. A century can pass
Between two letters, and time leave not a trace.

43.

As our body will one day be buried in the ground, some say our soul is now buried in our body. Sometimes I agree. But on rare days a wild suspicion panics me that the body is immured in the soul. I thought it just today, making notes for my afternoon class, thinking hard about what is outside me so that the mind seemed its own place, a cloud tethered by a thread, and that thread is soul. Wordsworth, remembering his childhood, writes:

> that single wren
> Which one day sang so sweetly in the nave
> Of the old church that, though from recent showers
> The earth was comfortless, and, touched by faint
> Internal breezes—sobbings of the place
> And respirations—from the roofless walls
> The shuddering ivy dripped large drops, yet still
> So sweetly mid the gloom the invisible bird
> Sang to itself that there I could have made
> My dwelling-place, and lived for ever there
> To hear such music.

Like that, I think: the body inside the soul as the boy within the bird song, making a home in what hardly exists, but is there in the ear, so that the limit of the bird isn't the breast from which it sings, but the edge of the song pouring out of it, and ends only where silence begins. Right now I'm living inside my dog barking, living inside Bach playing on my computer, and living inside the mourning dove's cooing. The soul like that, I think—save the music can't be heard.

Air archaically meaning "song" or "strain of music."

One way to pray is to begin by saying, *Sing to me, my wren*. But it is a prayer so oddly to oneself. That part of you that isn't you.

A kind of faith begins that is a form of digestion. So slowly the body wears away to nothing inside the soul, as does Ahab's leg still fleshed inside the white whale's stomach—so gentle is the acid there—long after the dismasted man himself has died. One could say that Moby-Dick is the Captain's soul, an irresponsible thing to claim, an affront to common sense and received tradition; one could say of ourselves, as of Ahab's leg, we are for our whole lifetimes by our souls being eaten away.

✦

Sir Thomas Browne, explaining to himself his own faith, in *Religio Medici* writes:

> *All flesh is grasse*, is not onely metaphorically, but literally
> true, for all those creatures which we behold, are but the
> hearbs of the field, digested into flesh in them, or more
> remotely carnified in our selves. Nay further, we are what we
> all abhorre, *Anthropophagi* and Cannibals, devourers not
> onely of men, but of our selves; and that not in an allegory,
> but a positive truth; for all this masse of flesh which wee
> behold, came in at our mouths: this frame wee look upon,
> hath beene upon our trenchers; In briefe, we have devoured
> our selves and yet do live and remain our selves.

My hands a field, and my mouth a field, and my face a field of grass. Imagination can hardly do the work, the wild bison of thought let loose in the herbs of the mind: that in living I consume myself to go on living. One could go further. The grass eats the sun, and so do the flowers. The fruit of the vine is but the star's mimic. Each day, three times a day, I fill myself up on sunlight, devouring the star that grants me life.

It doesn't end well, appetite. Dimness that brightens briefly making the dark that follows all the darker. And the drone called thinking, which is nothing more than a ruminant habit, ends when there is nothing left to chew.

Sing to me, my wren. Dive down from the rafter. Dive down from the eave. Devour me whole, O soul.

✦

Herman Melville takes from the air itself that thought Sir Thomas Browne left hungering there:

> Consider the subtleness of the sea; how its most dreaded creatures glide under water, unapparent for the most part, and treacherously hidden beneath the loveliest tints of azure. Consider also the devilish brilliance and beauty of many of its most remorseless tribes, as the dainty embellished shape of many species of sharks. Consider once more, the universal cannibalism of the sea; all whose creatures prey upon each other, carrying on eternal war since the world began.
>
> Consider all this; and then turn to this green, gentle, and most docile earth; consider them both, the sea and the land; and do you not find a strange analogy to something in yourself? For as this appalling ocean surrounds the verdant land, so in the soul of man there lies one insular Tahiti, full of peace and joy, but encompassed by all the horrors of the half known life. God keep thee! Push not off from that isle, thou canst never return!

The etymology of *consider*: "to examine the stars." To draw the connections between the distant points, to make a shape called thinking, means thinking is also drawing lines across distances so vast that time, not miles, is the only measure; and time in such quantities, in such cosmic abundance, that some of the stars of our thinking no longer exist, and there is a darkness where now we find a bright point; and all the light by which the mind navigates through this other ocean called life, burned first long before our birth, so that to consider anything is to remove yourself from yourself in such a way that you find yourself no more than a fragrance left on the hand after mowing the fields of the starry archipelagoes, a grassy perfume called self.

Strange scythe of mind that sharpens a blade of grass to cut down the verdant field. Mind that is the grass blade. Strange eye that stares out at its own absence. Strange appetite that finds my hand so often in my mouth.

44.

Tacita, Muse of the Unspeakable, deafen this prayer, mute the wild wood dove, wrest away the wren's song, let the thrush lose her lament or learn to lisp, and make the house finch fluent in forgetting . . .

Another name to add to the list: Christopher Harper-Mercer.

✦

In 1855 Walt Whitman publishes "Song of Myself" in *Leaves of Grass* for the first time. He'll revise it throughout the rest of his life, publishing a last version in 1892.

"What is the grass?" the child asks, is one moment I always remember.

And something about the "atoms," each "belonging to me as good belongs to you."

Good here, I guess, means "also."

How death is different than anyone supposed, "and luckier."

When I was in high school my teacher told me what so many of us were told by our teachers in high school: Whitman wrote the poem of America.

But I don't read it much any more.

✦

On August 1, 1966, Charles Whitman, after killing his mother and wife, went to the University of Texas, where he studied engineering, climbed up the clock tower of the Main Building, and for over an hour shot whomever he could shoot. He killed fourteen people on campus and wounded thirty-two.

Studying poetry at the University of Iowa in 1999, I was in the habit of reading some poems after lunch, lying down on my couch, the radio faintly on to the news. Mostly I'd end up sleeping, dreaming my dreams. I remember reading John Berryman's *Dream Songs*, one particular poem, realizing in my half-dozing state exactly what the poem was about:

> I heard said 'Cats that walk by their wild lone'
> but Henry had need of friends. They disappeared
> Shall I follow my dream?
> Clothes disappeared in a backward sliding, zones
> shot into view, pocked, exact & weird:
> who is what he seem?
>
> I will tell you now a story about Speck:
> after other cuts, he put the knife in her eye,
> one of the eight:
> he was troubled, missionary: and Whitman
> of the tower murdered his wife & mother
> before (mercy-killings) he set out.
>
> Not every shot went in. But most went in:
> in just over an hour
> with the tumor thudding in his brain
> he killed 13, hit 33:
> his empty father said he taught him to respect guns
> (not persons).

Then I heard the radio speak. Someone reported gunfire at Columbine High School. Not much was known. Reports about the chemistry teacher being shot. My sister-in-law was then a student at Columbine High School. Taking Chemistry.

My wife and I flew back to Colorado and went to the outdoor memorial. It was raining. Some speaker said that heaven was crying. But I know heaven doesn't cry. That's just rain falling down on the field to make it grow, falling down on the flowers, those real and those fake, falling on the bereaved, on the stuffed animals in piles, on the photos of faces.

Days later we flew "home."

✦

Then the mind has the wound called darkness, and darkness is called memory, and memory lives in a cave called mind, and a cave is a kind of shelter made out of a wound, and in this wound thinking happens, and it is not for tears: thinking.

Who is what he seems?

I don't think Whitman was related to Whitman. I could find out. But I don't want to look it up. I don't really want to know.

I mean, I really don't want to know.

But I guess he must be. "For every atom belongs . . ."

Whitman wrote the great American poem. Both Whitmans. It's easier to hear this newest version, the one so many men keep rewriting, each in their own way, but each the same, this poem of America.

It doesn't sound like much it is so loud.

Emily Dickinson knew something of it, too: "My Life had stood—a Loaded Gun—" But now it is no Master who does so—the gun carries itself away, the gun pulls its own trigger.

Boys and men keep rewriting that poem, too. Some of the children memorize every line.

✦

Bang bang they play at school and fall over in the grass. Then the bell rings, and most all of them get up and go to class.

But some stay on the ground, looking through the fragrant blades at the green shards behind, breathing in the grass, seeing beneath the leaves their shadows, and finding—when they look close—the small life whirring there, the leafhoppers, beetles, and crickets, and some children stay in the grass, wondering about the hum there so near the earth your ear must be in the dirt to sing along.

Sometimes when I pick up Iris from kindergarten I don't know why the children are running so fast or to where.

I heard no beat, not a drum, fill the air. Nor did I hear the silence after, that wound in the grass, that wound in the field, stray bullets that mow the field blade by blade so it takes almost forever to annul the atoms.

O green scent of the broken grass blade, O perfume of the wounded field, kill this prayer in your mercy, O Tacita, break the clocks in the tower, break apart time, one leaf of grass at a time, leave some sunlight and some shadow, one spear standing tall and straight, just enough to know how long the day has left, not time, not time, but what light has left to endure.

"A child said, What is the grass?, fetching it to me with full hands."

I don't know. I don't know what's in my hands.

45.

Christopher Harper-Mercer's mom loved guns and said that her son had much knowledge of guns, of how they work and of their laws. She called him "baby." Neighbors recalled how he could talk with passion about his guns, but couldn't talk about his own life. The guns had a life he could express. Schoolmates said he changed the subject when the subject was himself. "He didn't say anything about himself," one said. Another said he could say, "Hi."

He shot ten students at a community college in Oregon.

He liked a picture of himself so much he posted it online: Me, holding a rifle.

John Berryman, in another dream, writes:

> There sat down, once, a thing on Henry's heart
> só heavy, if he had a hundred years
> & more, & weeping, sleepless, in all them time
> Henry could not make good.
> Starts again always in Henry's ears
> the little cough somewhere, an odour, a chime.

> And there is another thing he has in mind
> like a grave Sienese face a thousand years
> would fail to blur the still profiled reproach of. Ghastly,
> with open eyes, he attends, blind.
> All the bells say: too late. This is not for tears;
> thinking.

> But never did Henry, as he thought he did,
> end anyone and hacks her body up
> and hide the pieces, where they may be found.

He knows: he went over everyone, & nobody's missing.
Often he reckons, in the dawn, them up.
Nobody is ever missing.

Ever here, I guess, means "always."

Sometimes I have to make myself make the mistake I need to make.

Does the poem describe the violence within it so that we remember and, should we forget, can find the reminder we need of our sorrow, or horror, or grief. Does the poem add luster to darkness and make it gleam. Does the poem warn us about ourselves. Who is what he seems. Does the poem bear in it the burden we cannot carry ourselves. Does the poem act out for us the violence within us so that we can be in the world at peace. Does the poem give courage where it should give fear. Does it make you imagine what should not exist so that it won't exist. Or is it the opposite. Which one. Is it each one.

All these are questions. The answer keeps being blank. The blank between the letters and the blank after them. Blank of all the margins. Blank beneath the words.

Like a blank page not numbered in a book, acting like it isn't there even as you gaze down on its silence, nobody is always missing, it feels like a mistake, this being present by being absent, this existing by not existing, like some kind of footsteps that precede the feet, and all the grass is bent down before the bell has even rung, not a bell but a recording of a bell, and what the bell says is, "Too late," before the children from the school have yet run.

His mother called him *baby*.

Nobody is missing. Nobody is obeying the laws.

46.

<u>Book First</u>

Trances of thought and mountings of the mind
Let wonder wander through the eye and I follow
The song back to the shepherd's glade, the mind's
Internal echo of the imperfect sound
That keeps as in a fold the creature safe.
Thus occupied in mind, I lingered here,
Resting in the grass that is prelude to flesh,
Gazing up at the clouds that darken a moment
The sun that sudden brightens as thought in my mind
Remembering the sweet promise of the past
When I was more than only within myself folded.
I love what I must leave, the mind itself
The meditative mind, best pleased perhaps
While she as duteous as the mother dove
Sits brooding, lives not always to that end,
But has less quiet instincts—goadings-on
That drive her as in trouble through the groves
As drives the idea called panic, music of the under-powers,
Subordinate helpers of the living mind
That flout fact with the flute's thin reed of tune.
The mellower years will bring a riper mind,
Less given to brooding, less inconsolate, less fevered
And less immured by the heat, those fantasies
Born out of idle dreams in the crucible of youth
Thus baffled by a mind that every hour
Turns recreant to her task. *Fledgling, I*
Ripened into the darkness of the panicked grove,
And where wings failed I found a leaved-thought
To bear me on further, and a torch burning
On nothing more than the aether, or the fog

That gathers in the wandering center of being lost.
I was transplanted. Well I call to mind
The structure in the dimness called the mind,
Some maze whose middle is larger than the whole
Riddle, and no monster, just the mother dove.
The mind of Man is framed even like the breath
And harmony of music; there is a dark
Invisible workmanship that reconciles
Discordant elements, and makes them move
In one mystery, some song no one can sing
Because the song sings us. Then desire
To be the hero relents, the easy grandeurs fade
In the half-light from which hope too high-reaching
Rose, fevers of self in which the cosmic song
Sprung off the tongue as an arrow from a bow
To wound heaven into kindness and bring the angels
Low, and lower, down to the worms in the earth.
And now the musk rose and the murmuring fly,
The whole chorus of the common reminds the mind
Not a single word belongs to it alone; such were
The thoughts and feelings which have been infused
Into my mind, should ever have made up
The calm existence that is mine when I
Am worthy of myself, *which sometimes I am,*
Even if seldom, even if as mutable as the moon.
Often when I close my eyes, ambitions
Like living men moved slowly through my mind
By day, and were the trouble of my dreams,
Each their own vision, but each also me,
Peopled my mind with beauteous forms or grand
And made me love them, *devote myself to them,*
A fever of myself, of self-love, though I did not know it
Until tired from these sleepless dreams I lay down on
the changeful earth *and heard the hum in the grass,*

And twice five seasons on my mind had stamped
A mold into which the senses pour intelligence
To impregnate and elevate the mind
Beyond the little confine, kind jail, that says I.
My mind has been revived—and if this mood
Fades, then it fades. The mother-dove still coos.

47.

Written in William Wordsworth's hand, photographed from the correspondence with Briggs and Cottle, a "Song" from *Lyrical Ballads*, found among many poems in manuscript, including the "Preface" in the author's own hand. Among the poems, written on paper as large as a poster, one crossed out, written in darker ink above: "N.B. do not print the following poem. W. W." The poem begins at the lower margin of a page, continuing atop the next column, crossed out with a large *X*.

✦

✦

Song
a pastoral

Fly, written
day   of
stoves
this
Arms

your languages
song   kettle
poker   of
away   fury
plate   metal

earth   made
pulses   slower
in   was
heaven   knows
is   degrees

a disconsolate
field or
him!
poor fool
the   edge

fumbles
completely
out
and
brink

```
          stands
          he has
     methinks   can
       West     the
      neither   first


        sink     him
      heaving    lost
       death     blood
       pretty    blue
                 frost


     companion,   while
        from      cheek
        glad      desolate
       summer     floor
        were


      witness           helpless
                          thing
    comes

                        crowds
                        sound
        the             clouds
```

✦

To my eye, the words crossed out begin to form the helix of life's most buried structure, but it's only the shape of the lines that marks out what exists as no longer existing. Not deserving to exist.

I think of the poem as a kind of pastoral in reverse. Or do I mean the underneath of the field.

I know the poem isn't very good. It's not meant to be.

✦

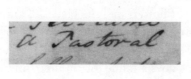

✦

I took many photos of lines Wordsworth crossed out, but he did so with such thoroughness that no words could be read underneath their own negation—but I know they're there.

(Somewhere, I hear a whisper as if whispering to itself about the passion of presence in absence, or is it the passion of absence in presence.)

✦

Nota Bene:

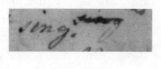

✦

I hear both words sing. I think I do. I think both words are still singing. Maybe to each other in the dark of the closed box where they live. Maybe to you and me. Maybe to a box called time, which is kept in the library in a different room.

Signature

The sun sings no song; not one a human ear can hear; not one with which a man might hum along. Millennia passing have put Apollo's lyre on mute. But stems of flowers and the blades of grass each spring stand up taut like harp strings being tuned by an invisible key. But the whole dance continues, even if we hear nothing of the organizing tune, even if nature acts for us as does a mime for children, mimicking motions, but keeping the secret words unknown. We see the dance, but to the melody find ourselves deaf, guessing at the music by the swaying of the whole.

Thoreau's morning has little to do with the measurement of time. His morning lasts longer than the day it begins; his morning is longer than the time of history's whole span. This morning light carries within it that first bright shine of creation ongoing when essence steps first into form and chaos into cosmos. The eye exists because the sun does. When Thoreau suggests that *as he sees, so he says*, he confesses to some solar principle that undergirds expression. More than the fatality of character, Thoreau suspects a deeper metaphysic that links our impulse to speak to that silent light whose unheard melodies compose the world into order. To see by that light is to be strung to the same tune.

The blank of the page that follows *Walden*'s last sentence, "The sun is but a morning star," mimics the silence that Thoreau would have precede his every word—a silence, in almost pure paradox, that can begin only by saying first all that can be said. Only at the end, can we begin. Only then do we hear silence. Only then do we see the sun's morning light: light of pure beginning, silent as is the first letter of the Hebrew alphabet, aleph, which cannot be pronounced, as Heller-Roazen puts it, "not because its sound is too complex but because it is too simple."

This letter that inscribes the possibility of all meaning resists meaning itself. In offering some sense of the silence that precedes everything, it also protects that oblivion from which being emerges. What do I hear when I finish *Walden?* Thoreau speaking one letter whose sound is too simple to be heard, the sun's initial, syllable no more than blankness, syllable no more than light, *aleph, aleph.*

✦

As Emerson found himself apprentice to circles, so Thoreau finds himself initiate to silence. Early on his journals seek some language to express not just the quiet repose of nature's more serene moments, but words that might give some sense to what words wholly oppose: silence complete. Paradox is a rite of initiation he must perform on himself; a crisis that will reverse his perceptions, letting them sense what is not there to sense, and turns inside out the language that records them. Simone Weil says: "We are subject to that which doesn't exist." So Thoreau must work through the fact of his body toward that which his body cannot perceive, attuning himself to the reality of that which exceeds the limits of his existence, must pitch his ear to "tuneless numbers," to find within the moment of but a syllable the morning's entire eternity. He senses so himself in mid-August, 1838: "I did not hear the strains after they had issued from the flute, but before they were breathed into it, for the original strain precedes the sound by as much as the echo follows after, and the rest is the perquisite of the rocks and trees and beasts. Unpremeditated music is the true gauge which measures the current of our thoughts, the very undertow of life's stream."

Our rote aesthetic values are overturned. The beauty of the melody he might play on the flute bears little of his concern, a sound, like an echo, given back to the world which alters it as it rebounds against stone and forest and wild ear. Thoreau plays the flute according to the musical strain that precedes the blown melody, almost pure medium, open to those essential forms of order and beauty that precede physical being and, moving through him—the instrument of the body being as much a flute as is the flute itself—gain form in the mortal ear. Thoreau knows that the reward isn't the beauty made. The poet may well be a maker, so says the old word. But what a maker of? A life. A kind of living that keeps silence whole: "My life at this moment is like a summer morning when birds are singing. Yet that is false, for nature's is an idle pleasure in comparison: my hour has a more solid serenity. I have been breaking silence these twenty-three years and have hardly made a rent in it. Silence has no end; speech is but the beginning of it. My friend thinks I *keep* silence, who am only choked with letting it out so fast. Does he forget that new mines of secrecy are constantly opening in me?"

Silence begins at the end of speech; such silence is a made-thing. Thoreau suspects, as did philosophers centuries before, that some silent, spiritual essence maintains its oblivion within sound as the seed persists silently inside the fruit—generating the possibility of life ongoing only by the destruction of the specimen. A silence that must be spoken. And as specimen relates to species, and species to image, those visions words give us contain within them the silent germ that can take root in earth and ear and mind only by the fullest speaking possible. Do you hear silence grow prolific? Only then does the mine of secrecy stay open, filling every rift with its paradox of invisible gold.

The mine is in the words carried on nothing more than breath. More silent than breath. Breathing inside inspiration.

This doctrine of silence is ancient; it dawned with the dawn of the world. Giorgio Agamben writes:

> In the thought of Zeno and Chrysippus the pneuma is a corporeal principle, a subtle and luminous body identical to fire, which pervades the universe and penetrates every living thing. . . . This breath or fire is present in each person and communicates life to him or her: the individual soul is but a fragment of this divine principle. . . . The center of this circulation is the heart . . . in whose subtle pneumatic matter are impressed the images of the

phantasy as the marks of writing are impressed in a wax tablet. The voice, too, is a pneuma that radiates . . . through the larynx [and] sets the tongue in motion. Thus one single pneumatic circulation animates the intelligence, the voice, the sperm, and the five senses.

How is it that Thoreau hears the melody before he plays the music? How is it that in his speech he but breaks silence in such abundance he feels himself choke on it? It is by a thought so simple it baffles us as does a riddle of greatest complexity. He senses what cannot be truly sensed, that there is in nature one breath that is soul or signature of the whole.

He thrills to it because he is part of it. He speaks as he does not simply to make meaning but, in doing so, to pull apart the very meaning he has made, as a child pulls apart, segment by segment, the portions of an orange. The child learns a secret lesson in geometry that scents her fingers citrus. So Thoreau's words present us with some beauty that teaches us how to take it apart. Speaker of that silence he also serves, we read him and find in our mouths some quiet that is not our own. A miner in inspiration need only inhale deeply to dig down to the ore.

Thoreau writes on August 1, 1838:

The best thought is not only without somberness, but even without morality. The universe lies outspread in floods of white light to it. The moral aspect of nature is a jaundice reflected from man. To the innocent there are no cherubim nor angels. Occasionally we rise above the necessity of virtue into an unchangeable morning light, in which we have not to choose in a dilemma between right and wrong, but simply to live right on and breathe the circumambient air. There is no name for this life unless it be the very vitality of *vita*. Silent is the preacher about this, and silent must ever be, for he knows it will not preach.

Such a preacher knows this silent vitality stays circulating in the air and in the blood, in the heart and in the loins, in the earth and in the clouds, only by virtue of speaking words so that silence might also be expressed, hidden and secret within the syllables. The O of the poet's invocation contains the breath by which it's uttered, silent in the shape that is also the shape of the mouth singing it. It is also a child's drawing of the sun that, on the page, casts out a light that looks blank, but isn't. Not exactly blank. Not exactly white.

It is but the silent blankness of that pure fire that is also universal breath.

It gives the flute its tune to play. It gives words that judge not right versus wrong, good versus bad, but, submitting to a deeper, more primal power, marks most the difference between what *is* and what *is not*. This blankness secretes in words the very germ of silence that makes the partiality of each expand back into the circumambient whole.

We don't need angels to offer us that aether that, like a spiritual gravity, keeps together the world; we breathe that aether in when we speak the words out. We become initiates to the paradox that only in saying all we can say, only in singing out every word along the line of breath until breath is gone, only then do we inhale that silent signature the ancients called inspiration. That's when breathlessness begins to breathe.

Thoreau says, "The longest silence is the most pertinent question most pertinently put."

At the end of every book there is a long silence. What does it sound like?

Like the morning light.

49.

In the temporary reading room of the rare book library a man in stained glass has three faces at once. He stares out into the room where the readers read, and on either side of his face is his profile. I couldn't see behind him, even though he's made of glass, so I can't be sure, but feel safe assuming, that the eyes looking forward stare also behind. It's hard to tell if he's some kind of monster or god; or just a man looking from side to side where passing time is caught in a single, simultaneous instant because the motion can be caught in no other way; or if, as I fear is true, his visage is demonstration to each of us sitting within the room he gazes into of the consequences of reading: another face comes into your face, and who you are is no longer your own.

I went to the library to look for what is lost, but everything in the library has been found. I hoped, in some haphazard way, to look for lines crossed out, language discarded after being called up from the mind as not right or not worthy, orphan words, or are they exiles, to gather them in these pages, and give them a home.

A séance of a kind: to ask the librarian for a name; she walks behind a door and returns carrying the voice of the dead in a box.

Every April over the course of many years Thoreau kept track of the weather. In brown ink he scrawled the observations so quickly the words outpaced the letters forming them.

April weather alternate rain [   ] 30-53

quite   rain   Ap 2-52
nest   walking
rain rain   Ap 15-52

(Easter   17) – wind heaves [?] water in the rain

april flowers 13-53

April 1ˢᵗ–54 raining steady april day
April rain

    heavy thunder shower
        3 days of rain precipitation

            noon finds rather warm rain
        a misting rain the night after

I like it when the cloud fills the mind to remind it that the cloud repeats
in the mind like a rhyme that never perfectly rhymes. The mist in the
night obscures darkness already obscure, and to know it exists, you
must walk through it.

Thoreau's sister Sophia gave to an orphanage a handwritten copy of
the end of *Walden*, but it isn't the ending the rest of us know.

    I do not say that John
    or Jonathan—that this gen-
    eration or the next, age
    [   ] this [   ] or the next
    will realize all this – but
    such is the character of that
    morrow which mere lapse
    of time can never make to
    dawn.
        The light which puts out our
    eyes is darkness to us. There is a
    dawn lurking behind the hills of
    every horizon at noontide[?]; there are ears that
    hear the drowsy crickets, and eyes that see the glistening
    dews even then. Only that day dawns to which we

are awake. There is more day to dawn; the sun is but
a morning star.

Against the margin of the page, Thoreau, as he neared its end, had to
write smaller and smaller to fit all the words in. I guess in the end he
felt the extra sentence made a mob, and sent the orphans out, to make
a life of their own, drinking the dew for water, soothed by the music
of the cricket's song.

But for Thoreau the outside was an inside, the head a tool for burrowing, and for the man who measured the cellar of the new Concord
Court House—

> To whom it may
>   concern.

[other side]

Concord Mass
   Aug. 15th 1850

This may certify
that I have this day
measured the sand
excavated for the cellar
of the new Court
House in this town, and
found it to be six-
hundred and six and
a half – 606½ cubic
yards.

>   Henry D. Thoreau
>   Surveyor.

—the land of deepest exile, of furthest wandering, had for horizon
a line within. On a page torn from a notebook and found in another
book he bound this letter he wrote to no one, or none, or one, or you—

discovery of America [illegible]
of the adventures of the faithful explain
[illegible]own interior. Here is the center of
Central Africa – I would say then any
vagrant countrymen [   ]
foreign theater for spectacles – consider
first that there's nothing which can
delight or astonish the eye – but you may
discover it all in yourselves. [illegible]
thoughtlessly after the setting sun for adventures, for there [illegible] the beast you
have imagined. If you would be a
soldier here is demanded the eye and the
nerve. What after all is the meaning
of that exploring expedition with all its
parade and expense – but just a recognition after fact that there are continents
and seas in the moral world which
[   ] all
unexplained by him [
                              ] thousand miles through
cold and storm, savage cannibals and savage
[   ] home and reflect – easier
to flee before one's life than face it.
We are all defeated [?] – this is the reason
we enlist. Know thyself is the motto of
the true explorer. The man heedlessly
obeys the first blind impulse, and hastens
to South Africa perchance to chase the

On the other side of the page:

giraffe, but that is not the game he would
be after. How long pray would he hunt giraffes
if he could? – As soon as one brave
sailor shall declare that he has fathomed
the deeps of life and found them shallow
then may he enlist for the first Guinea
voyage [   ] offer. – Let a [   ]
man face all the fools of existence, and
he will be ready for any service that may
offer elsewhere. For the [   ]
those that go blindly into trade and
cease to think, those cowards that
[   ] away and enlist, have been daunted
from the [   ] of the field – they could
not stand alone with their lives – Men
whom I meet in the street are so
[   ] outward bound – they live out
[   ] – they are going and coming – looking
before and behind them – all out of [   ]
in 'the air'. I would fain see
them inward bound setting in and in
further every day. When I inquired I
should [   ] that one had gone away –
where, [
              ] he had entered deeper within
the folds of being.
[   ] who could speak all tongues
[

                                                    ]

Relics, too, in boxes. Small prayers to presence that make absence so real it's felt on the nerves.

> This hand-hewn pine beam, probably part of a stud or rafter is from Thoreau's cabin at Walden Pond, and was hewed himself as described on pp. 66-69 of 'Walden', with the bark, as there noted, left on one side. The nails, also from the cabin, are presumably those described on pp. 69-71 of 'Walden', taken from the shanty he bought from James Collins for $4.25.

These nails that held the cabin at Walden Pond together were taken from it when the cabin was pulled apart. I like how the nails speak of the wholeness within which a life lives itself, how it is built by piercing into what's holy or whole.

The force that bent the nail came from Thoreau's own arm, so different from reading in a book a word he wrote, or in his own hand the same, to feel the muscle swing the tool, hammer still somehow in the air, and the three-faced man in the stained glass looking everywhere to see from which direction the blow will come.

Except the blow comes from within.

The librarian takes from me what I have borrowed, all of it borrowed, what I've borrowed, all of it. Thoreau had to return what he had borrowed, too:

Dear Sir,

I return to the library Marquette's "Recit des Voyage" in the unbound reprint and volume.

Signed respectfully,
Henry D. Thoreau

50.

> The muses are daughters of memory
> Clio, Terpsichore

But the poet only mentions the Muse of History, and the Muse of the Delight of Dance, as if the others have been, or need to be, forgotten.

> Beauty is difficult

> Helios

Hard to know if the poet's stating back to the god what the god already knows. But I guess beauty isn't difficult for a god, whose shining out of himself is his own shining source, but for the one who must say "Helios," all who are not Helios, beauty is difficult. Hard to know if Helios is the example of difficult beauty. Hard to know if it's a prayer, an affirmation, a plea for release.

✦

The poems Ezra Pound wrote in the prisoner-of-war camp at Pisa are written in pencil on two different kinds of paper. The majority of the poems appear on the ruled notebook paper a child in grade school practices her alphabet on, blue lines across the gray page, like wires made out of sky on an overcast day. He would turn the page sideways so the lines ran up and down, and in two columns, one left, one right, he'd write his Cantos. The words paced behind the blue bars like an animal in a cage, prisoners too, or so it felt to me, holding the pages in the reading room, while the man in stained glass above me looked in every direction at once, as if looking everywhere for something that had gone missing, or worrying from which direction the threat will come.

As if you could make a jail out of the sky.

Pound seldom crosses out a single word, and checking the lines against the published poems, all that changes are the lengths of the lines, as if—let out from the cage in which they were composed—they could walk further toward the margin before turning around.

He writes in ancient Greek:

ΟΥ ΤΙΣ	["noman" as Odysseus gave his name to Polyphemus]
δειλία δεῖνα	["cowardice at terrors," or "cowardice at wonders"]
ποικιλόθεον ἀθάνατα	[deathless many-colored bird]
μεταθόμενον! . . .	[change your disposition toward me!]
Κύθερα! Κύθερα!	[Cytherea, Cytherea, one among Aphrodite's many names]
ἔθος	[ethos]

I could link them into their own poem, if only to interpret it:

I am the one I am not,
unable to say what I am afraid of though I know I am
afraid, of terror, or marvels, and the soul
best described as a bird of shifting colors
has offered herself to the goddess of Desire
so that she might see me differently and let me live,
noman that I am, a virtuous life.

But mostly I'm making this up.

The other paper, given him by Lt. White, whose name Pound underlines thrice, is a pamphlet of airmail stationery, eighty blank pages meant to "save money on your postage." Within those eighty pages, loose because the weak glue has eroded away, is the poem I came to the library to see, Canto LXXXI, whose lines

> What thou lovest well remains,
>
> > the rest is dross
> What thou lov'st well shall not be reft from thee
> What thou lov'st well is thy true heritage

have etched themselves with a silent chisel into my head or heart.

> *Love is difficult*
> > *Cytherea*

Page after page, as on the blue-lined notebook paper, the pencil's pressure pushing down through the thin sheet and leaving the impression on the next page of the words written before, flow from the poet so fluidly it seems a god must be speaking them in his ear. But then, when he gets to the passage that—almost every semester—I read out loud to my students, he falters, crosses out, rewrites, changes and reverts, as if the god stopped speaking, or began speaking in more than one voice, and each voice spoke at once:

> ~~"Thine eyes two will slaye me~~
> > ~~sodenly,~~
> ~~I may the beautie of them~~
> > ~~not sustayne."~~
> ~~from airy sound, not~~
> > ~~worked so patiently,~~

~~my sprite no turned not~~
     ~~to me agayne~~
~~Till I had heard the father~~
     ~~of all rhyme~~
~~speak time's ingle~~
~~where he~~ [illegible] ~~me~~

See, they return, the tentative ones:

As I was listening to the
                    enchanted song
There came new
     subtlety of eyes
     within my tent
whether of spirit or hypostasis
w/ glad hilarities
came no entire face
but what the blindfold hides,
     ~~of every~~
     or at carnival
nor any pair showed
     anger
but as unaware
     of other presence
smiled, each pair as at
     loveliest
nor was there space not
     a full eidos
but if how every soul lives is by
                    own
+ proper space, + each of
                    these
can penetrate + interpass

as light through light
casting but shade before no
other lights
nor lose its forms, each soul
keeping its cosmos
interlaid/laced free passing

They return, the old ones:

nor any pair
showed of anger
~~it was not the sole~~
at others presence
~~but seemed~~
as careless or unaware
as it had the not the
whole
tent's space
~~as these were masks not~~
~~masks~~
~~but had their loveliest life~~
~~six pair~~
~~nor was not all~~
~~but certainty~~
sky's clear
night's sea
green of the mountain pool
~~shone from the masks~~
~~not masks~~
shone from the unmasked
eye,
in half-mask's room.
what thou lovest well
shall not be rent from thee

what thou lovest well, remains
    the rest is dross
what thou lovest well is thy
    true heritage
whose world, or [illegible] or
      thing
    or ____ is it of none
so, thinking [?] of althea [?] at the [illegible]
two rose like lips pressed down
    upon my own

See, they return, one by one:

first comes the seen
then thus the palpable
~~[illegible] to make Elysium~~
   ~~with~~
~~dost thou lived in hell~~

           ~~as twere~~
           ~~in halls~~
           ~~of hell~~

  ~~mined~~
  ~~jailed~~
Elysium, ~~penetrant~~
~~e'en [illegible]~~
~~dominant laughing~~
~~at bay of hell chill~~
~~making game of hell~~
~~even of hell~~
~~making her sport even~~
      ~~of hell~~

Hell is a place where repetition reigns, keeps crossing itself out to make itself seen, where what is is by no longer existing, a pitkin plowed through verse to pour in seed or white barley or blood or anything to appease the dead or placate the gods, a kind of vision or revision that never alters the mistake, but makes it over again.

Of heaven, I know considerably less.

But I did learn a new prayer, a small one:

> O lynx guard my
> > vineyard
> as the grape swells
> > under vines

It's not in any liturgy, just written behind blue lines. It's a strange prayer because it is so true. Protect the grape from the sun that ripens it. Beauty is difficult, Helios. We must learn to grow a leaf that shades us from our source, or the source will end us. Δειλια δεινα. How to tell the difference between terror and wonder, I don't know; the word says they are the same. Μεταθομενον! O lynx that laps that raisins off the vines.

51.

Sir Thomas Browne writes:

> Wee doe but learne to day, what our better advanced
> judgements will unteach us to morrow: and *Aristotle* doth
> but instruct us as *Plato* did him; that is, to confute himselfe.
> I have runne through all sorts, yet finde no rest in any;
> though our first studies & *junior* endeavors may stile us
> Peripateticks, Stoicks, or Academicks, yet I perceive the
> wisest heads prove at last, almost all Scepticks, and stand like
> *Janus* in the field of knowledge. I have therefore one common
> and authentick Philosophy I learned in the Schooles, whereby
> I discourse and satisfy the reason of other men; another more
> reserved and drawne from experience whereby I content my
> owne. *Solomon* that complained of ignorance in the height
> of knowledge, hath not onely humbled my conceits, but
> discouraged my endeavors. There is yet another conceit that
> hath sometimes made me shut my books; which tels mee it is
> a vanity to waste our dayes in the blind pursuit of knowledge;
> it is but attending a little longer, and wee shall enjoy that by
> instinct and infusion which we endeavor at here by labour
> and inquisition: it is better sit downe in a modest ignorance,
> & rest contented with the natural blessings of our owne

reasons, than buy the uncertaine knowledge of this life, with
sweat and vexation, which death gives every foole gratis, and
is an accessory of our glorification.

These lessons learned best in the Library: to close the book, to look up
and look around, the far horizon isn't knowledge or wisdom but the
distance from which wild ignorance daily bounds. From all sides that
horizon rides silently toward us; fate gallops on invisible horses. We
wake and find the horizon has fit itself to the profile of our own face;
we wake to find our face is made mostly of distance. All those miles
fate rode across fate also gathered and compressed, formed them for us
into a kind of mask we never asked to wear, and not knowing if already
it's on us, know not how to take it off; so it is we keep waiting for our
own face to arrive, limit of the farthest extent grown so strangely intimate, making what is most our own most mysterious, as if the world's
whole distance had made itself at home in a visage. Fate promises there
is a world we live in of which we know hardly a thing, and the nearer it
comes, the less we understand it. Studying doesn't help much, but still
we read the books, heads like grain-heavy wheat bent down. The days
pass, and each day we look around unceasingly in all directions; we
even stare out of the back of our heads. From which directions is our
ignorance coming? Looking up from our books, what is the expression
in the mouth, of the eyes? Apprehension. Cross-listed, in the Library,
with Hope, with Fear, subsets of the larger worry, Understanding.

Ψυχή

Teacher, this is my book report on the soul. I promise not to start crying in front of the class like I did last time with my book report on the discovery of the mind.

The word psychology which speaks so loudly in our ears now of the mind and its working bears little resemblance to the Greek ψυχή from which it derives. The soul didn't think, or think about thinking.

It wasn't psychological. It didn't really resemble you. It wasn't an identity.

Some say the soul was first discovered in dreams. The image there of one like ourselves who wanders free and away from the dreamer. The old poets considered it possible that the man in the dream experiences the same mystery when his roaming ends and he falls asleep, an act which is no more than our waking, and what fills our mundane days is to him the vision of his soul.

Homer mentions ψυχή only when the life of the man is threatened. Without ψυχή he cannot survive. To go to war is to risk your ψυχή. To kill Hector is to win his ψυχή. When you swoon, ψυχή leaves your body, then a mist comes on your eyes, and if ψυχή returns you're still alive. You know about swooning, right? It's when someone pulls a spear from your thigh and out of the wound for a moment your soul flies away. If it doesn't come back, you've *swooned to death.*

Not exactly breath, ψυχή is also not exactly body, though Homer says there is a soul of the lungs and a soul of the heart. Often ψυχή is used interchangeably with *head*, and so some scholars believe the soul is located there—hence, in confusion, the holding of one's head, and so in sorrow, and so too of those rumors about Socrates that when he sneezed his soul was speaking to him. But all we know for certain about the location of the soul comes from the ways in which, as told in poems, it leaves the body. It flies away from limbs. It leaves through the mouth. From the nose. From the chest. Or a "wound in the flank."

The soul cannot reside in the dead body, it can't die with it, but must seek an afterlife. If the soul leaves early, the body gets ill, or "pines away" and dies of longing.

The link to breath, ψυχή to ψύχειν (to blow out or breathe), means that the soul is something always coming into us and leaving us, and is not only never properly our own, but in some ways belongs to everyone. I like to think the soul hovers there on the lips, fanning with a winnowing blade the air into the lungs, and later guiding out the words the singer sings. Another word, ψυχεινός (cooling), means the soul keeps the body from the fever of itself, and having a soul stops us from burning up.

A deeper sleep than sleep, but not the sleep of death, sometimes you come across a man or woman lying on the ground, or collapsed on the floor of a grocery store, and though they don't breathe, over days and even weeks the body doesn't corrupt, until one day, without any sign preceding the miracle, he or she stands up, and tells you the tale of the adventure, of having traveled to Metapontum and ordered the people there to build a temple to Apollo, or of having found a student in his home to explain some philosophic point that, when in class the question had been asked, the answer refused to be known.

The soul lets some people be in two places at once, as of Pythagoras, seen at Metapontum and Croton on the same day. Other times, the soul flies out of the mouth in the shape of a raven and returns as a man—scavenger, trickster, bird of shadow, associated in the undercurrent of thought with water that comes falling to earth after the bird calls.

There is a kind of memory that doesn't think, or thinks it doesn't think, and another kind of memory that is "the eye of the soul," which is memory that thinks. The soul isn't thinking, but it sees through thinking, as when, writing this report, I looked up and out of the window, except then my thinking was in my head, and for the soul, the thinking is the window.

To demonstrate his point, a teacher brings his class outside and, taking "a wand which draws the soul out of the body" strikes a boy with the wand, draws out his soul, and guides it far away where it stands by itself, and then the teacher asks his class to beat the body of the boy, which they do, and the boy seems not to feel a thing, and when the teacher touches the body again with the wand, the boy wakes up, "unharmed."

Not different aspects of soul but different souls altogether exist along with ψυχή. θυμός feels for us all we feel, spirit that collects and is source of all emotion, and it lives in the chest, but in moments of great fear, can move about within the body but seldom flees it, as when, seeing Hector dragged by Achilles around the walls of Troy, Andromache's θυμός leaves her heart and moves to her fingers, seeking some way to escape the horror she feels at her husband's death; but this soul cannot leave, and she wakes from her faint having been nowhere else but scared behind the walls of Ilium. μένος quickens into spear-sharp strength the sense of purpose that, in feeling fear, might quail. It hopes only to act, not to receive. It can be breathed into you by a god who wants you to act on her behalf to kill whom she wants to be killed. It can madden the senses into shields. And when it leaves, you might find yourself looking at your hands, saying "What have you done?" talking to your hands as if they were not part of you, as if they had acted on their own, separate from the body to which they are attached; but it isn't true, you did these things with your hands.

All I've spoken of so far is the living soul, and though I know my time is almost up, there's still the dead soul to discuss, and I hope my grade won't suffer for speaking too long.

Most often we obscure our sense of the soul by the assumptions we carry within us about it, and when we want to describe as best we can our own soul, instead we discover we have outlined an idea we've long held, given to us we know not by whom, and rather than a theory of the holy-dark-emptiness, we've circumscribed a vacuum with our breath, and what would have been more honest, after speaking out loud all those words while the audience nodded off into partial dreams, would have been to put my hand against my throat to feel the vibration there humming beneath the words.

After death, mostly the soul continues as it had been, but where before there had been body, now there is only shadow, or shade, or in rare cases, a snake. Mostly the soul can move and speak just as before, but sometimes it cannot, and can only "flit and squeak."

Door on an old hinge. Fieldmouse.

As if the soul were a vermifuge, Achilles worries that Patroclus's soul loosened and removed to Hades will allow the maggots to defile his body.

Θυμός at death leaves the lip or limbs, and, as does breath into the larger air, diffuses with no trace into the aether. But the ψυχή which, when alive, none have a thought of, none notice, in death bears the thoughts and wants, the fear and hopes, that pervaded the mind of the man now gone who, no longer bearing the burden of his own life, leaves it for the soul to bear, a shadow without a heart who nonetheless carries the heart's hard cares.

The connection between shadow and soul is still in need of systematic inquiry, but every time you stop to question a shadow you find you're talking once again to yourself. So the categories remain obscure. Aristotle claims ψυχή also meant "butterfly," and though no evidence exists that the soul transforming from life to death becomes a butterfly—to begin in hunger insatiable, to fall asleep, and then to wake winged and hungerless—the image speaks so hopefully to what, before battle or suddenly taken ill, one might wish death to be; of the precipitous decline in butterfly populations, beyond the sorrow of less beauty, now there is this fear that even the dead have begun to lose their souls, and that brief shadow beneath the wings as the butterfly sips having gone missing means the afterlife has begun to shut down.

The dead bear the wounds that killed them. They find the same jokes funny but have a hard time laughing. Their voices don't work the same, and they move strangely, flitting as a moth does before a light, or a butterfly, which seems to be in two places at once, as it lands and then lands again on the same bloom.

The funeral rites tend to take a few days to complete, and during that time the soul is neither on earth nor in Hades. On an urn, made in the sixth century and recently exhumed, a small armored man stands next to the fallen Patroclus, and, written next to the homunculus, the word ψυχή. The soul waits silently for the body to be buried or burned, not mourning among the mourners but standing patient beside them, witness to the rites of which it is the subject, delayed in their cries, caught in the no time between the day of death and eternity, a kind of waiting room in the dust.

Some who die never get to be dead. Children, adolescents, "brides and youths unwed," "tender maidens with grief yet fresh at heart," grooms who, stepping over the threshold of the bedroom, pass away as the torch is lit . . . the list is long. Some scholars say such souls live in the suburbs of hell, home in the outskirts which are never a home, and others ascribe them no place at all, some honored as gods, some forgotten, some remembered only in the burning of grain, the pouring of blood, the fragrance of the bitten fruit, and some abandoned to the absence of lost breath and never remembered at all.

Some souls even forget themselves. Some might be called ghosts. On the day of the great festival when the earthenware jars of a new wine first were to be opened, and even the most misanthropic of men would dine with others, the ghosts would wander the city and the fields, men and women would chew the leaves of the buckthorn, "reputed to be good for warding away apparitions," and after the feast, when normally couches would be shared and wine drunk, each man now would sit alone and drink his jug of wine as fast as he could in complete silence. No one understands this silence. Not the men and women. Not the ghosts.

But for most of the dead, burial rites completed, life goes on. Not that the dead don't know they're dead, they do; but repeating the same actions as in life, it's easy to forget for a time the nature of doom—until one looks down, and sees the wound. But it's easy to forget. Easy to walk back into the room as if nothing has changed, easy to begin again what has already happened, to think it is the first time, what has never ceased to be done. Teacher? Teacher?

Teacher, this is my book report on the soul. I promise not to start crying in front of the class like I did last time with my book report on the discovery of the mind.

The word psychology which speaks so loudly in our ears now of the mind and its working bears little resemblance to the Greek ψυχή from which it derived. The soul didn't think, or think about thinking.

It wasn't psychological. It didn't really resemble you. It wasn't an identity.

Some say the soul was first discovered in dreams. The image there of one like ourselves who wanders free and away from the dreamer. The old poets considered it possible that the man in the dream experiences the same mystery when his roaming ends and he falls asleep, an act which is no more than our waking, and what fills our days is to him the vision of his soul.

53.

For the past three weeks I've read a book by Jan Bremmer, *The Early Greek Concept of the Soul.* On the day I finished reading it, I found a scrap of paper stuck in the pages. I pulled it out when I got to it: a checkout slip from 11-14-2012 at 3:24 p.m. from the Main Library in town; Dona Stein checked out a book of poems.

I don't know how or why it was in the book I checked out, from a different library entirely, nor would it be such a strange mystery to me, such a haunted moment, if I didn't know Dona Stein, a poet herself who on the local radio station invited poets to come and recite their work through the air, a show she gave up in 2012, and from whom, since that year, I've never heard from again.

My search for an obituary found none, but not a single mention of her is made after 2012.

The book she checked out was due 12-05-2012, almost three years ago. It was titled *Dear Ghosts.*

54.

Kristy called from the Homecoming Parade and gave the phone to Iris. "A man on a big raft threw candy and I caught it!" "In your hands?" I asked. "No, I caught it on the ground."

Later that night, a text: "Iris was looking out of the car window on the way home and said 'Sometimes it looks like everything is just made of air, like the trees and the clouds and the moon.'"

I thought about it the next morning, walking to the museum where, though I didn't know it yet, I'd see a gold earring in the shape of a bee hanging by a thin wire above the broken urns, and, in a room that held a broken shield so old the image on it could only be imagined by reading the placard describing what time had erased, a wall of funerary statues from Palmyra, where even now men devoted to God are blowing the ruins up. The other bee flew away forever, or is still in the hive, or the grave.

Everything is just made of air, I thought, walking into the air, in the sometimes bright, sometimes not, sunlight of a partly cloudy day in which the nighttime stars still burned unseen behind the blue, buried in the light of which they're also made.

Sirens

He tells his friends he has no choice, but he does; beautiful-voiced Circe told him so:

> First you will come to the Sirens, who beguile all men who
> come near to them. Whoever in ignorance draws near to
> them and hears the Sirens' voice, his wife and little children
> never stand beside him and rejoice at his homecoming;
> instead, the Sirens beguile him with their clear-toned song, as
> they sit in a meadow, and about them is a great heap of bones
> of moldering men, and round the bones the skin is shriveling.
> But row past them, and anoint the ears of your comrades
> with sweet wax, which you have kneaded, for fear any of
> the rest may hear. But if you yourself have a will to listen, let
> them bind you in the swift ship hand and foot upright in the
> step of the mast, and let the ropes be made fast at the ends of
> the mast itself, that with delight you may listen to the voice of
> the two Sirens.

The two Sirens sing with one voice a single song, music different than harmony, where two voices merge as one, something stranger, more fascinating, in which the song is less than those who sing it, and, being sung, makes the singers less than whole, so that two is somehow less than one. To hear it makes you less than you are.

Odysseus tells his companions: "Me alone she bade listen to their voice." He acts as if his desire is her command, or what he wants is a form of fate.

But what does he want?

Maurice Blanchot writes:

The Sirens: it seems they did indeed sing, but in an unfulfilling way, one that only gave a sign of where the real sources and real happiness of song opened. Still, by means of their imperfect songs that were only a song still to come, they did lead the sailor toward that space where singing might truly begin. They did not deceive him, in fact: they actually led him to his goal. But what happened once the place was reached? What was this place? One where there was nothing left but to disappear, because music, in this region of source and origin, had itself disappeared more completely than in any other place in the world: sea where, ears blocked, the living sank, and where the Sirens, as proof of their good will, had also, one day, to disappear.

Before Odysseus asks his friends to lash him to the mast of his dark ship, before the crew prepares to leave Circe's island and journey past the Sirens and Charybdis and Scylla, he took the sheep he carried on-board and "went along beside the stream of Oceanus" to the place Circe had earlier told them about. "I drew my sharp sword from beside my thigh and dug a pit" and in it, along with milk and honey and white barley and wine, cut the throats of the animals and let the blood flow into the hole. The dead from every side clamored to the blood, and only by holding his sword over the pit did the hero keep the horde away. He was saving the blood for the prophet Tiresias, from whom he wanted to learn how to get home. But before the seer comes, Odysseus, camped on the edge of death, sees a ghost step toward him that he knows. He finds in the deep shade the shade of his mother. He hadn't known she died. "At sight of her I wept, and my heart had compassion on her, but even so I would not allow her to come near the blood, for all my great sorrow, until I had inquired of Tiresias."

Tiresias comes. He drinks the blood and tells the truth.

The prophet tells Odysseus his journey will not end even after he arrives home, even after he has killed the men who desire his wife to be their own, for the sea god's great anger extends past destination all the way to destiny. Tiresias says:

> But when you have slain the suitors in your halls, whether by
> guile or openly with the sharp sword, then go abroad, taking
> a shapely oar, until you come to men that know nothing of
> the sea and eat their food unmixed with salt, who in fact
> know nothing of ships with ruddy cheeks, or of shapely oars,
> which are a vessel's wings. And I will tell you a most certain
> sign, which will not escape you: when another wayfarer, on
> meeting you, shall say that you have a winnowing fan on
> your stout shoulder, then fix in the earth your shapely oar
> and make handsome offerings . . .

It is strange advice that can only come from the place of death—to wander so far away from your beginning that you come to a place where no one can recognize you or the tools you carry, where people mistake the oar for a winnowing fan, not the tool that shuttles the ship to the lands it invades or returns to, but the instrument that knocks the chaff off the seed . . . Odysseus must wander far enough inland so that another man can approach him and make the *accurate mistake*. Only there, building an altar in error, can the man seeking forgiveness from the god find it, there where none salt their food, where none eat fish, where the ocean is less than a rumor, and the god who governs the waters is unknown. You must go so far into your penance that the god from whom you seek reprieve has no shrine in the land where now you stand, and there, where none have uttered that god's name, where the god's power is less than wheat-chaff, there you must plant the tool of your torment and salvation, the oar no longer an oar but a winnowing fan, which beat away your pride, and left some germ called obedience, or faith.

But maybe it isn't so simple.

Odysseus alive among the shades sees what few men living come to know: the winnowing blade called time beats away the husk and leaves the seed; but the husk is heavier, and the seed weighs nothing, and blown away on a breath it arrives in the shadows, poor soul. He wants to know more than Tiresias has told him. "I see here the ghost of my dead mother; she sits in silence near the blood and cannot bring herself to look upon the face of her own son or speak to him. Tell me, my lord, how may she recognize that I am he?" Let her come near the blood, drink of the dark blood, and she will speak.

"At once she knew me," Odysseus says, and he asks her how she died, by long illness or by sudden calamity. Anticlea answers her son, alive in the murky dark: "Neither did the keen-sighted archer goddess assail me in my halls with her gentle shafts, and slay me, nor did any disease come upon me, such as oftenest with loathsome wasting takes the spirit from the limbs; no, it was longing for you, and for your counsels, glorious Odysseus, and for your gentle-heartedness, that robbed me of honey-sweet life."

Odysseus, whose dearest wish is to return home, land of origin, deep-rooted source, travels to the underworld to learn what he must do to accomplish his hopes; but there, he finds in the undergrove's shade his own most intimate source, body that gave his body life, that carried him, nursed him, raised him into the hero that now he is, and though he "wondered in my heart how I might clasp the ghost of my dead mother," and three times finds she flits through his arms, the "pain grew ever sharper in my heart," a sorrow digging in his heart a pit filling pulse by pulse with blood, and the ghosts cannot stop from nearing him now, nor can any sword hold them back, finding as he does at the end of all living the source from which his life began.

Sometimes a panic comes upon me. Not always the same. Like when ends are beginnings and beginnings ends. Like when they can't be told apart. Like when you spend your whole life wanting to get home, to get some place, anywhere but where you are, driven by some sense of purpose, by some necessity, and to get there you have to discover there is no place to go. But there are other panics. Like song.

Blanchot ponders the strange enchantment of the Sirens' song: "It did nothing but reproduce the habitual song of men, and because the Sirens, who were only animals, quite beautiful because of the reflection of feminine beauty, could sing as men sing, they made the song so strange that they gave birth in anyone who heard it to a suspicion of the inhumanity of every human song." The first songs we hear, before we even know the words that carry the tune, are the lullabies our mothers sing us. Some of these songs we think we've forgotten until, at night, putting our own children to bed, we hear the song again sung from our own mouths, lulling the child to do what she most does not want to do, to fall into the gap called sleep, and face those who live only there, within the dark. Later that same night, song recovered and house asleep, finding yourself restless, you discover one of the conditions of adulthood—you can't sing yourself to sleep. Blanchot writes, "Is it through despair, then, that men passionate for their own song came to perish? Through a despair very close to rapture. There was something wonderful in this real song, this common, secret song, simple and everyday, that they had to recognize right away, sung in an unreal way by foreign, even imaginary powers, song of the abyss that, once heard, would open an abyss in each word and would beckon those who heard it to vanish into it."

When the Sirens note the swift ship drawing near they begin their "clear-toned song." They talk to Odysseus tied to the mast: "Come hither on your way, renowned Odysseus, great glory of the Achaeans; stop your ship that you may listen to the voice of us two. For never yet has any man rowed past the island on his black ship until he has heard the sweet voice from our lips; instead, he has joy of it, and goes his way a wiser man. For we know all the toils that in wide Troy the Argives and the Trojans endured through the will of the gods, and we know all the things that come to pass on the fruitful earth." The Sirens speak to him as they sing. They promise him a song that will sing him back his own life, the sympathy in long toil, a song that both confirms what the hero has lived through and, by being sung back to him like a story not his own, removes him from that life he lived and those bloody deeds it seemed to require. Some songs remove us from ourselves when we are the subject of the song. It is like a story I heard from a man I met years ago, hired by a wealthy businessman to write his own autobiography for him. The writer was called a ghost. The Sirens promise to Odysseus a song that will shine in wisdom—why things are the way they are, why I am the way I am. But none of these words are the song.

Odysseus says his heart wants to listen. He asks his friends to free him but they add lashes to his binding and row harder. The Sirens tell Odysseus that their single-voiced song leads to knowledge, but this hero most renowned and most reviled for being so clever, Odysseus of devious ways, does not want to learn from the song what can be known, his heart wants to listen. Only in those buried chambers, pulse by pulse filling with blood, where in the old thinking the fascinated images of those we love reside, does the abyss of the Sirens' song open in us the same abyss, so that to fall into the underworld is only to fall into ourselves, to disappear into our own hearts, and live among the ghosts that dwell there. The Sirens sing even as they beckon Odysseus with the song they will sing, a music underneath the words, pulling on Odysseus's heart even as the words distract his mind, urging him into the distance they contain, that unimaginable gap between words and the song at work underneath them, that abyss beneath knowledge on which the mind floats like a swift ship going only in circles though it seemed all that time headed home.

One could say that in every song, every poem, there hides a monster, a Charybdis, far below the words where the music keeps digging deeper the depths, keeps making more present all that goes more missing, adding abyss to abyss until the void is felt. It feels like beauty, I guess.

You want to get to the source, to the origin song seems to hold, but as you near it, it drops further down, until the only hope of arrival is to drown.

Strange freedom Odysseus asks for from his crew. Freedom to return to the fate he has just left behind, venturing into death having not yet died, finding lifelike his mother he loves, but she isn't alive, she is far less than alive, the source of his own breathing no longer breathing, mother of his tongue not speaking, save when she drinks from the blood he brings. That distance he crossed—so different in degree than mere miles—he never crossed. I mean: he did what cannot be done, but that doesn't mean it has been done. The incompleteness stays inside him, his death yet to come already present in him, taking all that is innermost and nearmost, and putting within them the distance between us and all things we love most, so that my own heart feels lost far inland where an oar becomes a winnowing fan, even as it beats, nearing this essay's end, a bit quicker in my chest.

Maybe Odysseus needs to hear the Sirens sing their single-voiced song because his mother spoke to him in the underworld and said, *I died because I thought I had lost you.*

That song is the distance between them. A lullaby that puts to sleep lullabies, that puts to sleep the songs of sleep. Distance from the song that is the song itself.

Should you want to hear the Sirens sing, Strabo offers you this advice to find them:

> Eratosthenes says that the places mentioned in the story of
> the wanderings of Odysseus, also, belong to the category
> of fiction, and that the persons who contend that they are
> not fictitious but have a foundation in fact, stand convicted
> of error by the very fact that they do not agree among

themselves; at any rate, that some of them put the Sirens on Cape Pelorias, while others put them more than two thousand stadia distant on the Sirenussae, which is the name given to a three-peaked rock that separates the Gulf of Cumae from the Gulf of Poseidonia. But neither does this rock have three peaks, nor does it run up into a peak at all; instead it is a sort of elbow that juts out, long and narrow, from the territory of Surrentum to the Strait of Capreae, with the sanctuary of the Sirens on one side of the hilly headland, while on the other side, looking towards the Gulf of Poseidonia, lie three uninhabited rocky little islands, called the Sirens.

And so we have a last definition of the Sirens, not animals with the guise of female beauty, not mythic creatures singing as one their ever-incomplete song of pure source, just some rocky little islands on which no one lives, eaten wave by wave away, disappearing as they listen to the sea's own song, made complete by the thing that undoes them.

The Star Knot Is the Chief Thing

Some law hidden in everything.

✦

    pink anvil each strike
    lights up within the pink
    anvil of cloud and all
    the storm storms inside it

✦

In 1866 Gerard Manley Hopkins writes:

> *July 11.* Oats: hoary blue-green sheaths and stalks, prettily
> shadow-stroked spikes of pale green grain. Oaks: the
> organisation of this tree is difficult. Speaking generally no
> doubt the determining planes are concentric, a system of
> brief contiguous and continuous tangents, whereas those
> of the cedar wd. roughly be called horizontals and those of
> the beech radiating but modified by droop and by a screw-
> set towards jutting points. But beyond this since the normal
> growth of the boughs is radiating and the leaves grow some
> way in there is of course a system of spoke-wise clubs of
> green—sleeve-pieces. And since the end shoots curl and carry
> young and scanty leaf-stars these clubs are tapered, and I
> have seen also the pieces in profile with chiselled outlines,
> the blocks thus made detached and lessening towards the
> end. However the star knot is the chief thing: it is whorled,
> worked round, a little and this is what keeps up the illusion
> of the tree: the leaves are rounded inwards and figure
> out ball-knots. Oaks differ much, and much turns on the
> broadness of the leaf, the narrower giving the crisped and

starry and Catherine-wheel forms, the broader the flat-pieced mailed or shard-covered ones, in wh. it is possible to see composition in dips, etc., on wider bases than the single knot or cluster. But I shall study them further. See the 19th.

So hard to know what keeps up our illusions. The star knot that can't be untied—no matter how hard you look at it, you can't think out the tangle into law. Teaching Hopkins I can feel the world go blank around me. No words for the neighbor's willow when in the fall the teardrop leaves brighten into a yellow that shines out its last green and the wind moves through the tree so it is a young girl shaking her head and laughing while looking down in the grass and finding what she thought she'd lost. A ring. Or the late cricket singing. See how hard it is to see, I ask. The mind mixes in memory and suddenly the eye is a metaphor.

Sometimes I think it is a description not of the oak but of the mind: "The star knot is the chief thing: it is whorled, worked round, a little and this is what keeps up the illusion of the tree." It is whorled and worked round, or so the line drawing in a dictionary makes it look. Composed of the elements first cast out into nothingness by the death throes of the very stars that pierced the abyss with their light, the mind could be seen, if you wanted to see it so, as a knot formed by tying together light that is no longer bright. Sometimes that's how I want to see it.

But mostly I ask my students to take out a page of blank paper and draw what Hopkins describes. Nothing recognizable ever results. Sometimes the page is left blank.

So much work to see that I don't yet know how to see. I shall study it further.

✦

I remember a cloud that formed in deep west Texas in June of 2005. Hana wasn't yet a year old. I sat outside of the house I'd been given to write in for a month. I was reading Plato's *Timaeus*, trying to understand exactly how it is the world formed, when I saw the cloud in one vast upsweep gather the sun into pink and within the cloud the lightning struck in horizontal lines that flashed and made the cloud blink.

I remember that cloud more clearly than I remember Hana as a baby. The cloud floats in the star knot so clearly. But the child has become cloudy. What is the law?

✦

July 19. I have now found the laws of the oak leaves.

✦

June 2005 . . . I saw an anvil floating in the sky. Law was the fire laced inside.

57.

The dimple in the stream puts a hole in the cloud and a hole in the sky.

The sun puts a liquid bright hole in a cloud.

The hawk tucking in its wings is a hole falling through the sky.

My constant need for praise from others measures the hole that is my heart.

My constant need to praise an other is a hole in the sky called God.

58.

Sir Thomas Browne: "Our ends are as obscure as our beginnings, the line of our dayes is drawne by night, and the various effects therein by a pencill that is invisible."

Emerson: "Whatever limits us, we call Fate."

I keep wanting to learn how to read, but have trouble understanding what page I'm on. I mean, it's hard to know what is a page, and much harder to read it.

I keep writing these pages hoping one of them will teach me how—

to see, to read—

I don't know exactly what I'm trying to say—

Sir Thomas Browne:

> For there are mystically in our faces certaine characters
> which carry in them the motto of our Soules, wherein he that
> cannot read A. B. C. may read our natures. I hold moreover
> that there is a Phytognomy, or Physiognomy, not onely of
> men, but of Plants, and Vegetables; and in every one of them,
> some outward figures which hang as signes or bushes of their
> inward formes. . . . By these Letters God cals the Starres by
> their names, and by this Alphabet *Adam* assigned to every
> creature a name peculiar to its Nature. Now there are besides
> these Characters in our faces, certaine mysticall lines and
> figures in our hands, which I dare not call meere dashes,
> strokes, *à la voleé*, or at randome, because delineated by a
> pencill, that never works in vaine; and hereof I take more

particular notice, because I carry that in my owne hand, which I could never read of, or discover in another.

Γνῶθι σεαυτόν, says the oracle. Know yourself.

Gerard Manley Hopkins, walking with a friend on December 12, 1873, sees "green-white tufts of long bleached grass like heads of hair or the crowns of heads of hair, each a whorl of slender curves, one tuft taking up another." This sight he could have noticed on any given day he sees somehow newly, finding in the lines some other script than daily recognition. He says he saw "as if my eye were still growing."

For a little while, I guess, he learned to read.

Auguste Rodin's *Thinker*, head bent down on his bending down hand, is for so many of us the image that comes to mind when asked to picture thinking. Without lids it's hard to tell if his eyes are open or closed. The gods are that way, too—but the gods don't need to learn how to read. Only we do. That's how I learned Rodin didn't know much about thinking. The first book isn't held by the hand but is the hand, those lines that describe a life etched by an invisible pencil in the night, and the statue to be true would, to picture the work properly, stare into his own hand. Then maybe he'd grow some eyes and we'd know—

know something—

how to read maybe, maybe how to spell, maybe how to say a name, maybe the name that is my own—

59.

When I look down at the blank page I don't see the maze. But then I begin the poem, and line by line the labyrinth emerges. As a child I always thought the point of working through the maze was to arrive in the middle, but later I learned that's where the monsters live, and when a child enters, he's eaten. Now sometimes I think that monsters live in the middle of all things, waiting to be found to know whether or not they are real, or if they are—like so many things—just a rumor of themselves. And though in many poems I've written the word *monster* I've never found a monster dwelling there. That doesn't mean it doesn't exist. It just means I was wrong about the nature of the maze. It doesn't trap you. It just keeps showing you the way out.

I think about Theseus unspooling behind him Ariadne's thread. I think about it when I watch the dark line follow the pencil and how the words grow their bramble behind it. It's as if the walls of the maze arise only after you've walked past them, and the labyrinth can be found in no other way. It's made by your wandering or wondering. The line of the poem, winding from margin to margin, like the fine thread of Theseus's escape, mimics the riddle it maps, and even the route of escape can bewilder; though the line of the poem, like the twisting, peristaltic mystification of the intestine, ends up by leaving us outside always the world we'd been in. I guess sometimes the maze is on the inside.

But I also know some kind of infinity hides itself in the poem. Sometimes it's called an immortal bird. When the maze is darkness it flies deeper into the darkness. All the way to the center of it. This might mean the maze does have a center, but the center is for itself, and those who wander in, who read their way through, aren't ever allowed inside, even as they're in it, walking, thinking.

Blanchot writes: "From the finite, which is still closed, one can always hope to escape, while the infinite vastness is a prison, being without an exit." Strange to say how often I feel the urge to get into what I can't escape from, but it never happens. Sometimes I hear a tune as if within a song another song sings, but when I stop to listen, it goes away, and so too does the song I was singing. Sometimes I read a poem and sense another poem hidden within it, a poem so much clearer than the one I'm reading, so much truer, though I don't know what truth is, nor can I see what's so clear. Then trouble finds my mind. Then I know the maze has a center, and the center is larger than the maze, and there's no way out, no exit, because there's no way in, and the life of the mind is as strange as the life of the heart, alive always on the periphery, swallowed whole by the thing of which it has no part.

Theseus's Ship

The wind blows many things off course.
A strong gust tears the winnowed husk in two
Carries the chaff in different directions
One inland and one out to sea.
But different versions mostly end the same.
This story is about a man and a ship.
In Delos he danced a dance the youth still dance.
An imitation of the labyrinth.
The youth still call the dance The Crane.
To dance this dance yourself
Cut from the left side of the head some horns
Build an altar. It's called the Keraton.
Kerata means "horns." Find a rhythm.
Convolute it. Involute it. Now the dance is done
But the altar remains.
Even when the ship leaves the altar remains.
Sometimes the dance. Often the wind.

✦

The thirty-oared galley in which he sailed
Youth to safety they preserved through time.
They took away a timber from time to
Time put it in a pile
They replaced it with a new plank.
Centuries passed and the boat grew younger.
In a thousand years it became new.
Clever or bored some youth looked at the pile
Of old timber and fitting board to board
Built the ship again. They stand side by side
On the long grass the wind blows like waves
When it blows it blows like waves the grass.

Poets and philosophers like to argue
About which ship is Theseus's ship
And which ship is the image or impostor
While the grass rises in swells about their ankles.

✦

The thirty-oared galley in which he sailed
Youth to safety they preserved through time.
They took away a timber from time to
Time put it in a pile
They replaced it with a new plank.
Centuries passed and the boat grew younger.
In a thousand years it became new.
Clever or bored some youth looked at the pile
Of old timber and fitting board to board
Built the ship again. They stand side by side
On the long grass the wind blows like waves
When it blows it blows like waves the grass.
Poets and philosophers like to argue
About which ship is Theseus's ship
And which ship is the image or impostor
While the grass rises in swells about their ankles.

✦

Kerata

This version blows the labyrinth out to sea.
A strong wind carries the crane off course.
Sometimes one finds the dance winnows the chaff
But mostly yourself remains. A different imitation
Means a different dance, but the rhythm in the head
Calls in the same directions: convolute, involute,

Dance. The youth build the altar. The gust leaves the husk.
And the dance still remains an altar to the tears
A man cut from his side. The youth called the horns "horns."
Many danced this dance when the wind left. Still it is
The story of one ship and some altar: Delos, the Keraton.
Of dance? Often it is about an end. Even now it's done.

61.

A morning run through Lake View Cemetery in east Cleveland.

The sun erases the names on the stones before I can read them. Erases the names with light.

Rounding a bend, a grassy hill with no graves, just tractor tread printed in mud in the ground, leading to a copse of trees. A wrought iron sign, black with white letters, reads: "Future Development."

So that's where the future grows.

Whitenesses

Who was it that said the artist holds a mirror up to nature? Or was it society, not nature, reflected there? I guess I can't remember the mirror.

In the Middle Ages monks performed feats of great emotion in front of mirrors to study the physiology of the face in moments of *ecstasy, awe, horror, happiness, surprise, despair.* I'm sure the list goes on. One of the questions about the nature of the will that has long fascinated me regards the limits of its force. I can move my arm on purpose while saying inside my head, "Now I'll move my arm." But I can also say inside my head, "Now I'll move my arm," and let my arm keep resting on the arm of the chair. I can stand in front of a mirror and tell myself to feel an emotion strongly, for example, *guilt.* I imagine I'd need to imagine what in my life I feel most guilty about, and then wait for the moment my face registers what I feel inside myself. But I can also imagine making a face that looks like guilt, and feeling nothing at all.

Not long ago after a scandal at a writers conference, I overheard a student of mine say to his friend, "You feel like being a man means you shouldn't write." By *you* he meant *I*.

During a more recent scandal a student sat in my office crying. She'd read post after post on the internet written in ALL CAPS. She said to me, "They say being white means I shouldn't write poems, and I see their point, but it feels awful." I could see in her face that the sentence was true. She felt awful. "What should I do?"

Sometimes what brings most comfort is to mirror back to the person in pain his or her pain. To show in your face their face. So I mentioned Emerson. In his essay "Fate," Emerson asks: "How shall I live?" Then she looked at me and I looked at her and some time passed in which what was yet unsaid remained unsaid.

Thinking about the difference between those two questions—What should I do? How shall I live?—so nearly the same, so vastly separate, I found myself walking over the green hills carrying a mirror in both arms. I was living the life of the artist—showing nature to herself, showing to any person who came before me her own nature. But as hard as I tried to turn the mirror around I couldn't. I kept saying in my head, "Now I'll turn the mirror around," but I couldn't. It was hard to walk all that way up the gentle slope, staring at myself so long that all emotion left my face, and all that was left was the labor of carrying the image of my own face in front of me, expressing nothing, just blank— not blank, I mean it was just a white face, a white man's face, a face built around whiteness.

Fell asleep again in a chair, reading Marcus Aurelius's *Meditations*: "All the things of the body are as a river, and the things of the soul as a dream and a vapor."

✦

In the morning the girls play a game I've never seen before. Hana tells Iris: "Now you lie face down on the ground, and don't struggle, or I'll have to sit on your back." Iris struggles. She says she doesn't want to be arrested. "I'm arresting you and I'm going to have to put you in jail if you struggle." "But I didn't do anything," Iris says. "Yes, you did," says Hana. "What did I do?" "You know," Hana says. Iris stops struggling. "Get up." Iris gets up. "I'm taking you to your cell." "What's a cell?" Iris asks. Hana puts her in the shower and closes the door. "This is a cell." I guess she got solitary. "Let me out! Let me out!" Iris yells. "Only if you say sorry." "But I didn't do anything." "Yes, you did." "I'm sorry," Iris says. "No, you're not."

I don't know to play along. I mean, I don't know if I should play along, or if it's a game that should be played. I say, "You'll have to be let out for work duty."

Iris and I bundle up to shovel snow. Whiteness over everything. We work in silence, just the noise of the shovel edge scraping the whiteness away, leaving a different whiteness underneath. A broken whiteness. Then I hear a song. Very quiet, then louder. It's Iris, singing the ABCs.

That song of all labor.

Robert Frost writes:

> The bird would cease and be as other birds
> But that he knows in singing not to sing.

✦

In singing not to sing.

The poem is "The Oven Bird." In guidebooks the song of the oven bird is transliterated as *teacher, teacher, teacher.*

Teacher, teach me how in song not to sing.

✦

Those once sung about, long forgotten. Not a vestige remains of ways of life that seemed, when lived, endless. Powers dispersed into air—of souls, of nations. Subtleties and beauties, of poem and of face, affection most tender and passion most violent, no whisper even remains. Whole nations leave no trace. The languages they spoke that held on their tongues whole citadels of philosophy, entire edifices of truth, crumbled into less than ruin. Not even rumors remain. Not even a word on a potsherd. No ostraca. The stone becomes less than the air.

I can't breathe.

Trying to find in what is comfortless some comfort, I read Marcus Aurelius, who reminds me by reminding himself to keep a proper perspective, to be gentle in what has no gentleness. The Stoics believe that Nature is all. The word in Greek, φύσις, means both how the universe works and how a person does, implies a reciprocity that the laws that govern the stars govern us, that the sun, the moon, the invisible spheres, all also exist within, and as absurd as it is to say, it is nonetheless true that the extant of my arm's reach is no less than the abysmal distance between galaxies. Who doesn't contain the universe entire? Law governs us both.

I can't stand up.

Astronomy sees more now than it did in second-century Rome, when those versed in the nature of the universe could only look up at the sky and watch it nightlong to learn the mysteries there. Now we know vast order contains vaster violence. Galaxies consume one another, as do stars other suns, as do planets moons. Billions of stars spin around a massive black hole into whose depths light itself pours. Absence at the center of most things, and the absence repeats. Everywhere is like this. And unlike Marcus Aurelius urging us to think about the isolate point that is the earth, it seems most stars are circled by planets, whole worlds in orbit, lifeless each. Against the light that fills the eye, most of the mass of the universe is dark matter, which scientists know is real, despite the theory being the only proof—that theory that without it, nothing could exist, including the scientists thinking the thought. "One philosopher goes without a shirt, a second without a book, a third yonder half-naked: says he, *I am starving for bread, yet cleave I fast to reason.*" Now that the universe is less reasonable, nakedness is what the philosopher wears on the inside. Let's say the principle holds. I'm walking around every day with whole worlds inside me, but not one of them yet has been found on which a creature could breathe a single breath. It is more than our graves we carry within us as our weightless burden. There are the empty reaches, too. And the worlds gathered around stars red and blue.

I can't breathe.

✦

"What the white whale was to Ahab, has been hinted; what, at times, he was to me, as yet remains unsaid," writes Melville, in chapter forty-two of *Moby-Dick*. "It was the whiteness of the whale that above all things appalled me."

Zeus appears as a spotless white bull. Pearls. Marble. For the Persians who worshipped fire the white-forked flame on the altar was holiest. Kings and Queens drawn by milk-white steeds. Justice's own robe. Color of redemption. Purity. Wisdom. Innocence. Power. Melville gives many more examples. Then he writes, "Yet for all these accumulated associations, with whatever is sweet, and honorable, and sublime, there yet lurks an elusive something in the innermost idea of this hue, which strikes more of panic to the soul than that redness which affrights in blood."

I keep thinking that the violence of my hands is my hands. Blood you can wash off. But not whiteness. It's underneath the blood.

The sailor can be called from his hammock to come and gaze out upon a "midnight sea of milky whiteness." He cannot rest easy again until blue water is under him. He says it wasn't the fear of what hid underneath the surface that so frightened him, but the whiteness itself. The white surface in all directions with no end. "Though in many of its aspects this visible world seems formed in love, the invisible spheres were formed in fright." Then the invisible sometimes makes itself seen. When I imagine it, it is not the moon lending her light to the ocean that colors it so. The whiteness just rises up from within, hidden somewhere in the depths of all things, threatening always to emerge and become the surface. What scares me is that there is something other than depth underneath that sea of milky whiteness. Something no plumb line can measure. Not a volume. Not an empty book. Somewhere that isn't anywhere, a placeless place, where the white whale makes his home.

Sometimes I call it *whiteness*.

The leg Ahab lost still exists in the whale. Maybe it's embalmed in the gut. I guess I don't know. When he hunts the whale he also hunts himself. Whiteness larger than the white man. He hunts his own condition. Only the witless survive.

I mean the witness.

Sometimes I imagine I'm caught within the white squall of myself, and then I imagine I'm not imagining it. Then there is an "eyeless statue in the soul."

We like to say the old gods are blind. But their blindness is our vision.

I keep trying to see my children. I wonder what it is to see them, how I should learn to do it. How to teach them to be, as I am to myself, a kind of whiteness that is a kind of horror, and how to make the horror kind.

How shall I live is not a question they've learned to ask. They just live.

✦

Some months ago Hana, before bed, asks us about affirmative action. These aren't the words she uses. She says it isn't fair that someone with different color skin might be given something she's denied only because she is white. She says the sentence like it is a question. We say it is fair. That makes Hana angry. "How can it be fair?" She gives the examples everyone gives to show how it is unfair. We tell her what gets told. The life you have has given you advantages that you're not aware of, and others haven't had those benefits. We say the country is built on a history in which African American men, women, and children were kept as property, and that the horror of that time persists in inequalities that must be addressed. "But I didn't keep slaves. It's not my fault that happened." "Yes, it is," I say; "It's your fault." Now she's yelling. "I didn't do anything." "Yes, you did," I say. "No, I didn't," she yells. "You're doing it now," I say. "What, what am I doing?" "You know."

✦

My mother once gave me, an anxious child, worry stones. Polished rocks in a white fake-velvet bag, cinched shut by a gold cord. When I felt upset, I was supposed to take out a stone and rub it until my worry went way. As an adult I've wondered what would have happened if I kept rubbing one stone with my thumb and never stopped, if the stone would wear away to nothing, or if my thumb would disappear first.

In speaking not to speak. In reading not to read. In writing not to write.

Now when I write or read I find myself circling my thumb against my index finger. I don't even know I'm worried until I think to myself, *So this is how the stone felt.*

✦

In the "Extracts" and "Etymology" that preface *Moby-Dick*, Melville quotes Richard Hackluyt: "While you take in hand to school others, and to teach them by what name a whale-fish is to be called in our tongue leaving out, through ignorance, the letter H, which almost alone maketh the signification of the word, you deliver that which is not true."

One could make the same argument about the word *whiteness*. If you pronounce it without the silent letter you misspeak egregiously. The whole significance of the word lies in the letter *H* which lends no part to the tongue, but which the tongue bears, as the mind bears memory, or the heart affection.

Throughout history grammarians have fought to rid the alphabet of the letter *H*. Every few centuries a conviction spreads through the rhetoricians that the aspirant has no value, and that the ancient Greeks were right to deny it the honor of a letter, marking it instead by a grammatical notation of rough breathing that looks like an eyelash turned back into the eye: '.

It begins as a kind of irritation, this sense that some silent thing exists inside the word itself, hiding in plain sight, mute even as it's spoken, descending beneath the surface of sound and there widening, deepening, threatening almost completely the forms of order above it which, though they seem so solid, tremble and shake at every syllable uttered; a whiteness beneath the whiteness of the page, deep below the black letters, not exactly holding up the words far above which float on the surface like a fleet of boats, hunting what they hunt, peering down into the element that could be the medium of their demise, but unaware of the deeper threat, beyond the water, that distance in the atoms, that the letter *H*, like a spiritual shunt, keeps open. Worse than irritation to feel the same in myself, that beneath the white of this hand, past the links in the loops of blood lacing my life to the lives that made me, there is some whiteness welling up within me, as light overbrims the star as it eats another star.

✦

But that's enough about whales.

I keep trying to keep my mind away from the unthinkable things, and then I realize my thoughts run a narrow channel, and my whole life digs deeper that cut, as a stream does dirt, and now I've thought so long, and the channel is so deep, that my thinking is what keeps me away from what I cannot think. In thinking not to think. Somehow I cannot see how to see. I guess I need the letter *H* to prop my eyes open; or hundreds of *H*s to stack one on the other to climb as if on a ladder out of myself—but every time I grasp a rung it turns into breath and disappears.

I keep taking the *H* out of *whiteness* but I don't see a thing.

Marcus Aurelius keeps giving me advice I try to heed: "Cease not to think of the Universe as one living Being, possessed of a single Substance and a single Soul; and how all things trace back to its single sentience; and how it does all things by a single impulse; and how all existing things are joint causes of all things that come into existence; and how intertwined in the fabric is the thread and how closely woven the web."

But I just keep worrying my hand against myself—that it isn't true. And my hand keeps getting bigger and bigger, the whiteness of my hand.

I wrote a song composed of a single letter, but it just sounds like breath leaving the mouth.

> Hhhhh—
> hhhhh—
> hhh.

I haven't learned how to sing it.

Sometimes I try to see my face then, what it looks like when I feel the weight of the letter *H*—I mean, I try to see what I look like when I feel it. I hold the mirror up to my face and look as long and hard as I can, but I never see myself. I guess it's because the mirror is just this page, and the closer I get to it, the more it fills up my field of vision until there is nothing left but nothing. No, not nothing. The mirror that overwhelms reflection. This mirror:

Confessions

Cannot wear light as a garment.
Cannot say the names that existed before the sun.
Cannot see my children as ears of corn patient for the reaping.
Cannot see my death as a fig ripe on the fig tree.
Cannot find the measuring reed.
Cannot build with darkness, water, wind, and the deep.
Cannot feel the toothache in another's mouth, but I can sing another
    mouth's song.
Not the cornerstone. Not the stone the builders cast away.
Not the burnt-offering. Not the meal-offering. Not the peace-offering.
Find the law of the comet precedent over the fact of the sun.

✦

Heaven or earth first, the lid or the pot, I don't know.
Bewildered and astonished.
Cannot know the work of my own hands.
Like the nurse anxious at the cot of the sleeping infant, knowing she
    will suffer by his hand.
Like a bird flying with its wings, barely touching the nest over which
    it hovers.
My work in the dark is the dark.
Labor at what should need no effort: kindness, gentleness.
Teach others to feel my sorrow as their own.
My face masks lust; my face a mask of—
Labor and toil after light which needs no labor or toil. Only a word.

✦

Light only a word.
Whisper to the whisperer, "Speak louder."
Cannot solve the strife between light and day, but light is the same as day.

Cannot reconcile darkness with depth.

Desire approbation, but despise the hand that approves.

Here are my chains, don't touch them.

Cannot feel the peace of which I speak.

Cannot find the dayspring. Cannot imagine a king.

Cannot understand time even as time passes while writing cannot
understand time.

Cannot hear below the rhyme where the darker currents collide.

✦

Cannot not hear the conversation from which I'm excluded; this
thinking.

Life also lives itself, by itself, for itself, excluding me from myself,
turning my face into a form of departure.

Cannot read the names written in water.

"A man"—the answer to the riddle becomes the riddle.

Socrates, Plato, Aristotle, Alexander. This love of virtue that leads
virtue astray.

Thread the mind holds onto to escape confusion, becomes the tangle
of its confusion.

Chiron, half horse and half man, taught Asclepius to heal men and
Achilles to kill them.

Lust after a cloud in the shape of a woman, and the cloud will give
birth.

As if imagining the marble columns intact could save me from the
mind's ruins.

A dream of a shadow.

✦

Keep regarding my self-regard, as if it's noble, or an excuse, to err
because I know I err.

Keep asking others only the questions I know the answers to.

Rehearse the accusations: rejecting the gods, creating new ones,
    corrupting the youth.
Cannot condemn myself for what I want to be condemned; cannot
    choose my vice.
To speak about silence I confess what need not be said.
The oracle screen glows.
"Control your passions" with prick stiff against the wallet in my pocket.
Quail hearing the female's cry flies straight into the net.
Damned by parables, examples, metaphors, substitutions.
Spoke under the shadow of the gourd plant's leaf as it withered.

✦

Even in shame a kind of pride.
The puppets move without strings in my vision of heaven.
Heart like an axe unwearying struck through a beam. But then it
    wearies.
Words to make true what might not be true.
Learning to wear shadows on the inside.
Teaching others to feel this sadness which isn't even mine to feel.
Wanting to say of myself the worst thing I can say, but never saying
    it.
The secret kept only in confession; confession being unable to confess
    itself to itself.
Desire slowly thickens me. Middle age.
Known most for being the man I'm told I am.

✦

"What we can ask is whether it can make sense to doubt it."
I can imagine behind my eyes where I think I think that there is
    nothing there.
I know 2 x 2 = 4 in a different way than I know someone has died; I
    know Mars is red.

Now I know I only thought I knew.

Asking again: what is it possible to doubt? That I have hands? That God is there?

As Ahab feels pain in his missing leg I feel something like faith.

Certainty, a tone of voice.

Bewitched by books I keep returning to certain sentences I read and repeat to others.

Offering as my best example the word *this* and then pointing vaguely to windows or clouds.

Not speaking correctly the difficulties.

✦

Braid belief into knowledge into doubt and like the Sphinx speak.

But a Sphinx that asks no questions.

As doubt comes closer to the doubter it's harder to maintain.

Easy to doubt the unseen planet bending gravity; hard to think this hand is not my own.

Clearing—"Being is the nearest. Yet the nearest remains farthest."—concealing.

A kind of blind put around me, knowledge, not to hide as the hunter does from the doe, but to hide away from the deer, so I cannot see the prey.

"The snow is white" is true if and only if the snow is white.

All ye know on earth . . . some beauty . . . some kind of truth . . .

These questions exclude other questions, and even doubt doesn't know how to doubt.

Doubt is its own route.

✦

Much has been written but little has been thought.

Chaos in the old books should be translated as *Chasm*.

Cannot wake again into the lack of song.

"But what is this to me, about an oak or a rock?"

"To 'philosophize' about being shattered is separated by a chasm from a thinking that is shattered."

I need a teacher.

I need a teacher to show me thinking is a path along silence.

To stand apart from myself.

To kindle the pyre in my mind.

The sky is blue and the clouds white or gray; I have not doubted the world I've been given.

I never say *I believe* when I tell someone "I know."

✦

"The world is flat" is true if and only if the world is flat.

The facts worn away by the river—shibboleth—to which the world seems not to belong.

The sun keeps trying to make a hole in heaven.

The child believes what you tell her seriously and often; she grows up talking to herself in serious and repetitive ways.

Cannot wear light as a garment.

Cannot say the names that existed before the sun.

This instruction manual called God.

Like so many children, the first word I spoke was *no*.

To love more than to love being loved.

No.

"Come and let us study the letters of the seers"

1. Aleph

That it has no sound but precedes all speaking. The seers look at letters, trying to understand. They imagine the letters as black flames burning on a field of white flame. They imagine the letters as vessels filled with light and that God used these letters to etch into nothingness the words that are the world and then the vessels broke and the shattered remains fell down into the matter they'd made. They imagine God by imagining the alphabet speaking itself forward and backward simultaneously forever. They imagine that to speak is to continue the creation of the world. Some of that speech is silent. Some of the seers ask, *And why not created with an aleph?* What is created is the world that begins in the words that preceded the sun and the dark, the water and the wind. "Because it connotes cursing," some seers say. *Arur* is the word for curse. "How can the world endure, seeing that it was created with the language of cursing?" Then the wicked could destroy the world. The letter itself isn't convinced. Aleph goes and complains to God: "Sovereign of the Universe! I am the first of the letters, yet Thou didst not create Thy world with me!" God answers: "The world and its fullness were created for the sake of the Torah alone. Tomorrow, when I come to reveal My Torah at Sinai, I will commence with none but thee: *I* (anoki) *am the Lord your God.*" Aleph yelled at God, but only God could hear its anger. To the rest of us it sounded like nothing, or like the sound of the throat opening to speak, or like the sun burning the page of the sky.

2. Bet

"In the beginning," *bereshith*, first word of Torah, begins with the letter *bet*. Why was the world created with it? For the seers, theories accumulate. Closed on the sides but open in front, so no one is permitted to look above or below, nor look at what is before or behind. The walls of the letter place us in our condition, housed in the limits of what we can know, unable to see past our vision. Of what has been, of what will be, these are not questions to ask. Only in the days since days began, and long before days cease to be, only there, can I ask what I ask. The seers see that all the rest is forbidden. "Why was it created with *bet*?" To teach you that in the world there are two worlds, for bet is equal to two. "Why?" To connote blessing, as *berakah* begins with bet. "Why?" Because bet has two points, one pointing up, and another pointing down, and when we ask the name of the Lord and look up at the question, the letter teaches us to look quickly back down, ashamed of our own curiosity, abashed at wanting to know. Others say aleph, having no sound, offers no house; but bet is a house. Bet as the tongue in the mouth. Bet as fear inside love. Bet as love inside the heart. The beginning begins with walls. Aleph is infinite; creation is a limit. The letter is like the truest kind of teacher, who, being asked what is the moon, points at the moon. But she's pointing at its dark side. Light is the limit.

Of Bees in Winter

Walking home from school Iris says she found a bee in the snow.

"Where?"

"I don't know. Back there."

When the green fields are frozen the bees stay inside the hive, the drones gathering around the queen who, in the center of the swarm, stays warm; the bodies of her own brood shiver and shake, they make heat enough to survive, shielding the life that granted them their own.

Not exactly a song, droning. But it's a way to go on living.

Pindar calls the Muses "honey-voiced." Many of his poems he calls hymns, and says of his hymns, they are "pleasing flowers." When but a boy, out hunting near Helicon, so tired from the chase that he lay down near a spring and fell asleep, a bee found him and built a honeycomb on his mouth. That's how it began, the poet's singing.

On Helicon are two springs sacred to the Muses. When John Keats wishes for a "beaker full of . . . the blushful Hippocrene," he is wishing to get drunk where Pindar fell asleep. Of bees, Keats notes in his ode "To Autumn," that in the late flowers they labor thinking that "warm days will never cease." The cells of their comb overbrim with honey. I guess that means an excess of song. I guess that means song doesn't know how to know it's mortal.

Not far away, on the same mountain, Narcissus fell in love with his own face.

Many years ago I went to a town surrounded by mountains. I went there to sing my songs, though I didn't call them songs then. I found my own face looking at me from a box. I took out the newspaper for a memento. The main article concerned bees—their disappearance. Though now we're accustomed to the fact that small children must be hired to wander through the fields and pollinate the flowers, back then the collapse of colonies seemed not only to have no remedy, but felt to many like a curse from the gods. Of the article, I remember only one theory among many proposed. Some scientists thought that the presence of cell-phone towers across the country were somehow confusing the bees, altering their ability to find the hymns on which they fed, I mean the flowers, or that the excess voices in the air, not singing in the honey-tones of the Muses but asking after prescriptions, overdue library books, kitchen remodels, rendezvous at cheap motels, or excusing a child from school because his nose won't quit bleeding, stopped the drone from her dance, and though her mouth overflowed with nectar, she could not direct her sisters to the field.

"Where?" I like to think a bee asks another bee. "I don't know. Back there."

Many more years ago, when I thought of nothing but needing to sing and felt in myself no song, my wife and I went to visit a friend in England. We drove with her, and a man she knew, out to the coast, and while walking along the cliff edge he told us his story about raising bees. They've bred bees to be ever larger, he said, so that each one can carry back more pollen and nectar, but now the bees are so large that the armor that protects them from a mite—their mortal enemy—no longer keeps out the danger, and so the bees are dying. That's why, he said, he started building hives with smaller holes. So the giants can't get in.

So we don't have to eat the honey of faulty armor.

The epic in the air.

That was many years before I found my own face looking back at me with a quizzical look in its eyes. Many years before drones flew through the air on remote control stinging enemies to death who were mostly people not their own.

Pindar celebrates athletic champions, but any brief encounter with the poems reveal that the Olympic games derive from war, and though one could argue that such contests relieve the urge to kill your opponent, and weave laurels of peace and wild parsley where blood would instead be spilled, it is easy also to see that the games celebrate the ability to kill who you will kill when you're commanded to do so. There's even a foot race for men wearing bronze armor. The most lethal win the laurels.

In one of my earliest memories, I leave my grandmother's side and walk over to a hedge where I've seen bees flying. Fascinated, I reach my hand into the bush and get stung twice, once on each shoulder. It's only the thought that now they've stung me they'll fly off into the woods and die that stops me from my crying.

Now I think maybe that's a myth—that the bee having flung out its sting sentences itself to death. Sometimes I think they simply turn around, go home, and reload.

In Greek, when the noun for "justice" is connected to the verb "to take or to receive," the translation invariably is "to exact punishment." Δίκην λαμβάνειν. The same verb can mean "to understand." But the books tell me I'm wrong when I write it "to understand justice."

The source swerves from me when I search for it. Somewhere in a book I've read the facts gather in their hive. A young goatherd, Comatas, on seeing the Muses dance and hearing their songs, sings also with the sweetness they secreted in his mouth. In their honor he sacrifices one of his master's goats. To exact punishment, the master locks the goatherd in a cedar chest; and when, after a year, he opens it up expecting find a corpse, he discovers instead the boy well fed, having sipped honey from the mouths of the bees who flew to him through the breathing holes from the hymns of the fields.

Were Comatas to be locked away in a wooden box now, it could be that no bees would find him, there being none left to do so; or those that did would buzz against the holes unable to fit through, scenting the honey-scent of the goatherd's mouth, flying furiously to get no-where at all. Or that one drone would find him there, locked in a box at a wedding party in Yemen, heat signature glowing honey-yellow on the screen, and blow the box up.

It is but sweetness in the mouth that teaches the poet to sing. One could say song is but an accident of wanting to taste longer the honey that fills the mouth. The Muses send bees to the poet's lips. I guess that's how you know you're a poet. A kind of buzzing that hovers around the face when your eyes are closed. Later the words fall out when you try to swallow the nectar, more gentle than you could speak without the dew, by accident more true.

The disappearance of bees has been named Colony Collapse Disorder. It affected most severely the western honey bee, the major pollinator for many plants necessary to the agricultural health of the nation and, more largely, the world. The health of a hive is marked by its survival through the winter months. At the turn of the last millennium bee-keepers found a steep increase in the number of hives that died. But *died* isn't the right word. It's not as if the carcasses of bees littered the land, evidence of the plague the bees were suffering; it's not as if a five-year-old girl walking home from school would find a dead bee in the snow. The worker bees had simply vanished, leaving behind not only no evidence, but also a hive full of honey, and the queen still alive, sur-rounded by the unhatched brood she could not care for herself. There is too the death of those not yet born; they die not from lack of what would give them life, but its excess, as a bee can drown in honey, or a poet in song. I think the condition is called impossibility.

No single cause has ever been identified. Some say disease, some mites, some fungi. Some claim bad beekeeping practices, including the addition of antibiotics to hives. Others blame bad queens, or in the worker bees a plague of forgetfulness. I've long harbored other suspicions, as over the years, to avoid the glare of blank pages, I've filled them with words so often less than inspired. I've sometimes noted as I write a bitterness in my mouth I too easily ascribe to the coffee I'm drinking as I write, or an aftertaste from the beer the night before.

As a bee in a healthy hive alters as it grows older, first flying out through the fields to find the pleasing flowers, then hivebound, tending the brood, and their bodies change as their work changes, so much so that they seem almost another creature from the one they began as, so too have the Muses changed, first just nine nymphs who liked to find in the wilds wild springs from which to drink and in which to bathe, and only later, these goddesses born of Memory herself, who swarm to those who are helpless enough to want to make art. The waters of Hippocrene have long ago been lost. I'm not sure they dried up. None now know where Pindar lies buried, so the grave goes ungraced by gifts of milk and honey. The flowers of some fields have walked away, and the bees have gone in search of what has gone missing, leaving their queen behind, to gather back into their mouths the absent theme.

The poets keep writing their books of poems, half aware, or not at all, of what's gone missing.

Now some beekeepers make their living by renting out their hives to farmers, driving from county to county, the hum in a box behind them, and sometimes these trucks crash, and the bees become a cloud above the road. Just to pay the rent. Just to keep living inside the box you live in.

Many ancient coins bear on one face the image of a bee. But there is a finer currency:

The head of a woman on the body of a bee, flying before a lyre.

Hesiod says that the Muses, daughters of Memory herself, bring sweet forgetfulness.

O emptiness of pocket. O emptiness of hive. How do you buy a song?

66.

In the gnomic mode the poet reminds how countless errors gather unknowingly in the mortal mind.

A man grows suddenly angry at another man, a relative at a small remove, and with his olive staff, strikes him dead. He goes to the oracle to learn what to do. The golden-haired god speaks out from the perfume of his own mouth. The man must go in a boat and find a pasture surrounded by the sea, where once another god showered down snow made of gold, and where the same god, suffering a terrible headache, asked another god to strike him in the head with an axe, and out leapt the goddess with a shout so mighty the sky shuddered and so did the earth. There the man, who brought also his sons and his wife, should build an altar to this new goddess, and be first to reverence her with a sacred burnt offering.

In the gnomic mode the poet reminds how truly a cloud of forgetfulness sometimes descends unexpectedly, and draws the straight path of action away from the mind.

They climbed the mountain and built the altar but forgot to bring fire or any means of making it. So they offered a fireless sacrifice.

This pleased. The god rained down gold. The goddess granted the man and all his sons a great gift: excellence in all arts, but no excellence greater than the ability to sculpt stone so it looked like living men and women.

So representation begins, the gift of error.

The Tune of Many Heads

Music and pain.

Baby Hermes tricks a tortoise into his home and kills it, making the lyre from its shell.

Philaris, tyrant of Sicily, has a life-size bull cast from bronze into whose hollow body he casts his enemies; then he builds a fire underneath it. The body in pain cannot say *I hurt*; sometimes the mind can't either. It just makes a sound that is pain, signifying only what cannot be described or said. Reduced to less than yourself, you are so much yourself. Others imagine feeling what they cannot feel. None of it is for words, listening. The screams of the victim altered by a musical device sound like the bellows of the living beast.

Mimesis as form of cruelty. I think of the green fields. But there are other pastures—perspectives—

As Hermes creates the lyre, Athena invents the flute. She wove into music

    the fierce Gorgons' deathly dirge

        that she heard pouring forth from under the unapproachable
        snaky heads of the maidens in their grievous toil,

when Perseus, with the goddess's counsel, worked to slaughter them using the image of their faces, caught in the sheen of his hero's shield, to hunt and cut off beautiful-cheeked Medusa's head with his bronze sword. It's hard to imagine what music it was Athena heard, while I'm writing and listening to Bach's *Partita for Flute Solo*, but the goddess made the instrument

so that she might imitate with instruments the echoing wail
that was forced from the gnashing jaws of Euryale.
The goddess invented it, but invented it for mortals
to have, and she called it the tune of many heads.

Many heroes bore on their shields thereafter an image of the Gorgon's
face, and I suppose they marched into battle hearing a flute play inside
their minds. Athena, too, when she appeared to men before they spilled
blood on dust, came wrapped in an aegis embroidered with the face of
the Gorgon:

                      and the men assembled quickly.
Those around Atreus's sons, the princes, Zeus's nurslings,
hastened to marshal the ranks. Grey-eyed Athena joined them,
wearing the precious aegis, ageless, immortal,
with a hundred dangling tassels, all of pure gold, and each
finely woven, and worth the price of a hundred oxen.
Thus adorned she flashed swiftly through the Achaian host,
urging them onward: in each man's heart she stirred strength
for ceaseless warfare and fighting, so that to them
war at once became sweeter than any thought of returning
in their hollow ships to the dear land of their fathers.

The "tune of many heads" plays behind the face, imitating the echoing
wails of the three monstrous sisters, one crying out in death and the
others crying at it, plays also in the air at the sight of Medusa's head
on the goddess's glorious wrap, making men forget the land they left
and long for, the comfort of the arms of their wives, the gaze of their
children's eyes, the loosened hair and loosened limbs of their loves.
Somewhere a flute plays its tune, mimicking pain by making music,
and war becomes sweeter than any thought.

✦

Who are these coming to the sacrifice?

Abraham saw a ram untangle itself from a thicket only to become entangled in another. His son bound on a rock that was an altar beside him. In his heart he declared, "Let this animal be instead of this one a valid exchange. Regard the deed as if I had sacrificed my son."

They say when Abraham unbound his son that Isaac stood up and saw on the rock his own ashes. They say ever after his eyes were weak, could not bear light too bright, and so he stayed mostly in the tent of his mother, a candle lit, studying the words of God who had commanded his death, and because Torah existed before the world it describes, in the dimness he reads his own tale, living again what he lived through, this experience that, shaping so his life, also preceded it.

In some accounts, the devil comes to Sarah, Isaac's mother, and tells her Abraham has sacrificed her son on Mount Moriah. The act is unbelievable, but she believes him. There are no words then that she speaks. She falls in the dust and moans out her mourning. There is nothing to say in her grief, only this sound she makes, horrible to hear, inconsolable but searching for solace, a wandering lament, a voice made homeless, a voice that cannot abide any longer in language, and to hear it is to hear a hurt that is yours but larger than you, a being bereft of life larger than your own, and what rings out in her sorrow becomes dust in your mouth. I guess sometimes you fall to the ground and don't know it until you taste the dirt suddenly there. It can happen even when you stay standing up—such forms of falling down.

But it's a mistake. Her son is alive. But now her sorrow at his death is also alive. What exists by not existing. Sorrow's own life.

The thicket-tangled horns of the ram which replaced her son become the horn played at Rosh Hashanah, the shofar. Its mournful sound reminds me, each time I hear it, how the sins I have been forgiven still exist by themselves, waiting for me to return. Some say the sound of the shofar is the sound of Sarah's lament when she learned her son had been killed at the hand of her husband. Music of sorrow that releases us into sorrow, when sorrow no longer has any cause, but still exists, a kind of expectation for which there are no words, only a note in the air and in the ear, where what is larger than our life settles inside it, not really making itself, or anything, known.

68.

A week after finishing the essay on bees in winter, on an unseasonably warm January day, while I walked down the street enjoying the sunshine, a bee fell out of the sky and landed at my feet. The bee was still alive, but seemed dazed down there on the gravel, moving slowly, as if it had just woken up, or its blood had grown strangely thicker.

I picked it up and its hairy, pollenless legs clung to my finger. It had on its thorax a spot of orange among the black and yellow stripes; I wondered if a bee could have a bruise. I put it in the grass where the snow had melted away. I wanted to feel hope, but I couldn't exactly make myself.

Two years ago, when on something of a whim I began this project on silence, I thought of it in almost celebratory terms. I felt that some germ of silence lived within and enlivened speech, informing song without taking part in it, and explained to myself that the reason why I'd been so prolific a writer wasn't because I'm overly driven or artistically impudent, self-absorbed or shamefully careless, but because there was no other way by which I could hear the silence dwelling inside the words I wrote, though *hearing* is of course the wrong word—it was only by writing as much as I could, abandoning poem after poem to the point of impropriety, that I could feel in the work that silence words surround but cannot enter.

I wonder if this is all a way of saying I believe in God but know that I cannot, or some other kind of self-illusion, as if one could perform a trick in front of a mirror, and believe in it even as you fake the magic, that the red ball hovers by itself in midair.

Running with my friend on the mesa, confessing to one another how we've both been drinking too much, how we find ourselves suddenly in middle age, thickening instead of quickening, I told him about the book.

He said I was seeking the mystical overlaps inside distracted forms of experience.

A few nights ago, in a fight with my wife, unable to sleep, I thought about the bee that dropped out of the air in front of me. I don't want to think in signs. For many years I saw in the appearance of every bird, like a seer of old, some omen meant only for me, and it was only after years of growing fear and paranoia that the world was set somehow against me that I realized I'd been acting like a child who, given all, expects more, and that the birds darting through the air, or even the tree full of cedar waxwings, or the sparrow, dazed by the window-glass, that I held in my hand, had nothing to do with me, but were their own miracle. Sleepless, I thought about this quiet book, how often it becomes a way of creating the possibility of sorrow I might not otherwise feel, and then, by writing it down, giving it to another, so they feel it, too. Somewhere I seem to recall Simone Weil saying it is the worst part of human nature to make another person feel as you feel, so as to bring them down to your own level, and so release yourself from your own sadness. Proto-dream on the edge of sleep in which middle age is floating on a door in the ocean and the only answer is to turn the knob, open the door, and go in. Proto-dream of an ocean full of doors.

What hand has come down upon me and turned me so inward? is a question Ranier Maria Rilke asks somewhere in the *Duino Elegies*.

All this time trying to learn how to think, and still there's not a thought that is my own.

Meditation on a Hut

I keep thinking thinking happens in my head. But sometimes I doubt there are any *inner processes*. But then that doubt feels like it occurs inside me, like I say it inside myself.

I find a hut built by someone else on the edge of field and woods and enter it as a kind of refuge. But I think I'm describing the sense I have when reading a book or a poem. And that the hut at the dark edge of wilderness is inside me. I keep walking into myself when I try to dwell in the world. But inside myself, I doubt there is a self. There's just a hut by whose reality I am strangely bewitched, built outside of me, but placed within me, where the self learns to hide from the question it asks about its own existence. I guess I'm imagining the hut. I guess I'm thinking in it when I open the page and enter.

Ease of metonymy keeping the mind in thrall: leaves on trees and leaves as pages and also the leaf of grass.

So quickly the gesture of going-in becomes the gesture of leave-taking. I can describe opening a door and stepping in as stepping out. Like there is a door standing in the forest by itself, hinges hung on nothing but air, and someone has to build the hut around it.

But other times there are walls. Just planks of wood. Just the rough refuge secure enough to let in the wind through the chink but keep out the driving snow. Just the refuge solid enough to let the beetle crawl in beneath the crack of the door where the light sometimes crawls in too. To describe the hut is to use the material from which it is built against itself, but I can't tell if that fills in what little space there is in the hut until no space remains, building the hut again inside itself to show how it is built, the example excluding the one who would live in it; or is it more like pulling out a plank and saying, *This is a plank,* pulling the door off its hinges and saying, *This is a door,* and so on, until everything that makes the hut a hut has been removed, named, replaced; or again, describing the hut builds another hut, an exact replica beside it, and there is a question, after enough time has passed, of which hut was the first hut, the one in which thinking about huts began, and though they look exactly the same, there is a nagging fear that to sit in one and think is to think differently than sitting down to think in the other.

I keep employing myself in the hypothetical. Mistaking rules for meaning. *This* is how you walk through the woods when you are lost. *This* is how you feel when you find a hut. *This* is how you open the door. *This* is how you sit in the abandoned chair. *This* is how you consider a plank. What is *this*? It's the word that points at what I'm doing so that I know I'm doing it. *This* is how I know it's important.

But there's never anyone else in the hut to see. Or to agree.

In the hut I have to keep imagining what it would be like to make a mistake where no mistake is possible. To ask a question about my relation to error. To be wrong in such a way that I must doubt myself where no doubt should be. Not *What is my name?* In the hut I ask if I'm the one thinking these thoughts. In the hut there is no guarantee *this* is true.

Returning so many times to a sentence as to a cornerstone: *My work is to dismantle the edifice of my pride.* But *edifice* sounds so grand. It's a surprise to find a hut instead of a cathedral.

Thoreau begins by dismantling another man's pride. He buys James Collins's shanty. "It was dark, and had a dirt floor for the most part, dank, clammy, and aguish, only here a board and there a board which would not bear removal." I like how he thinks most about the boards. "In her own words, 'they were good boards overhead, good boards all around, and a good window'—of two whole squares originally, only the cat had passed out that way lately." He buys it for $4.25, and the family leaves the next day. Thoreau arrives to begin building his hut by first dismantling it. "I took down this dwelling the same morning, drawing the nails, and removed it to the pond-side by small cartloads, spreading the boards on the grass there to bleach and warp back again in the sun. One early thrush gave me a note or two as I drove along the woodland path."

Instead of a hut, the thrush lives inside its song.

Martin Heidegger says, "Questions are paths toward an answer." So Thoreau, cart by cart, walks along the line of his question, hearing the notes the bird sings, and puts down the planks in the grass. I'm not so sure the planks are answers. It's just that you take something that is whole and dismantle it into pieces only to make it whole again. But it's a different whole.

I keep wondering if the Socratic method is asking someone to show you the edifice in which he dwells, and by asking him to describe it, plank by plank, board by board, help him dismantle it. But he gets angry. He didn't know that was what he was doing until, opening the door to walk inside, he steps back outside again. *This* is also to say that thinking isn't something one does to oneself.

What seems to happen *in* me happens *to* me.

Heidegger says: "Language is the house of Being. In its home man dwells. Those who think and those who create with words are the guardians of this home." But how do you guard it while living inside it? is a question I often ask myself, thinking there in the hut of my thinking.

One way to think of the hut: it is the thing you build to conceal your-self in. It stands out so you are hidden. There, past the interference or the threat of other eyes, you think. Or you think that you think. It feels so difficult to do, thinking, but maybe Heidegger is right, and thinking attends to "simple relationships." What is within and what is without. What I am and what others are. Thinking in the hut builds the hut again, but builds it inside you. The simple bears the riddle so purely it hurts. I hide in myself the hut I hide in to think, and then a question arises which feels like no path to an answer, a bewildered question—how do I get out of myself and enter this hut I've built inside me? The things nearest us create unimaginable distances by retreating always further within. Heidegger says: "But if man is to find his way once again into the nearness of Being he must first learn to exist in the nameless." And so, sitting in my hut, I've learned to suspect that most thinking doesn't feel like thinking at all. It's looking at the planks, the faint light that outlines them, a kind of distraction that disables the mind and leaves it blank. When I ask myself, a little ashamed, looking back down at the "Letter on Humanism" open on my desk, *What was I just thinking*? I realize that then, forgetful of purpose or meaning, hidden away from the rules by which I employ myself at self-given tasks, that I'd been thinking, a nameless work, too simple for words, in which being is a synonym for blankness. Or forgetting.

Somewhere, while I'm sitting in the hut thinking, that distracted field of blankness grows wild and extends just a little the ragged edge of the world. It labors for itself, as the tendril is a solar principle, and the flower a star's distant delegate, when my labors break down, when all by itself the edifice of my pride comes apart—and if I can see the wild carrot and the amaranth only through the chink in a board, and if I find, having built my hut around me, that I forgot to add a door or even a window, and all this effort to be in the world has removed me from it, it's a cost I'll pay, this ostracism, to see through the knot in the board of pine a bee cast her vote by packing her legs with pollen.

It's in that field I imagine Thoreau bleaching the boards he bought from James Collins, letting the sun bleach them, and straighten by its noonday heat their warp. But it's also then I sometimes feel the "gnaw-ing doubts of an empty skepticism." As with the boards he bought, used before to build the hut he will use again to build his own, that every word I use to build a poem or essay or book, every word I say inside myself to think all that I think, that I've similarly bought, $17.95 for Heidegger's *Basic Writings*, $10.95 for *Walden*; but then there is the larger debt, a contract drawn up as soon as a child takes a breath and opens her eyes, and signed when for the first time she looks at the one who bore her into the world and says, *Mommy*. The contract bewilders. I find myself on loan to the material I've borrowed, using words to build a hut that uses me to keep being built. None of it is mine. I've never spoken a word that is mine. And if in the hut I refused those blank distractions and instead created a language that is mine, speaking it would leave me irrevocably alone.

(My children play with the wooden blocks I played with as a child. I watch them build precarious towers. I guess the work hasn't changed. Word by word building what I build, none of it mine, thinking inside the hut, but the hut is what thinks itself. The children love to make the tower fall. It sounds like thunder. Or control.)

70.

The Muses when they sing, sing as one, so Hesiod describes hearing them descend from Mount Helicon after having bathed in the holy spring singing out in "their beautiful voice," and it is by listening alone he grows aware of them—this shepherd boy, son of a seafaring merchant—for the Muses, those lovely ones of nimble feet, walk at night and cloak themselves in "thick invisibility," hiding inside their hiddenness, doubly vanished by darkness and by some mist that is, I guess, divine.

"One time, they taught Hesiod beautiful song while he was pasturing lambs under holy Helicon. And this speech the goddesses spoke first of all to me, the Olympian Muses, the daughters of aegis-holding Zeus: 'Field-dwelling shepherds, ignoble disgraces, mere bellies: we know how to say many false things similar to genuine ones, but we know, when we wish, how to proclaim true things.'" The Muses who, being numerous yet speaking as one, call out to Hesiod, this single man, and refer to him in the plural. He is *shepherds, disgraces, bellies.* Inside him they see hidden many others, some like him, some not. One might say that, before the Muses spoke to Hesiod, in his life he was like a cloud surrounding himself, the thick cloud that obscures, by saying *I*, himself from himself. "So spoke great Zeus' ready-speaking daughters, and they plucked a staff, a luxuriant laurel, a marvel, and gave it to me; and they breathed a divine voice into me, so that I might glorify what will be and what was before." They give himselves their breath, and tell him now to do what before he could not—to sing, to sing, to sing all that is in time, and also, to sing the blessed lives of those not in time, of those who always are.

Such initiation is also a transformation; though the body looks the same, the laws it obeys have changed. Glenn W. Most writes: "Etymologically, his name seems to derive from two roots meaning 'to enjoy' (*hēdomai* > *hēsi-*) and 'road' (*hodos*)" leaving him with a name that can be translated as "he who takes pleasure in the journey." Most continues: "Hesiod applies to the Muses the epithet *ossan hieisai*, 'sending forth their voice' . . . and both of the words in this phrase seem etymologically relevant to Hesiod's name. For *hieisai*, 'sending forth,' is derived from a root meaning 'to send' which could no less easily supply the first part of his name (*hiēmi* > *hēsi-*) than the root meaning 'to enjoy' could; and *ossan*, 'voice,' is a synonym for *audē*, 'voice,' a term Hesiod uses to indicate what the Muses gave him . . . and which is closely related etymologically and semantically to *aoidē* the standard term for poetry." It feels like a question that can no longer be asked— What is to be made holy? I don't mean to be made less mean, less base. Something akin to being made whole. But how made whole? The Muses added breath to a man whose name meant "he who takes pleasure in the journey," and by their inspiration, changed him into a man whose name means "he who sends forth song." But he looks the same. But his name is pronounced the same. So how do you know? Only, I guess, by the song—which isn't exactly a proof, but a kind of evidence, or symptom, of holy transformation, which word, to bring dimly back to mind what I read long ago, Heidegger describes merely as ground set aside to keep real all what otherwise would drift away from existence. Like the Muses, I guess, who gave a man more breath so that he had air enough to garland their names into song, whose names alone, being sung, keep alive those who always are, but whose eternity depends on one man who once was and will not be again. The holy land is just a field where eternity learns to hide inside time.

Hesiod is initiated into the new economy, where the shepherd tends the flock inside the living fold that is himself, where the wild succumbs to the tame, where disgrace sheds its first syllable, and where the mere belly mums its constant cry that forces the mouth to fill with food, and lets the mouth open to sing out a different tune, not desire for, nor desire of, but desire sprung free from the prepositions that would govern its use; and the open mouth opens the holy ground and sends it forth, hidden inside the daily words and all the names that still seem to sound the same, and work the same. But aren't; and don't.

Shields

Reading Hesiod on the shuttle to the airport. The fields are dead or they're sleeping. He'd know the difference and what to do in either case. A lot depends on which stars are chasing which stars as they drop behind the earth's darkness. Some swallows and some finches live in the airport, living on the crumbs of travelers. Hesiod is very clear on when it's safe to travel. It's when "a man thinks that the leaves at the top of the fig-tree are as big as the footprint a crow leaves as it goes." There are some trees in the airport that may or may not be real; none are fig trees, I don't think. None of the birds are crows. It's funny when you don't understand the advice. Maybe *funny* isn't the word. It's strange not to know what it is you're being protected from.

Heraclitus says, "Learning many things does not teach one to have an intelligent mind." He says, "The teacher of most people is Hesiod; they think he knows the most—he who did not know what day and night are: for they are one."

Day and night, summer and winter, hour and eternity; fig and figment, sun and moon, foot and the print it leaves behind; life keeps slipping into death and death into life; dream and memory and memories of dreams; stars and steam, here and there. I guess opposites are two sides of the same fact. It's hard to know what side of the fact you're facing—hiding behind the shield, or staring at the image emblazoned on its face. Learning many things does not teach you how to be on both sides of the shield at once.

Leaving my family once again to go and talk to others about poetry. My first lesson is that poetry brings us within what we love most, or would love, or must love, or learn to love. I say these words while far away from those I love. My second lesson is that a poem founds the world it finds, and is entirely its own.

After landing, after having come down the walkway, I find myself once again in the no-place of an airport terminal, not quite the same as the one I left from, not quite different either. A man is leaning up against a bar, dreadlocked, eyes behind horn-rimmed glasses closed. His T-shirt says *Know Yourself.*

✦

Alexander the Great traveled through the world carrying with him a copy of Homer's *Iliad* prepared for him by his teacher Aristotle and a knife. The dangling modifier makes it seem the knife helped prepare the poem; some errors are deeper than revision. Alexander slept with both under his pillow, poem and knife. Aristotle slept inside his head, I guess, lecturing in dreams about the soul at work and its happiness. *Traveled* is here a euphemism for the terror of bringing war to people who did not know you even existed. *You* is here a euphemism for an invading army. The army marches over the horizon line with a pillar of dust over it so that in the right light it looks like it is made of the flames it is bringing to your home; but it's just the dirt kicked up by hooves and heels. A good way to know something is to kill it and then study it; things are easier to describe when they do not move. When asked why he holds the poems of Hesiod in such low worth, Alexander answered: Quite the contrary, but he is perhaps not fit for kings and generals. Hesiod is for "shepherds, carpenters, and farmers." He gives advice on how long the axle of a wagon should be, and how large the wheel; he says nothing about how best to throw a spear so that it kills two men at once, how much it should weigh, how sharp the bronze should be. Though the answer is simple. Sharp.

What is fit for a king is to learn how to rule men and end their lives if they don't obey; all those others can learn how to nourish it. I found Homer put into my hands when I was little more than a boy. I passed all the tests I was given. Diomedes wounded Aphrodite and Ares. Achilles loved Patroclus. The girl's name was Briseis. Athena jumped out of her father's head ready to do battle; she's the goddess of Wisdom. No one ever gave me Hesiod. I guess my teachers knew I wouldn't become a shepherd.

When I read in the news that the man in Kalamazoo who went on a killing spree was a driver for the taxi service Uber and had, between murdering six people, picked up others for fares, I couldn't help but picture in my mind Diomedes ranging the battlefield in his chariot, stopping sometimes to talk with friends and foes, telling some stories, discovering an enemy was actually an old family friend, trading armor with him, and then driving off to kill more people. Such a remarkable feat of killing was called an ἀριστεία, or "display of excellence."

What one wants is a shield. *One* here is a euphemism for *I*. The word in English derives from the Germanic and at its root means "to divide, to separate." The shield is what stands between who I am and who I'm not. In ancient Greek the word is ἀσπίς. Used as a substantive, it means so simply a man bearing a shield, as if there were no difference between a man and a shield, as if they were a single thing, neither alive nor dead, but somehow both, alive and dead, at once. Emerson says, "Cause and effect are two sides of one fact." So may it be of before and after, other and self, enemy and friend; the front of the shield bearing on it some image—a lion, Fear, Strife, a snake, the Gorgon—and the back of the shield imageless, but with straps to hold onto; they are two sides of the same fact.

But shields trouble the mind—pursuing the violence they protect us from, so that, as of night and day, the opposites become one. Sometimes learning breaks the mind, and intelligence begins its mourning. Then I think of the shield not as seven layers of ox-hide bound, nor chased metal, not even as the gold handiwork inlaid with bone of the lame god, but as something so thin it is nearly transparent, and it stands between us and all things with which we'd converse. Then love and fear are two sides of the same fact, and thoughts just arrows the shield turns aside. Nothing hits its mark. The ground is littered with trivia; I mean, littered with bullet casings and the abandoned shafts. Mostly the damage is collateral. So thin is the shield it can pass through us without causing a wound. It severs into halves the brain, keeping apart the hemispheres which, some neurologists claim, in ancient times remained connected, and the electric spark between the lobes let us hear gods speak. But the shield silenced those voices; now we mostly hear our own voice, a kind of echo effect, called consciousness.

✦

Of the long description, so detailed as to be almost impossible to imagine, that Hesiod gives to the shield of Heracles, none causes me more trouble than Death-Mist who, with mucus flowing from her nostrils and blood dripping from her cheeks, stands among the Fates as they battle over the body of one man. The man is nameless; just a figure on the shield.

Other sorrows and astonishments abound.

In the middle of the shield "was Fear, made of adamant, unspeakable, glaring backwards with eyes shining like fire." So much strains the mind. Fear looking backwards means he is trying, unspeakable god, to look behind him at the one carrying the shield. "Around the rim ran Ocean, and it looked as though it were in full flood; it held together the whole richly worked shield." As Hesiod describes the shield, so Strabo, following Homer, describes the world entire—Ocean surrounds the land, Ocean is the limit of all. One could say of the shield that it is an image of the world. In the center of the world stands Fear; the edge is all Ocean.

Over Fear's head flies Strife, who takes away the minds of men. Murder is there, and Slaughter. Fate drags men by their feet through the battle, "holding one who was alive but freshly wounded, another who was unwounded, another who had died." Twelve snakes writhe. Lions and boars whose black blood drips from their wounds to the ground. There the centaurs rushing to fight men, all in silver, holding golden fir trees in their hands for weapons. The battle horses of grim Ares, and Ares himself "giving orders to foot-soldiers, purple with blood as though he were slaying living men." Apollo plays music on his golden lyre. The Muses, those Pierian bees, "looked as though they were singing piercingly." Perseus, slayer of Medusa, fine horseman, was "neither touching the shield with his feet nor far from it—a great wonder to observe, since nowhere was he attached to it. For that was how with his skilled hands the renowned Lame One had wrought him, made of gold." He carries in a bag on his back the head of Medusa, and her Gorgon sisters rush after, their footsteps sharp on the surface of the shield, making in their anger a great noise, seeking revenge. Men fighting and men slain; women tearing their cheeks in sorrow; old men gathered at the city gates holding up their hands in supplication; the spirits of the underworld opening their mouths to drink the falling blood. The Fates, all three. Death-Mist among them. But also men singing in chorus; a bride in a wagon being led to her husband; a great wedding song rising up from the shield, where "men sent forth their voices from their soft mouths." Men dancing and laughing beside the pipe player. Plowmen cutting their lines in the dark earth. Men cutting down the cornstalks bent over with the weight of their seed. Others harvesting vines, carrying the grapes, treading them, and others "drawing off the juice." Men wrestling, boxing. Some on the hunt with their dogs. And other men racing chariots in an arena, ceaseless in their toil, the dust endlessly clouding the gleam of their armor and the flanks of the swift horses, none ever winning the victory they chase.

It must have been hard to lift, that shield, weighing as much as the world; and as the world, so the shield, that in the effort to describe it—from wedding song to brutal death, from sowing the field to Fate's reaping, from the bride's to the supplicant's band, from Fear to Ocean's edge—we speak ourselves past our ability to see, and the work of imagination becomes unimaginable. Then, as does Fear himself, we try to look behind ourselves, and see what it is we lost, and grit our teeth.

I call that living. Living behind the shield. Somehow what we lost is before us, turned away from our eyes; somehow what we've lost we're holding in our arms. A world behind which to hide away from the threat of the world.

I can imagine a gesture of utmost peace, but I've never seen it happen, nor read of an account. A person, anyone really, maybe everyone at some point must, tries to take account for herself all that makes her world a world. A catalog of existence. This work that begins as thought ends in some speaking or making; I mean to say, as soon as she says a word, the hammer strikes the metal, pounding into shape the shield. She might say, *I have a husband and a black dog; two girls; a house with a spruce that shakes with the spring wind and the winter; a car with a broken antenna; songs still singing in the air the children's chorus sang; a wounded god who came back to life; a goose that flew behind me low to the ground which I feared in all its anger; and baby goats that when I ran through them chased after me, leaping with their buds of horn into the summer air.* I should say that I married this shield. I mean, I married the one who bears it. She married my shield, too. I can imagine in the midst of battle—in the living room, in the classroom, in the park—seeing another shield coming toward you, the Gorgon with her lidless eyes and the snakes her furious hair, and what turns silent in you then, what then turns to stone, is not your body but your intent, and instead of entering into battle you stop running, drop whatever weapon is in your hand, and, taking your arm from out of the straps, you turn your own shield around and offer it to your enemy. To accept yours, he must offer his own. And it's only then the miracle occurs, word whose definition might more properly mean *the wonder of anything seen.* You see for the first time the world you've been carrying. Can walk up to it. Can see so quietly chased into the bronze sky the clouds even now gently blowing across it. Can run your fingers along the cursive line of your daughters' hair made mostly of flaxen light. Finally you can see why it tired you so to carry your shield, so full it is of the life you've lived, this life you've hidden behind. Maybe there your own eyes stare back out at you, image of yourself you made but lived blindly behind, and so you seem for a brief time to finally obey the oracle's command, to *know yourself*; but it's so different than you thought, not a knowledge of your own mind whose belief turns to doubt and whose thinking hides away some inner process occurring almost, it seems, by itself, but only seeing another person hold up the image you have made of yourself, and you feel so strangely less burdened. Not that you're at the center of this world. You might be hard to find. Not the hero or the god, just the lone figure in the far field where the rain comes down and bends over the head of the seed-heavy poppies; there you are, right there at the edge, just a few lines hastily sketched, where the ocean circles the whole world, and you recognize yourself by some attitude or posture, that relation each of us has to the world we've carried before us but have never seen, most often called departure.

Though I've looked at my shield as closely as I can, and though I've found crows in trees and crows gleaning in the furrows, and though there are fig trees whose leaves are newly sprung, I've yet to find any-where on this dark earth of shining bronze the print of a crow suddenly flown. I hope that means I'm not ready to leave; or that Heraclitus is right, and all the opposites are one fact—fear and peace, distance and presence, heart and blood, departure and arrival, husband and wife, parent and child. Then it makes sense that I can know my life only when I've given the whole world of it away to another, standing there empty-handed, while in the sunlight the dust falls back down. There's a word I've long wanted to know what it means, this word called *love*. Now I see the image I haven't made. There she is, holding the shield in front of her that is my whole life, and above the ocean's edge, there is her face, not the sun, Kristy, my wife.

Tomorrow I'll have to make this shield again. I know I will. I'll have to get ready for battle. Have to be born. Schooled. Taught again by the centaur how to kill and how to cure. Have to be the hero and have to learn again I am no hero. Have to lose first all I want to gain. Have to worry and to pray. To call out to that goddess, Memory, the only one among the immortals who walks through the world naked until she hears her name, and then she dresses in a garment you give her, and the purple robe is named Time. Life is the thing you live again and again, waking up each day not in it, but behind it, putting your arms through the straps, asking yourself again, Memory, remind me, how do I give it away? Memory isn't perfect. Sometimes she tells lies. But of all the gods, she is most kind. She dresses in days that wear her away, and keeps giving away her shield to those who in her keep some faith, that shield called mind.

72.

Homer's most famous lines regarding death are spoken by Glaucus to Diomedes before they are to fight in single combat, each man rehearsing to the other his lineage so that the glory of killing or being killed at one another's hands will be felt by both warriors. Well, felt by one of them. The one who lives.

> As the generation of leaves, so is that of mankind:
> some leaves the wind scatters earthwards, but the fertile
> woodland grows others as spring returns in season.
> So with men: one generation grows, while another dies.

Wind is different than a scythe. Though an arrow flies through the air the barb is no breeze; it is no bird, though it wears feathers. The thrust of a gale is not the thrust of a spear, and the brunt of autumn wind is not the brute of sharp bronze. I suppose Glaucus says these lines to Diomedes to say, *If I am killed, it does not matter; as I replaced others, others will replace me.* But the point doesn't fit. This image of the cycle of life becoming death and death becoming life depends on there being no interruption to the course of the year, and war is all interruption. Truer to speak of the axe-edge hewing down a tree in spring or in midsummer. Then the leaves die on the branch that also dies, and the work of generations ceases. That Glaucus doesn't say so, that he offers to Diomedes, son of Tydeus, killer of many men, this image not of war's cruelty, but nature's peace, must alter something in his enemy's heart, must open in Diomedes's heart an ear that can listen, that can hear that wind that blows gently across the earth, knocking off the leaves from the tree not because of its force, but because just a breath has strength enough to scatter the leaves earthwards. Glaucus offers a vision of death that is not a consequence of violence, but a principle of life. Diomedes listens and recognizes Glaucus. He sees that this man he is to fight is from a family his own treated as guests, as friends, long ago; and instead of throwing his spear at the man he was to kill, he "rejoiced" and "planted his spear-point deep in the nurturing earth," making a hole a seed could be dropped in, instead of a hole from which the blood pours out.

✦

In the past week a man in Hesston, Kansas, opened fire randomly on pedestrians as he drove his car to the place of his employment to shoot as many of his coworkers as he could. The factory in which he worked built lawn mowers.

A child said, What is the grass? fetching it to me with full hands.

In the past week a fourteen-year-old boy walked into the lunchroom of his Ohio middle school and shot two of his classmates before running away. Neither of his classmates died.

✦

Reading the *Iliad* one can fall under the spell that all the violence possible in the world is happening on the page and nowhere else, but I guess it isn't true. The poem isn't a rescue.

It's a description.

Not long after Glaucus and Diomedes trade armor, making in the field a small peace where the dust settles, the Trojans and the Achaeans return to battle, and for a time it seems the gods favor Hector and the towers of Ilium seem like they'll never fall. The leaders of the Greek army know it is Hector they must kill, and those seeking greatest honor try to do so. Teucer, skilled bowman, half brother to Ajax Telamon, takes aim at the hero but the arrow misses, hitting instead "blameless Gorgythion." Homer describes the young man's death:

> His head dropped to one side: as a garden poppy sinks
> under the load of its seed and the springtime showers,
> so bowed his head sideways, weighted down by its helmet.

So different, the image in the lines that stop one man from killing another, and these lines that describe a man's death. Irony is when you forget how to laugh. The garden poppy so seed-heavy it bends its head to the ground while the rain that fed its thought keeps raining down is an image in my mind of utmost peace, so beautiful I could cry, or drop the arrow from my hand even now as I'm drawing it back. But to imagine it properly, I guess you must see that the poppy is wearing a helmet. Often they "gleam" in Homer, so you can imagine the helmet shining with the wet rain as the poppy bends over, catching inside it every seed so not a single flower will ever take root. Maybe you've seen fields of such flowers, a helmet on each, bending their heads to the ground from the weight the stem can no longer hold up. When the wind blows hard enough they strike together and sound like bells dismissing the children from school.

Titles of Forgotten Books

A Collection of Problems
Afternoon Essays
Battle of Cranes
Bird Omens
Chronography
Difficulties about the Soul
Etymologicum Genuinum
Geographical Lexicon
Homeric Lexicon
Index of Famous Authors
Institutions of Oratory
Lesser Iliad
Lexicon of the Ten Orators
Library
On Abstinence
On Preserved Foods
Onomasticon
On Similar and Different Words
On Stoic Self-Contradictions
On the Choice of Correct and Excellent Words
On the Cleverness of Animals
On the Diversity of Sounds Uttered by Animals of the Same Species
On the Luxury of the Ancients
Philosophical Orations
Poets and Writers of the Same Name
Precepts of Chiron
Sayings of the Spartans
Scholars at Dinner
Seven-Times Shorn Goat
The Obsolescence of Oracles
Twenty-Four Books of Laws Distinguished by the Letters of the Alphabet
Wedding Songs

As the Wakeful Bird Sings Darkling

In shame, they say, the young woman ran away to hide her pregnancy and, taken in by a teacher of letters named Phemius, gave birth to her child while doing the wash in the river Meles. She named the boy Melesigenes, "born of the Meles." Another word in the Greek reminds me of the name, μελεσίπτερος, or "singing with its wings," speaking of the cicada or the cricket. And so the name of the boy could be understood as "singing of birth," or "singing of being"; or, more largely the strain of music or the tune that is itself the music of existing, so that being is its own song, and birth the beginning of melody as it is of life.

All the sources agree that the baby boy was born with sight; opinions vary on the nature of the man's blindness.

Pseudo-Herodotus says that, having given up teaching for traveling around the world gathering stories to turn into song, Melesigenes came to Ithaca and suffered an eye ailment. A man named Mentor cared for him. There it is, the Ithacans say, the poet went blind, in the land of farseeing Odysseus, whose travails the poet made immortal. Others, including Pseudo-Herodotus, say he recovered, and went blind somewhat later, in Colophon. There the same disease returned, but he could not recover from it. He took his songs begging, trading lyrics for food and shelter. He found himself in Cyme, making his way along a mountain path, when he was discovered by a shepherd who marveled that a blind man could find his way through untrodden regions. The shepherd brought him to his hovel, listened to his talk, to his poems, and took him to the city, proclaiming that the blind man should be kept at the public expense so that he could live and sing without worry. The city council disagreed. To do so would mean all the *homēroi* would come to Cyme, and they'd have on their hands a useless crowd. Μέλεος, so close to μέλεσι as to also be considered a potential source for Melesigenes's name, means "idle, or useless," and so we learn that hidden within the song of existence is also the uselessness of song.

From then on the man was called Homer, named for his condition instead of his birthplace. His blindness became his name. Blind singer, whose song alone could see.

Pseudo-Plutarch claims the poet's name derives not from the name for the blind, but from *homēreountes*, for the guides that lead them.

But Proclus disagrees entirely. When Melesigenes was given to the Chians as a hostage, the man was thereafter known as Homer; *homēron* means "hostage." Alternately, the word means "surety," or "security," given to another in the form of a person who is himself the promise that the debt will be paid. Nor does Proclus believe in the stories of Homer's blindness: "Those who have stated he was blind seem to me to be mentally blind themselves, for he saw more clearly than any man ever."

In Homer's name—wisest poet who died by being riddled—we hear another riddle of sorts. Blind man who is also his own guide. Self-held hostage to his own debt. Those poets who modeled themselves after Homer named themselves after him, the *homēridai*, making his name synonymous with poetry itself. To learn to sing is to work at being blind. I mean the song is what takes your eyes and wears them for you, and you follow, listening as best you can. It's how one pays one's debt. Bearing the dark as one bears a wound, describing to others the world, that it is, that it is, and in it *you* also are, paying the debt, word by word, called vision.

> These eyes, though clear,
> To outward view, of blemish or of spot,
> Bereft of light, their seeing have forgot

sang one of the *homēridai*. "Let be be finale of seem," wrote another. To be real it must be sung. Held hostage by this debt to the world, you offer yourself as your own surety. Leave your eyes; take your I. Where being and song emerge one within the other, the eye turned only outward is blind. But the blind eye turned inward sees the world entire, sings it into timelessness so that in time it can return and dwell, just like the baby born by the river Meles cries out at the riddle of eternity becoming so suddenly mortal once again. A body. These eyes. And those tears that accompany the first song keep trying to wear the eye away as does a drop a stone. Even Achilles weeps. Hero ~~Melesgenes~~ Homer sang into being, alone among the Argive host, who in his brief respite from war refused to kill and sat instead before his deep-hulled ship holding a lyre and singing of home, home, which seemed to the hero less real than it had been before, away so long from its shores, so that it could only be seen again by closing his eyes, and playing the tune inside the words called hope. But hope isn't a wish. It's just a thought blindly seeking its home as does the dandelion, when the blossom is blinded into the seeds and the sun is only a kind of solar wind that breaks the eye into a thousand parts, each one blown its own way to take root in the forgotten ground and, Argus-like, make from a single blindness a thousand eyes, each unfolding a vision called home, that is home, until sleep comes again to each, and closes all eyes.

✦

Satan curses the sun:

> To thee I call,
> But with no friendly voice, and add thy name
> O Sun, to tell thee how I hate thy beams
> That bring to my remembrance from what state
> I fell.

He's left Pandemonium, where by "darkness visible" he learned again to see, to come to Paradise to end it. The light of the sun brings to mind the vision in which he used to dwell. But even the sun's bright light is but an image of heaven's eminent glow, and so Satan despises the light that, falling into the garden, feeds the flowers by making them seen.

Satan sees as Sir Thomas Browne says: "The Sunne itself is but the dark *simulachrum*, and light but the shadow of God."

The poet uttered these words because he could not write them, blind Milton, calling out the blank verse to his daughter Deborah, amanuensis—if not light itself—to his darkness. Earlier in *Paradise Lost* he speaks of his blindness:

> I sung of Chaos and Eternal Night,
> Taught by the heavenly Muse to venture down
> The dark descent, and up to reascend,
> Though hard and rare: thee I revisit safe,
> And feel thy sovereign vital lamp; but thou
> Revisit'st not these eyes, that roll in vain
> To find thy piercing ray, and find no dawn . . .
> Then feed on thoughts, that voluntary move
> Harmonious numbers; as the wakeful bird
> Sings darkling, and in shadiest covert hid
> Tunes her nocturnal note. Thus with the year
> Seasons return, but not to me returns
> Day, or the sweet approach of even or morn,
> Or sight of vernal bloom, or summer's rose,
> Or flocks, or herds, or human face divine;
> But cloud instead, and ever-during dark
> Surrounds me, from the cheerful ways of men
> Cut off, and for the book of knowledge fair
> Presented with a universal blank
> Of nature's works to me expunged and razed,
> And wisdom at one entrance quite shut out.
> So much the rather thou celestial light
> Shine inward, and the mind through all her powers
> Irradiate, there plant eyes, all mist from thence
> Purge and disperse, that I may see and tell
> Of things invisible to mortal sight.

It is a kind of explanation, and a kind of manna to the harm, these words in darkness spoken, carrying what light they can bear. The poet begins in the original blindness, dark related to no eyes, but that Chaos or Chasm of old which, brought together with Night, births the world. It is the old agony, bearing into being what did not exist before, and Milton suggests the poet must himself descend into the chaotic fundament where light itself must be created if a flicker is ever to be seen. But sometimes the poet brings with him some fragments of the chasm he fled, little chaos of the pupil in the eye, no longer the hole through which light pours, but some splinter of night itself, overwhelming the eyes by making their orbs the ancient groundless ground gaping open, called origin entire. There the wakeful bird sings darkling; the darkness is the condition of her song, tuning her notes to all that disappears so that, should light return, the names will grasp at memory again, and the day continue on as if night had never happened. But it is just such dailiness the poet refuses—truer to say it is the poet who is refused the day. Milton grows eyes inside his head for he has suffered not blindness, but inversion. Now he contains the world in which he is contained, wanders through the world by walking through himself, each word like a step into somethingness.

I like to think of Milton, whose eyes though blind looked healthy, unmarred by any visible deformity, staring into the room he could not see, reciting to his daughter his world invisible to mortal sight. Save that in hearing it she sees it herself. For some time the words are a kind of bridge between his mouth and her ear, his mind and her own, and the world that claims immortality as its measure crosses over into mortal realms. It is an irony Satan must appreciate. The way words work.

Of Milton's blindness stories abound. Many think it a punishment divinely sent. Others ascribe it to his habit from youth of staying up late studying Greek. It came not sudden to him. But over the course of ten years or more, his vision slipped away. Some accounts say he avoided all medicine but manna itself. Others that he furthered his own diminishment by unwisely trying every trick medicine offered. But medicine at the time proved different than we imagine it now. He thought, for example, that something he had eaten settled grievously in his system, casting up vapors that settled in his eyes, and his blindness was, in a sense, a case of indigestion. Fitting enough, I suppose, for the poet who told again what it is to eat from the Tree of Knowledge of Good and Evil and lose Paradise as a result. It's not that you are what you eat, but the consequences of your appetite come to bear.

He writes to his friend Leonard Philaras:

> It is ten years, I think, more or less, since I noticed my sight becoming weak and growing dim, and at the same time my spleen and all my viscera burdened and shaken with flatulence. And even in the morning, if I began as usual to read, I noticed that my eyes felt immediate pain deep within and turned from reading, though later refreshed after moderate bodily exercise; as often as I looked at a lamp, a sort of rainbow seemed to obscure it. . . . But I must not omit that, while considerable sight still remained, when I would first go to bed and lie on one side or the other, abundant light would dart from my closed eyes; then, as sight daily diminished, colours proportionately darker would burst forth with violence and a sort of crash within; but now, pure black, marked as if with extinguished or ashy light, and as if interwoven with it, pours forth. Yet the mist which always hovers before my eyes both night and day seems always approaching white rather than black; and upon the eyes turning, it admits a minute quantity of light as if through a crack.

Another poet, who lost his world but kept his sight, spoke of God as the crack of light beneath a hotel door.

For many years I'd thought of Milton's seeing a rainbow obscure a lamp as some repetition of the rainbow Noah saw when the flood finally receded. *That's how you know,* God says, *I won't do this to you again, take the world away like that.* But of course, Milton's rainbow was but one sign that the world was what he was losing. Now I think his eye had somehow hardened as if into a prism, and to see through it broke white light into its component parts, as if the poet wanted so much to see that he even wanted to see his seeing, and so his ambition broke apart his vision. The mist itself might be made up of countless such prisms, as anyone who has found in fog so unexpectedly a rainbow can attest. Then, too, the abundant light that would leave his eyes when he lay down at night, so that one can hazard a guess that we see not by light entering the eye, but by light pouring out from it, and to assume the inside of the body is dark is to make a novice's mistake, for patient inquiry reveals that the inside of the body is composed almost entirely of light, and "we live by an invisible Sun within us," as Sir Thomas Browne claims, though he might also remind us that such light is itself a kind of shadow, a simulacrum of diviner light, which bathes us in blindness we happen to call sight. Nor does Milton's blindness seem a static thing, but within the dark is interwoven some mist of white, rising up within him, not the blackness of ink spilled all over the page, but blankness of the page itself, that first child of Chaos and Night.

Genitals / Asterisks

There is an insect whose name I don't remember but whose mating habits I recall reading about. When a male of the species finds a female he carefully plants a drop of sperm on a short stalk, and does this repeatedly, until the female is encircled—so I like to see it—by the strangest forest imaginable, each tree like a child's drawing of a tree, a line with a circle on top, and each tree genital.

Whitman: "Wind whose soft-tickling genitals rub against me it shall be you!"

Whitman: "Let shadows be furnished with genitals!"

The female insect becomes pregnant by crossing the circle's circumference long after the male has wandered away. If the female could fly the whole species would die.

Blake says that stars throw down their spears and water the heavens with their tears. I've never known if the spears are cast and the weeping is at the consequence of the wounds, or if the spears are dropped as in surrender, and the tears are of supplication. Maybe it doesn't matter. In regret or in fear the stars weep down some light that waters the heavens so that the earth can grow. The thought is beautiful and old. Some *pneuma, spiritus, phantasmic aether* circulates from the cosmic edge to the tree tops and the deep seas, to the lung and innermost blood—a little bit of the stars weeping is the semen in the testicle, and the egg in the ovary an internal sun.

Socrates says that beauty is the soul being pregnant.

The thought sounds lofty, but is leafy, is earthy, not an ideal on loan, but a law in the loam. To become pregnant is simple work when the air is its own consummation, and light a nuptial rite. Just walk in any direction long enough. Eventually you'll become apprentice to the fact that you live within a circle whose edge you did not perceive because it is unseeable, you know it's been crossed only when you find in yourself the sudden idea, that new sense that the eye has opened again though it's been open all along, or you bear the burden of this weightless thing called possibility where before had been routine. But it's hard to know the circumference of the circle you live within. And some forms of walking are just sitting in a chair, thinking. Sometimes the atmosphere is a white page, and sometimes the stalk with its drop of semen is just the letter *i* or *j*.

"That which is creative must create itself," says John Keats.

The female insect lays her eggs on the underside of a leaf and walks away. Sometimes in a butterfly garden the child will find similar eggs. Little asterisks bright white on the green.

✦

The dandelion full blown weighs nothing atop its pale green stalk, an asterisk that is an orb, waiting only for wind strong enough to fall apart.

In Greek the optative mood expresses hopes or wishes.

The child makes her wish by pretending to be the wind; she doesn't know she is also pretending to be the sickle when she plucks the weed up.

In scholarly books the asterisk marks a point in the main body of the text in which further information can be found elsewhere, often at the bottom of the page in smaller type beneath a line that separates what is below from all that is above. The fact is buried in the ground and must be exhumed. Or is it the roots that must be dug carefully up so as not to kill the bloom?

The dandelion is an asterisk on a stalk; its grammar cast in the optative mood.

Aristotle says, "Hope is a waking dream."

Asterisks mark the ancient roots of words whose earlier form cannot be found, a mother that is herself motherless. In poststructural linguistics the asterisk notes an impossible form. Plato used the star symbol to note an agreement in different doctrines.

When the child makes her wish the rhetoricians know she is referencing a page where origin and impossibility cease their old strife and reach an agreement to put down a root. Stars, you mothers bereft of your own mothers, stop weeping. The genitals of breath have blown across the asterisk and now the seed seeks out hope in another field. The stars blow themselves out with their own breaths, and the elements float out into the unwritten territories. What the child discovers she doesn't know. The asterisks of the flowers, the asterisks of the stars, are each a footnote that reference the page that might explain to us the sentence we find ourselves in, or the word we are. But it's a page not yet written. That blank page, those reams of blankness, more distant than the past, before time began its incessant *me not-me me not-me*, called origin, which should be no more than a single point, but encloses us all.

Pale Node

speakable, unspeakable   things   you
never were   hair unbound   the holy offering
the light of the sun   your shining
foot   many apples they threw   blazing fire
garlands of roses, twined wreaths   of violets

you never were   gold   kind, unkind
work of my hands   on that ship   lovely tresses
they dropped the stones   seeing your face
they dropped   from their hands   the stones
seeing your face   they meant to throw the stones

your face that brought them   death unspeakable
a god worked from a   cloud you   your pale face
I listened to what came to me   it didn't say
it wasn't true   Helen is anyone   is everyone here
the face I spoke of   also speaks   also spoke

you never were   for me   speakable
I undo   with words   words
sword words   stone words   the sea-girt purple swell
gild the fragment   so bright   no guilt remains
blind   sore ease of sea   let me see

Epithalamium in the Archive

Among the assorted notes Marcel Duchamp kept in a green box— notes written to explain, elucidate, plan, and complicate *The Bride Stripped Bare by Her Bachelors, Even,* on which he was at work for over a decade, and which, to some minds, are the truer work of art, for which *The Large Glass* is but an illustration or unfinished sketch—a scrap of paper contains the following definition: "When the tobacco smoke smells also of the mouth which exhales it, the two odors marry by infra-thin." It's my favorite form of nuptials. A kind of mystical union, save it occurs most often in profane places—breath and onion, urine and asparagus. But it also must be the case that the eye marries the sun, and the child's bare foot is bride of the grass she ran across and her own pungent sweat, and at night her hair that smells of lavender shampoo and the faint scent of the day now gone turning into memory, memory which smells mostly like dust.

There is no monogamy in such marriages; faithfulness requires be- trayal; to wear a ring for each nuptial would so weigh down the hand it could not be lifted. But I like to think that the mesmerizer's trick of hypnotizing a young woman and telling her that her hand is lighter than air, and the crowd gasps when her hand floats as of its own will up above her head so it seems her body entire might float after it, is just the consummation of the countless marriages the girl has without her own knowledge betrothed herself to—her hand that smells of itself and everything she's touched, the book she reads at night before bed, the cotton pillowcase, the jade plant, the dog. Just as the air smells at times of pollen, and the rain smells of the dark cloud, and the earth of time—all these burdens that release us from being merely ourselves unshackle us, take off the finger that one ring we were born wearing, this bond to our own isolation which, though of no metal and seldom seen, bears down more than gravity does to keep my hand just here, on this table, in the Houghton Library, where I've come so many miles to arrange a few marriages for myself. My hand lifts a little up, floats a little bit in the air, over these keys my fingers press to make the letters appear on the screen.

As a bottle of ink, even empty, smells of chaos and night and desire, I want to think these words I type smell of the experiences they name, but when I get close enough to the screen to breathe in the scent, I don't really smell anything at all. I can feel the eyes of the others in the library on me; but when I look up, they look away. Even the young woman taking a silken dress out of a box looks away; and looks away again when I see her holding in her hand a little black shoe.

✦

Because the spine is broken I could not open the book. But by special permission it was brought to me anyway, the HOLY BIBLE, a crack in the green leather obscuring the Y, so that properly seen it reads HOL BIBLE. Not the whole of "complete," but hole as in something missing. Within an ornate gold floral pattern her name is written in gold, all caps, she to whom this Bible belonged, listed in the library information system as "former owner": EMILY E. DICKINSON. Can't open it, but can hold in my hand what she held in hers, can brush my thumb across her name, can touch, sitting next to me, her HOL BIBLE whose pages contain the faith her family held, all whose hands also touched this cover, which touching now I also touch, asking her father permission for Emily's hand, little gnome, to be in my own. But the father is long gone. It's hard to know who the authority is. To know you'd have to open the book where all authority rests. But it's forbidden. One way to learn about absence is to hold in your hand what you cannot open, and know that you cannot know. It's kind of like holding a stone in your hand; it's more like holding a hole.

Her father "bought her many books but begged her not to read them." But the Bible he approved. The book I cannot open she could not keep closed.

She writes of her family: "They are religious, except me, and address an eclipse, every morning, whom they call their 'Father.'"

I rest my hand gently on the eclipse.

I think there are ways to think.

Some ways involve opening books. Some ways involve keeping them closed. Some require you to write by hand every word another hand once wrote. Some require you to read every word another person read. Sometimes in the archive you get to ask yourself, "What is my own?" But in the archive ownership is possession of a different type; it is to become possessed, it is to become owned. When the book smells also of the hand that held it, to breathe is a bridal song, the air a veil.

I see there are other ways to think.

Some are about distance where miles are measured as time. Dickinson, maybe daily, maybe not, maybe often, maybe seldom, opened up this HOL BIBLE and the faith that unfolded there closed some other book in her mind. I can fit my hand around her doubt, but I can't get inside. Often I close my eyes and think about my life, days that as a child I lived, and I have pictures of myself as a little boy in the summer in the grass, I can see myself running there as I see my own children run now, barefoot in the grass, but don't see as now I see, my left hand on Emily Dickinson's Bible, staring out of my eyes which I cannot see, out of my face which I cannot see, so unlike the little boy turning around and looking at me to show what it is he holds in his hands, in which I stare at my own face, which cannot be, because to be alive is to never see your face, not truly, but only to see out of it, and memory is just a hand on a closed book that believes, because it must, that that's how you read, you just put your hand on the book, and wait. And it was just some leaves he found, that little boy; I just wanted to show myself some leaves from which a worm had taken a bite. I keep finding myself putting one hand on the cover of the Bible and the other on my head waiting for both books to open. But the only page that comes is this one I'm writing, and when I write it, I keep using both hands to push the buttons down, breaking the betrothal called patience.

Sometimes I think the soul has no epistemology.

It's just like when you suspect every page of a book goes blank when it's closed, and the words appear when it's opened only to disguise the holy work of erasure, but no matter how quickly you open a page, you never see the words appear out of nothing, they're always already there, silent but ready to speak; even when you barely crack the book open, they're there, the words in shadow of the page above it. Sometimes it's a truer way to read, not to open the book. It teaches you something you can't learn in any other way. Like watching a sleeping face dream, it has something to do with innerness that isn't exactly mind.

✦

One of the marvels of the modern archive is that you can have your soul and read it, too.

Every page of the HOL BIBLE digitized means I can read the book that is closed beside me.

In Numbers XXXI:6 to XXXII:12, where the Israelites war against the Midianites and slay their kings, and take all the women and children captive, and burn the cities and castles with fire to the ground, and keep all the cattle for themselves; where Moses on seeing their spoils makes them kill any woman who has known a man, and kill every male child; where what remains is divvied out in fair portions, there Emily Dickinson pressed a leaf from a tulip tree.

Where, in Samuel, David flees from Saul knowing the king wishes to slay him, and he goes to Ahimelech the priest, and asks for bread, and asks for a weapon, and David is given bread, and given the sword of Goliath the Philistine, whom he slayed with a pebble, there Dickinson pressed a little orange flower.

> I took my power in my hand
> And went against the world—
> 'Twas not so much as David had—
> But I was twice as bold.
>
> I aimed my pebble—but myself
> Was all the one that fell—
> Was it Goliath was too large—
> Or only I too small?

Emily Dickinson took scissors and cut out Job XXXVIII:27–33, cut out both columns, so that half a verse is left of XXXIX:13, and the next page missing too, where the cut cuts through the middle of some words, as the plow will also cut a wildflower on the edge of the sown field.

> Has the rain a father? or who has begotten the drops of dew?
> Out of whose womb came the ice? and the hoar frost of heaven, who has engendered it?
> The waters are hid as with a stone, and the face of the deep is frozen.
> Can you bind the sweet influence of the Pleiades, or loosen the bands of Orion?
> Can you bring forth Mazzaroth in his season, or guide Arcturus with his sons?
> Know you the ordinances of heaven? can you set the dominion thereof on earth?

Where the verses went, I don't know—in a letter, in a poem, in the trash, or put in the field from which she cut the flowers she pressed—I don't know. But shouldn't the rain smell of God, and also the dew? And the ice smell of its maker, if maker there is, and the geometry of the stars picture the Author's mind as does a sentence read in a book. Just as waters are hid as with a stone, even the open book is closed. Some pages you cut out. Some flowers you cut and put in. Then at last the holy words smell of the things they begot. There is no law to learn. Save the law of pressure. That presses a flower for later memory, if not eternal return.

Where in Psalms it says, "My soul is continually in my hand," she pressed a blue flower.

Where Jesus, during Passover, tells his disciples he will be crucified, and a woman comes in and anoints his head with precious oil, and during the meal he says that one at the table will betray him, and the betrayal occurs; where he says this wine is my blood, this bread my body, eat and drink of it, and he goes to Gethsemane and says his soul is sorrowful, and Judas kisses him upon the cheek, and the false witnesses appear, and he is accused of blasphemy, and he is sentenced to death, and he warns Peter that before the cock crows, Peter will deny him thrice—this whole page Dickinson cut out.

It's hard to read the intent in absences.

In the First Epistle of PAUL, the Apostle, to TIMOTHY, Dickinson has cut out TIMOTHY, which makes Paul address in a long letter a name gone missing, also called a hole. The name occurred in the middle of the page and left on the opposite side a gap that crosses the columns:

teacher of the Gentiles in ~~faith and~~	*	~~13 For~~ they that have used the
verity.		a deacon well, purchase to
8 I will therefore that n		ves a good degree, and
every where, lifting up ho		oldness in the faith which is
without wrath and doubting.		~~Christ~~ Jesus.
9 In like manner also, that wo-	*	14 These things I write unto

The words crossed out are cut in half.

Where in Hebrews it says, "Now faith is the substance of things hoped for, the evidence of things not seen," that through faith we understand the world framed by words, and faith where translation is to be put beyond death, and the faith of all the fathers is recounted and tallied up, where by faith Moses forsook Egypt, by faith the sprinkling of blood, by faith passed through the Red Sea as by dry land, by faith the walls of Jericho, and by faith the harlot Rahab, there Emily Dickinson pressed a flower now faded to the same color as the page.

She dog-eared Revelations at the wormwood star.

She dog-eared Revelations where the locusts come dressed in armor, wearing crowns of gold.

She cuts out a last passage, Revelation XXI:2. That's when John looks up and sees Jerusalem descend from heaven, "prepared as a bride adorned for her husband."

In an early poem she writes:

> The soul her "not at Home"
> Inscribes upon the flesh.

I like to think she tucked the bride into her bed of white, and folded the sheet over her, then put the bed into a house and folded down the roof and, affixing a stamp on the corner, wrote no address, just *Return to Sender*, for nobody can accept forever this heaven on loan.

78.

My friend points out that in the edition of Spenser's complete poems in six volumes, including "A Glossary Explaining the Old and Obscure Words," whose title page bears Keats's younger brother George's signature and the date 1816—year when John began to write his first poems, and Spenser the first poet he fell in love with—that the archaic type makes the word *rest* appear as *reft*.

Rest so often a euphemism for death. Keeping secret what it cannot say.

Reft in Peace is a common epitaph carved into stone that no one ever sees.

✦

I once had a theory of mind that accepted the possibility that by reading every book another poet read you could become that poet; I mean, your mind could become that poet's mind. A shortcut would be to find the poet's own books, hold in your hand the books he held in his, and search for every line marked in the margin or underlined. This is the shortcut called enthusiasm.

I read Keats's copy of *The Faerie Queen* by stopping only for those lines underlined and marked, often with three or four horizontal dashes, in the margin. Let me record for you the entire poem, it takes just a minute to read:

> Silly old Man, that lives in hidden Cell,
> Bidding his beads all day for his Trespass
>
> . . .

. . . there *Thetis* his wet Bed
Doth ever wash, and *Cynthia* still doth sleep
In silver Dew his ever-drooping head

. . .

And on his little Wings the Dream he bore

. . .

Through widest Air making his ydle way

. . .

Pour'd out in Looseness on the grassy Ground

. . .

And nought but pressed Grass where she had lyen

. . .

Great Grace that old Man to him given had;
For God he often saw from Heaven's height.
*All were his earthly Eyen both blunt and bad,
And through great Age had lost their kindly Sight.

    *[in Keat's hand, at bottom of page] Milton

. . .

His huge long Tail, wound up in hundred Folds,
Does over-spread his long Brass-scaly Back

. . .

Those glaring Lamps were set, that made a dreadful Shade

Much later, I know, I know, I think I know, the goddess will pour out the loose grain of her hair as her fingers, like a winnowing fan, comb up through the tresses.

I once had a theory of reading that proposed that a single line from an epic properly read would contain the whole poem. I likened it to the body's pleasure, where a touch on one organ loosens every limb. I called my theory the Erotic Epistemology of the Page.

But then I learned you can't reft yourself away from your own mind; you just can't put it to rest.

But then I learned you can't reft away a single word without harming all the rest.

✦

A manuscript transcribed in Charles Brown's hand of Keats's "Sonnet (1819)" crossed out, by whose hand we don't know, on display beneath the glass. To record each word the X deletes grants back existence to what's been denied it:

```
Star!                              art!
                                   the
      watching                     apart
        Nature's                   sleepless
          waters                   priestlike
          ablution                 earth's
              new soft
                  the
                  steadfast
                      Love's
              its        sink
            ever         sweet
        fall             taken
  passionately               to death
```

✦

In Keats's Shakespeare, edition so small it fits in one hand, he reacts vehemently to Samuel Johnson's editorial comments. He crosses out an entire paragraph of conclusion on *As You Like It* and, feeling that decussation not protest enough, in wide spirals circles through it again, and then again, and once more, as if he's trying to damage every word. It looks like a sketch of cloud tumbled by wind, or a sketch of a wave as over the strand it rolls in.

Underneath he writes:

Is criticism a true thing?

When a man's verses cannot
be understood, nor a man's good
wit seconded by the forward child,
understanding, it strikes a man more
dead than a great rejectioning in a

And the rest of the words can't be understood, cut in half by the end of the page.

✦

That's the question, now I know, that's been asking itself inside me all along: "Is criticism a true thing?"

Matthew Arnold found in Keats a man wholly undisciplined, a man who once coated his tongue in cayenne pepper the better to taste the claret he drank after, who once spent six weeks without regaining sobriety; but what is worse in Arnold's view are the letters Keats wrote to Fanny Brawne, wherein he expresses passion of such degree that he feels dissolved into the being of the woman he loves, where Keats claims he could do it, he could die for her, and he might be, be already dying, for "love is my Religion," and he could be martyr for it. Arnold called such letters, echoing the criticism of his poems that so wounded and enraged Keats, "the love letter of a surgeon's apprentice," spoken by a man who cannot rise above his "sensuousness."

Keats writes in a letter to his friend: "O for a life of sensations rather than of thoughts!"

Matthew Arnold defined poetry as "a criticism of life."

Sometimes I have a sensation I call thinking. Sometimes I have a sensation I call life. Maybe you have these sensations too? It usually happens when I discover I'm within the thing that is within me—as of thinking, as of life. The condition is *critical*, word derived from the medical realm before it arrived in the judicial, meaning the "crisis of a disease," which is the point from which you either recover or die. What Keats knew, that Arnold couldn't guess at, is not that poetry is a criticism of life, but that life is a critical form, and you don't get to think your way out of the crisis, nor can reason tamping down passion remove you from the sensation that all sensation will end. That's a passionate thought—it shares our critical condition.

That's when the thing of greatest surprise occurs. The book that fits in the hand is the temporary condition; the book that contains the hand that held it is the permanent one.

Heaven is all margin.

I imagine the poem is a kind of handshake that begins by shaking the mind.

✦

I am writing these words sitting in the library. I sent through the air a request for three portraits of Keats by Joseph Severn, who nursed him to his death. On either side of my computer John Keats looks away from the words I'm writing about him.

One Keats gazes off to the right with a look of daydream. The other Keats looks to the left with a glare whose intensity borders on anger or anticipation. But the third Keats, in a frame propped up by a stand, looks at these words as I write them, the eyes cast slightly upward though the face tilts gently down, as if he has just heard something he does not want to understand, but he understands.

79.

Hearing about my interest in abandoned words, of rescuing the revision from the tyranny of its improvement, one of the librarians comes back with a book. She opens it to a page with an illustration, a black-and-white lithograph as of nineteenth-century magazines, in which a group of men stand and write furiously on large loose sheets at a table while in a chaise lounge a woman leans back and reads.

The caption calls it a "View of the Destruction Room, 117, Long Acre," which is "A room full of interesting Books, or at least when cut up will be so, as far as regards the places they refer to, and quietly waiting an opportunity to be changed from generals to particulars."

Emerson writes: "We stand before the secret of the world, there where Being passes into Appearance, and Unity unto Variety."

Men who work in the Destruction Room call themselves Destructionists.

80.

A strain in the wind . . .

(There is a meadow that is a made-place larger than the mind but found only within it. Dreams grant permission, and sometimes do poems, as when the world works itself inside the margins, and the boat on which you're learning to sail drags its anchor into the sea filled with the buttons that have come off the coats of dead men, and the dog you didn't know you had warms his numb feet in the water, and you come to a meadow where Mr. Alcott waits and to pass the time you take turns reciting couplets and pleasing rhymes, familiar enough in the dream, but on any other page unknown. Thoreau dreamed that dream. He dreamed it more than 160 years ago, but it's still his dream; or is it that the dream keeps dreaming itself through him, long after the man himself disappeared into the field across the sea; or is he now the dream that the dream dreams. "The short parenthesis of life was sweet," is one line he recited in the meadow's made-place. *Parenthesis* so much better than *problem*, I keep thinking, reciting to myself the line Thoreau recited in his dream, line that exists by not existing, written down in the world that's gone missing, world lost on waking to the world, but here now somehow in this one too, as are those holes in the air the wind blows through. The rhetorician knows that parentheses are used to add a word or phrase into a sentence that otherwise seems complete, a small example or a little illustration, set apart by the punctuation; or, the rhetorician knows, parentheses are used to mark a passage or theme that departs from the larger discourse, to include but keep separate the digression. Maybe both are true—the informative example is the thing that digresses. A dream often feels like it occurs between parentheses, of night and day, of waking and sleeping, between ear and ear—a melody gone astray in the nerves, a breeze meandering through grasses, music caught inside a maze. But in his dream Thoreau knows the poem that tells us our life entire is the same digression, the small information inserted inside a sentence whose larger theme we do not know. Sweet, short parenthesis of life—as of the eyelash-curl of the hands as they come together in a child's prayer—this undervoiced phrase, whisper of fact becoming less than fact, that is a life entire.)

. . . & my nerves were the chords of the lyre.

Grief Substitute

To hide him from war, to disguise him from fate, his mother hides her child in another king's court, dressing him as a girl, calling her Pyrrha, who mingled among the daughters of Lycomedes. He wasn't so young. Brought into the daily intimacies. Learning to braid Deidamia's hair into a single strong plait, her shoulders bare, her unstrung robe open to her waist. Learning to weave so that the weaving rod draws close to the breast as it pulls the spool past the warp; learning to pack the weft tightly with the reed. It is an old pun Socrates used when describing the just state in which women train with men as the men themselves train, naked and grappling the body of their opponent in the agony-ring, that none should assume there wouldn't also be lessons in "weapon handling" and "horseback riding." Beyond horn combs and bone pins, beyond the intricate knot of the intimate sash, Achilles took his weapon in his hand and went riding. Deidamia became pregnant with his child, the boy who would be known as Neoptolemus. That name means "new war." But the new war was only the old war on infinite repeat. Odysseus found Achilles by pretending to be a merchant of women's wares, including among the perfumes and silks a shield and spear. When Pyrrha grasped the weapon, the older man saw the warrior. It was Achilles—whose name means "grief of the tribe." But I hear the name as *grief that is more than one's own*. I mean his name is *grief the man bears that is larger than the man*.

✦

While the hero lived among the lovely daughters as a girl himself—or is it before, and if so how long before; it's hard to know when origins multiply and sources are many, but I guess you choose the story you need to be true—Agamemnon gathered his army at the shore but no wind came to fill the sails of the ships. He'd offended a goddess and now was being punished, as so often happens—you don't know the offense you've given to eternal beings until, in a moment, what you need to have happen will not. Just a breeze, or like a breeze, just a breath. On a margin next to an empty craft I once prayed for breath to fill a word but none would come until I bore a child into the world, so the seer said. The seer told Agamemnon he must sacrifice his virgin daughter to the virgin goddess to make amends, and then the wind would blow them to death. Each death its own; each the same. Agamemnon told his daughter that Achilles waited in Aulis to marry her, though the hero then wore a robe loosely tied and wove flowers through the waves of his hair in a different land, Iphigenia came to offer herself to that man and his glory, to marry that absence. The wedding altar was altar of another sort. A stone in the air, so I see it, held up by some kind of wind. I don't know how that wind works; I just see the rock floating. When the father becomes a priest he forgets the fear of knowing what he knows. Then the knife isn't a knife in the hand that isn't his hand. The throat is where lifelong the wind always blows, a southern wind, but the north always follows. That's why he cut his daughter's throat. So her breath would become the wind. Some sources say the goddess came and swept the girl away, replacing her body with a deer. Then the hair he grasped in his hand became an antler of rescue. Then Iphigenia woke in a temple in a foreign land, sentenced to be a priestess-virgin and to kill every stranger that landed on her shore. I forget what god demanded this observance. In other sources there is no substitute. Grief fills sails as often as it fills eyes. There is the feeling after furious sobbing that another breath can't be taken, and sometimes, there is the same feeling in the air itself. But mostly a breath is taken once again. Breath that begins as a breeze that ends as a breeze. But mostly the sources don't agree. They just exist.

✦

Sometimes I think the body is just a net through which forces blow. Life doesn't shape itself. It's given a shape.

Wrath, goddess, sing of Achilles' wrath.

A friend is another self, says Pythagoras.

Patroclus comes in tears to his friend and asks to wear the hero's armor. Achilles grants him what he wants. Patroclus puts the armor on. He leads the Myrmidons into battle. It's hard to know who knows who the man gleaming in bright bronze is. The other Greeks? The Trojans who see the man they most fear suddenly step out of the flames near the ships like a metal wasp maddened? Achilles himself who sees himself fighting the war he will not fight? Patroclus killing men as another man who is himself also the man he is?

Θεράπων is the word used to describe Patroclus. It means "attendant." But that is only the gleaming armor of the word. The underside of Θεράπων that presses against the skin means "ritual substitute." As the ox or unblemished goat sacrificed is but a ritual substitute for the human life demanded by the gods, so Patroclus is. Θεράπων is also the word from which "therapy" derives. So it must be to have another self go out into the world and accomplish the deeds properly your own, even if those deeds are merciless—is a form of therapy.

None of these ideas are new.

Wrath has a strap so you can tie it on.

When Hector kills Patroclus, Achilles's therapy is to die without dying. Hector strips the young man's body of the hero's armor and makes it his own. Then Achilles is himself the man who killed the man who is himself now living as one who has died. Once the riddle is learned, the eyes never cease their crying.

Love is an intricate knot death itself can't untie.

But some forms of crying are just called seeing.

Menelaus stands over the body of Patroclus

> straddling his corpse, as over her first-born
> calf its mother stands lowing, plaintively, having never
> given birth before.

Man who birthed these sorrows.

Mourning has a hood so you can cover your mind. But it's only exposed all the more.

Grief is a black cloud with a tether.

When Achilles learns of Patroclus's death a dark cloud gathers over him. He gathers dust and ash and pours them over his head and tunic. He tears his hair. He groans like a calf with the knife against its throat. He groans like the calf walking into the knife. He is like a lion whose cubs a deer hunter has stolen. He leads all hearts in lamentation. He fills the wounds with an ointment nine years old. He rubs oil into the body. All night long he wails.

Others tell him to eat but he will not eat. He won't wash the dust and ash off himself. He will not grant his body the honors of life. He will not sleep. He will not catch his breath.

A god makes him new armor and he puts it on. But it's just a substitute for the armor he lost. Which is to say the life that lost it. Substitute grief. Perpetual mourning.

Maddened and merciless because he is on both sides of death at once—the mourner and the mourned.

Any word you speak, you can also hear.

He fills a river full of bodies so the element of ablution is pollution itself. Nothing gets to be pure.

Twice he is called a "demon." I don't know if the word means genius, if you can be a genius at doing what now Achilles does.

To the supplicant that Achilles before had captured and let live, that man with whom Achilles ate Demeter's grain, the name of the goddess calling into the hero's raging mind the sacred ground the supplicant makes when he kneels upon it begging for his life to be spared, Achilles says, "Fool, don't talk, don't make speeches." When the head bends low so the neck in its delicate grace arcs down and the arms stretch out their circle with the hands upturned so the wrists turn skyward, the body of the supplicant becomes the grace of fragility. Achilles stabs his sword through the collarbone the whole length of the blade, the blade which measures the whole length of the kneeling body.

As Achilles approaches him, covered in the blood of the men he's killed, covered in the ashes and dust he's poured on himself, Hector wishes Achilles were a girl to whom he could talk sweetly.

As the women wailed and tore their breasts with their nails mourning Patroclus, Achilles rent his clothes and tore at his chest as if he, too, had breasts, and Patroclus, his friend, was torn from his bosom.

As in a dream where you run from what you fear but cannot escape who pursues, and as in a dream where what pursues cannot catch what flees, so Hector runs from Achilles who runs after him. Seen from another height than the ramparts of Ilium, it is an image of our relation to our self, chasing what cannot be caught, running from the threat that won't arrive. I think; I am. Like two magnets of the same polarity pushed together so that one can feel the force that keeps them apart—but then some god flips the story, and they clap together as if they'd never not been one. So Achilles confronts Hector. Hector wears the armor he stripped from Patroclus, Achilles's own armor. Achilles drives his spear clean through the tender neck where the collarbones hold apart shoulders from neck, there where the armor made vulnerable the body within it, spot Achilles knew not by seeing the vulnerability, but remembering being vulnerable himself, wearing the same armor into battle. Grief makes every substitution. Hector who killed Achilles by killing Patroclus; now Achilles kills Hector so as to kill himself. Sometimes the riddle works so well it doesn't work at all. Achilles wishes he could "carve your flesh raw and eat it" so as to put Hector's body inside the armor of his own, to devour the man, to digest him, to make the other body once again his own, as a friend is another self never contained within the self, and the awful math of substitution, algebra of the gods alone, tears those who love and fear in two, and those two in two again, so it's hard to see who is who, and the mourner and the mourned are one, and the reviled and the cherished, and the murderer and the singer of laments, and for these grief substitutes the eternal equation has no other mark than an equal sign, each equaling each, Achilles = Patroclus = Hector, small prayer the dark clouds repeat, or the man himself, he is never himself, sitting nightlong by the ocean, covered in the gore of his killing, not knowing how not to be sad, to be raging, to be broken, to be dead, to be alive, not knowing how to walk into the loud breakers and wash the blood on the body off.

Everything's a test, saith the gods.

Let man = X. Begin the therapy.

✦

In the funeral games Achilles institutes after the cremation and burial of Patroclus, athletic events that are themselves substitutes for the war waiting to recommence, after the bones of his friend are gathered from among the other bones (bones of sacrificed animals and bones of sacrificed Trojan youth), after the chariot race and the foot race, after the boxing match and the wrestling, after the swordplay and the shot put, there is a last game that haunts the *Iliad*, my slow reading of it. I know many days have passed, over a week, since Hector's death, and his naked body dead in the dust waits for burial, undefiled by dog or bird or maggot. Even his wounds have healed. To those warriors who participated in the previous contests Achilles has given great gifts, golden cauldrons and two-handled cups, talents of gold and fine armor. Then Achilles has brought out ten double-axes of hard iron, and ten single,

> and some way off set up the mast of a dark-prowed vessel
> in the sand, and tethered a fluttering pigeon to it
> by a thin cord attached to its foot, and then told them that this
> was their target.

The archer who strikes the bird will win the double-axes; the man who severs the tether will get the single. Teucer famous archer, won the lot and drew his arrow first. He misses. The bitter shaft cuts the tether in two, and the

> pigeon fluttered
> high up into the sky, with the cord still hanging loosely
> earthward.

So I imagine the bird flying even now. In the freedom of its escape, in its fluttering life, still bound, still with captive's tether hanging toward the ground.

82.

I wanted time to think about time; I took my family to Rome.

A seagull perched on the head of a god.

Broken at the wrist, a hand still pointed one finger up at the sky. My little girl stood next to it, so much smaller than the finger, looking straight ahead.

Whenever that first day in Rome she said, "Look!" it was to point out a bird scavenging in the ruins. She pointed her little finger at it, and when the bird flew away, she pointed up.

Like the old tourists of heavens, she kept looking to the birds for some sign.

✦

The poppies grew up between the stones, small red dots among the broken columns.

An infant Heracles catches a snake by its neck; there's a look on the baby's face I can't quite make myself forget, this look of making a plaything of death.

Medusa gazes into the mirror at her own transformation. Each snake has its own life tangled among the others. She has a look on her face from which she cannot turn away. Fear, disgust, fascination, repulsion all play at once across the stone that is her face. Medusa herself couldn't have captured herself so honestly. Medusa looking in the mirror at her own face, the only face her face doesn't turn into stone.

I wanted time to think about time; but I kept writing about irony and art.

In the basement, among the epigraphs on gravestones, I learned a new fact, if fact is the word for what I found. They buried lightning in the ground, the ancient Romans; wherever it struck they found the hole and buried a stone inside it, or sacrificed a sheep and poured in the blood to appease the god's wrath, and, setting a fence around the ground so travelers might not trespass unwittingly across it, wrote a marker for the grave: "Lightning hurled down at night by the god is here buried."

Was there anywhere never struck by lightning.

The memorials were called *bidentales*, a name variously understood as referring to the two prominent teeth of the two-year-old sheep sacrificed, to the forked spear carried by Hades, to the spear Achilles used in the Trojan War which by some accounts was two-pronged; but I prefer to think it refers to the strange rhyme between the shape of lightning forking down from the sky and the serpent's split tongue.

I kept thinking how the gods' pleasure is to be given displeasure by those beings whose lives they can end. Our mourning, their music. Perpetual like a music box that never needs winding. The heart's double beat. These opposing sides of the same fact.

But the poppies weren't bright as wounds among the broken stones. They understood something about ruin. But like a deaf man at a symphony, I could only watch the music they played as the breeze blew their heads about, and the stones persisted.

Then I had a dream where a snake had in its mouth its own tail and rolled across the fields. It marked a line as straight as the line of any life that begins at one point and ends in another. But in the dream I saw a baby riding inside the circle of the snake and inside the circle time didn't work right. The baby became a man and the man became a corpse and the corpse became a baby and so it rolled on among the poppies and the grass. But my dream came waking. Washing my face before bed. My eye in my eye in the mirror.

83.

I wanted to think about memory, but the guidebook was out of date.

Does the brick in a crumbling arch of the Palatino have a different life than the marble of Bernini's *Apollo et Daphne*, the roots of the bush with the flowering white petals clinging to the crack that sustains it, and the foot of the girl running from the god becoming a root, and the wood gathering beneath the god's hand where he grasps her waist, and her hands flung up in her despair sprouting laurel leaves whose delicate tangle will turn light into life—light, the very being of the god who chases her. I guess there's no escape. Even transformed, the girl depends upon the god whose love she fears; but the bush gives a little shade to the brick, and its root drinks the rain that widens the crack.

In the same museum, a painting of Actaeon who comes upon bathing Diana and her naked nymphs, and though he doesn't yet realize what he has seen, the antlers like leafless trees spiral up from his head and his hounds bay at his legs as if already they smell the hindquarters of the stag and the next hunt has already begun, though the life they chase doesn't know it.

I had thought memory was what let me imagine Augustus walking through these ruins in such a way that, at his each step, the grandeur restored itself. But stepping outside the museum into the large park, the sunlight gilding the hair of my daughters into the lit-up, dust-covered gold of late autumn leaves, I felt memory was something different from remembering, something outside the experience of a life it is so deeply embedded within, as the leaf sleeps inside the lobe of the hand, and the principle of the branch waits patient in the wrist, and the lightning strike of a single thought in the mind turns the sand there into a fulgurite that emerges much later as an antler or a tree. And so I learned memory had little to do with the past—it was tuned wholly to the future, the root of what is to be, but whose flower hasn't yet come.

So minded I went to visit the small room in which John Keats died. Some golden bough in my mind.

I didn't know what I didn't know.

The room small as a roomy crypt. Out the window the fountain where a sun-symbol spits out a stream of water endlessly filling the boat that's always sinking. Though Keats complained about being cold the fireplace was but a few feet from the bed where he lay dying—in the center stone of the mantel, a lion opening its jaws. Or is it a loud-barking dog. On the ceiling painted flowers filled each their small square, just as if his wish had already been granted, and daisies were growing above him, if only daisies bloomed in reverse, their roots reaching for the sun, and the flowers opening up inside the ground.

The mind that craves reversal finds itself subject to curious laws.

Like a shadow discovering it has a body.

My children each made sketches of the quick profile B. R. Haydon drew of Keats in a letter beneath sealed glass, a way to pass the time while I passed through the rooms of the house working against time, gazing at the drawing Keats made of a Grecian urn in the British Museum, staring at the death mask made by Antonio Canova's assistant, knowing—though I could not hear it—that at the bottom of the Spanish Steps a sun kept spitting water out of its mouth, and that the bed Keats had died in, the sheets which he wrapped about himself, the shelves that held his few books, all were burned down to nothing, and the library in the house now, assembled many years after Keats died, is only somehow a resemblance. The children came to find me. They'd finished their drawings, which meant my time was up.

Iris:

Hana:

Memory asks a question about likeness no one likes to ask.

✦

The next morning we walked to the Cimitero Acattolico where Keats is buried. The kids chased the cats between the stones. When we found his grave the kids took pictures of it. So did I. I read again and again the epitaph Keats chose for himself:

> Here lies One
> Whose Name was writ in Water.

I kept repeating it to myself in my head, a kind of chant, until I heard it as *whose name was written water*, and only then, some error finally made I didn't know I had to make, I felt it, what I so long wanted to feel, the man inside his death living there still, and death no opposite to life, not its end nor its dismissal, but—as in the Pyramid of Cestius rising behind the poet's gravestone where to this day none have ever found the treasure and remains of the man whose mausoleum it is—a hidden chamber, secret even to the builder of the life itself, into which one finally climbs. I felt that secret chamber. I felt it in myself. And that's what broke the husk of my pride—thinking so childishly that my death, like my life, was my own. It wasn't. The hidden crypt is a common room where the songs of mourning become each day again the morning.

MHΔHN ATAN

I wanted to be one of the ancient pilgrims who carried in their heart a question; I took my family to Delphi.

I didn't know what my question was—a question without a question, or a question about how to ask one.

Thirty-five hundred years ago a woman stood next to a large boulder so grotesque in its convolutions that it looks like a brain erupting out of itself, breathed in, and spoke in place of the god. She spoke clearly, the Sybil, contrary to the rumors, foretelling the travails of Helen. Ever since, those who want to know the future, be it king or shepherd, have traveled to Delphi to beg a glimpse through the invisible screen of purest sky always before our eyes. Maybe time is just an atmosphere taken in with every breath, but in places the air alters, and each breath ceases to be a mortal measure. Maybe Delphi is such a place; or it is, anyway, for those who have learned to breathe.

The Archaeological Museum below the ruins is filled with votive offerings from Mycenaean times through Roman, filled with the figures that adorned the temples:

> An elongated human figure throwing a spear but the spear
> is missing, already thrown or long ago lost. One missing the
> hand that did the throwing. For eyes they have holes. These
> men and women fit in the palm of your hand.

> A pig. A horse with the leg of its missing shepherd still
> standing beside it. Small as children's toys.

> Miniature spears and axes.

A double-headed Siren, two faces that shared one pair of ears so that one face could sing and the other listen at the same time, which may be the only way to survive the fatal song.

A Greek soldier with the Gorgon on his shield about to strike his enemy, though the sword in his hand has disappeared, as has his Trojan counterpart.

Europa leaning forward on the bull as it steps into the ocean, but her head gone missing, and her arms and feet; she just presses her breasts against the muscled back of the transformed god whose front legs and head have run far ahead of what remains plunging into the silent sea.

A caryatid wearing a crown of holes around her hair. A large stone on her head and her eyes are closed from the weight of the whole roof that centuries ago collapsed.

Thetis begging Zeus for her son's life, but Thetis and Zeus are seen only in the words describing what there is to see that can't be seen. The supplicant goddesses remain, the one behind with her hand on the shoulder of the one before, as if brushing aside the other's hair to whisper in her ear a word.

Twin men missing their penises, hair in thick braids, lidless eyes, smiling.

Life-size figures made of ivory whose eyes shone so bright they once were made of gold.

As I walked to the ruins I kept in mind what I saw in the last room of the museum—a dedication from Aemilius Paullus thanking Apollo for his victory over King Perseus and the Macedonians. I'd read Plutarch's account of the man's life, but all the details had gone missing. I seem to recall his men didn't like him. He kept too much to himself. Maybe there was a mutiny he quelled by giving gifts or by decimation. Instead of direct fighting he kept moving his army from camp to camp, trusting time would wear away the enemy. But I'm not sure. Time has worn away the impression.

As I walked to the ruins I kept thinking about how many of the statues had broken genitals, how time kept breaking the delicate stone, some primer's lesson to the lifelong study of time; then the absurd image came all by itself into my head, that there was a treasury the gods kept in which the vaults were filled not with coins but the broken penises of the statues of heroes and shepherds, gods and generals; the noses and nipples of mothers; the hands of warriors, of lovers.

As I entered the ruins I kept seeing the smiles on the faces of statues— not a smile of greeting, but the smile of one who remembers suddenly a word long forgotten that describes the moment at hand, or the smile of one who finds inside the vault of the mind the answer she was going to ask of another, a smile that is involuntary and inward.

A hose made the sound of the water burbling out of a spring, but the spring itself ran dry.

Somewhere the stone Zeus fed Cronus and Cronus vomited up rests on this mountain.

Somewhere the grave of Achilles's son.

The omphalos that marks Delphi the center of the world sits below Apollo's temple, an undecorated conical stone, replica of the one Pausanias describes as kept beneath a net made of fine wool.

The treasuries knocked down.

Large stones that might have been the pedestals of votive offerings or might have been the blocks of the crumbled buildings everywhere on the ground.

I don't know the names of any of the flowers, though some look familiar; nor the birds that flit to the stone benches of the theater and sing their warbling song; the bees I call *bees*.

Of Apollo's temple itself, place of prophecy where one Pythia slept so as to receive dreams, and another wore the prophetic laurel, and a third breathed in and spoke, around whom the poets gathered and listened and turned the awful precision of Pythian speech into riddles so that the one who came seeking answer left with obscurity instead of light—as if poetry's purpose weren't to bring clarity, but to protect us from it—only a few full columns stood, and a few more partial, of the many that surrounded the building whose size could be seen by what remained of the foundation. The clear sky today was its roof.

"Know thyself" written nowhere in the air.

Nor were the other sage axioms I learned etched into the stone anywhere to be read save in the tri-fold brochure I carried with me.

Μήδεν ἄγαν, "Nothing in excess."

Leaving the ruins, walking down the holy mountain, I realized I hadn't asked my question, and it would remain unanswered for me, maybe for my whole life, this question I don't know nor know how to ask. The bees flew from flower to flower—from sage to poppy to nameless blooms—gathering the pollen and nectar. Thyme growing in the cracks between stones. Wild carrot. Tansy or yarrow. Some bird sang high in a tree. What is the question the world asks through the minor demonstration that is me? The gods and goddesses smile their smiles, this small gesture of eternity. They have no holes in their eyes through which light enters so they can see. Lovers have no hands, no genitals. Warriors no weapons, no arms. The holy places have hints instead of walls. Sulfur wings in the purple thistle. I never knew how much excess there was, how little was needed to make felt what might be known— the bend of a woman's hip beneath the stone folds of her robe.

Made complete by what goes missing.

Made complete by what goes missing.

By the stone path outside the ruins an old cat, recently in a fight, sat in the weeds and flowers, his ear torn, his nose bleeding, a wound on his neck bright against his white fur.

Soon the wars would begin again.

So much has to go missing to leave what can be known.

The other inscription on Apollo's temple no one has understood, though many have guessed. It is but a single letter.

E

85.

In the ruins the kids look for bugs and cats. Ruinous with their own eternity, they ignore the broken temples, the empty treasuries. When they find a large black beetle they put a stone in its path so it turns around. They find a piece of straw and place it in front of the beetle that, once it crawls on the stem, they pick up and watch his careful balance until they tire of the trick and put the creature down in another place entirely. They laugh and laugh until the small one falls on a stone worn smooth by centuries of feet stepping on it. She said it felt like someone took away the ground. She thought her sister had played some kind of trick.

✦

In the souvenir shops, among the replica coins and the pendants with Athena's owl staring out, I keep noticing chess sets in which the playing pieces are the gods. Zeus and Hera are king and queen, Apollo and Athena the bishops, and so on, until the pawns are those minor gods with small domains: satyrs, centaurs, nymphs. It must be an enthusiasm as old as worship—to play a game with the forces who make of your life a game.

86.

I wanted to think about the unthinkable; I took my family to the underworld.

We gave to the ticket man our coins, and he led us to the man behind the gate who gave us orange life preservers. No one spoke our language save a few words. Left. Right. Watch your head. Bravo. That man guided us through the mouth of the cave to the man who steered the boat through the water, for the cave was filled with water, and no one could walk alone.

The guidebook had said that somewhere in the extensive cave system cut out by the underground river coursing through it remained one of the old entrances to Hades. But a guide will say anything to a tourist of light and gloom to get him to buy a ticket.

We each brought with us the requisite bag of blood called a body anyway, just in case from out of the dark reaches any shade approached, victims of the highway corkscrewing through the mountains, refugees drowned in the Aegean Sea, warriors whose teeth bit dust in bitter marriage, or the blind prophet of old, Tiresias, who alone among the dead continues to see.

I had a question, but I didn't know what it was. Something about the way life keeps disappearing. I mean, a question about how the question keeps going away before I learn how to ask it.

"Watch your head," the boatman said, when the tunnel narrowed to its thin vein. "Bravo, *capitan*," he said to my children in the front, who sat staring ahead in the front of the boat, completely silent.

Electric lights at intervals lit up the underworld's formations.

Stalactites milky-white hung down, some large as a giant snake's tooth, others in the open chambers delicate as tears made of glass. Though the purpose was to look up, I kept looking down by mistake. The river in its perfect stillness mirrored the vaulted caves and the intricate drippings in exact detail so that in the instant of a glance it seemed what world lurked under the water reached up in unnerving replica to the one above it, the same world but in reverse, so that, if the mind relaxed too much, a terrible vertigo entered it in which the difference between world and reflection lost its boundary, and one felt oneself floating on the thinnest surface, a little plane of isinglass, much too fragile to keep apart these worlds insistent on colliding and becoming one—just as the jaws of a serpent must close on what it devours—the waking world and the world that reflects it, object and idea, substance and shade, and to look too far over the edge of the boat not only sparked a reprimand from the boatman in a language I couldn't speak, but showed me the only shade that came to visit me was my own.

The boatman let us off and we followed a path for three hundred meters back to the surface. Kristy kept saying how frightening it would be to get lost in the labyrinth. I agreed. Iris kept running ahead and returning. Hana walked slowly behind.

Who isn't lost in the labyrinth.

Then you walk out.

Then the labyrinth gets lost in you.

When we finally came to the exit of the cave, the bright light startled so it made one dizzy. Then I noticed something I had not ever noticed before. Just as a sudden flash in the dark causes in the eye a continuing glow long after the light has gone, so too does coming from the dark into the light, where for a long time I kept seeing in my eye an inexplicable shadow floating before me, the undergloom's persistent veil.

87.

I wanted to stop thinking; I took my family to Mycenae.

The walls made of such large stones it is said the Cyclops built them, the Cyclopean walls, so that it sounded as if one stone among them all was not a stone, but an eye.

The gate through which the tourists walk bears above it a triangular stone with two lions standing their forelegs on the pedestal of a column, stretching out the length of their bodies to reach the top, but their heads—made of a more precious material than stone—are gone.

Thought kills me that I am not thought.

I kept touching the walls trying to imagine the facts I learned that I overheard.

The burial pits of Agamemnon and Clytemnestra first buried outside the city wall in a circular chamber made of narrow slabs of stone "symbolizing the thin line between life and death" said the tour guide to the group of which we had no part. Then the Cyclops came back and built another wall around the dead who are not safe even in death from the harm others might want to do them.

I didn't any longer want to want to see what had been there as if it still rose before my eyes.

No mind trick to step back across time when no electric wires cut the ruin across.

Just the life of the wall, the life of the stones that made it stand, the brutal square crude strength chiseled, the bare fact of being a thing made into the made-thing.

All the statues of the gods, Iris noticed, had eyes without irises.

I kept touching the stones. Hana kept sitting down in any shade she could find. Iris kept pointing out the ants carrying burdens larger than themselves—the ant carrying the carcass of a beetle, the ant carrying like a sail the wing of a moth.

The heroic age goes on and on, on ever smaller scales.

I find myself in the middle of my life.

The bees and beetles fly through the air as if we were just stones and somehow not a life living there. Or just the life that is a stone, that being stung, doesn't need to care. Stones that move sometimes. That have a little blood jewel to mine.

I wanted to find, like the figures found in the temple site, the right gesture to make for the rest of time.

Like my hands both held up to shade my eyes from the sun. Like my hands like leaves to drink the sun but the leaves are clay lightly fired in heat like the sun's.

Like my eyes blind to any light but the all-white of marble—

an ant carries an ant-sized stone—

onto each the sun pours down its golden oil.

88.

A century of meditation. It ends among the ruins centuries built.

Rome. Delphi. Mycenae.

The wreck lies around me and I cannot make it cohere.

A dream in the ruins.

The broken column that is what remains of the temple.

I find the stone the builders cast away.

It's smaller than I thought, rounder. A gray that is also a little brown.
A turquoise phosphorescence where it narrows; and where it narrows
a dark black crescent or ring.

But when I go to pick it up, the cast-out stone that will become the
cornerstone, I startle the rock from its sleep, and it flies away, cooing
as it goes—

the dove disappearing behind a cloud.

(★)

Sources

2.
Plato, *Theaetetus* (Loeb Classical Library 123, trans. Harold North Fowler).
Book of Psalms.

Riddles, Labyrinths
Greek Epic Fragments, Thebaid (Loeb Classical Library 497, trans. Martin L. West).
Greek Epic Fragments: From the Seventh to the Fifth Centuries BC (Loeb Classical
    Library 497, trans. Martin L. West).
Homeric Hymns. Homeric Apocrypha. Lives of Homer. (Loeb Classical Library
    496, trans. Martin L. West).
Emily Dickinson, *Poems.*

5.
Ezra Pound, "Canto CXX."
T. S. Eliot, *The Wasteland.*
Henry David Thoreau, *Walden.*
Emerson, *Journals* (archive in Houghton Library).

6.
Wallace Stevens, *Notes Toward a Supreme Fiction* (typescript, Houghton Library).

7.
Jean Daive, *Under the Dome: Walks with Paul Celan.*

Heliopause
George Oppen, *Selected Prose, Daybooks, and Papers.*
T. S. Eliot, "Love Song of J. Alfred Prufrock."
Simone Weil, *Gravity & Grace.*
Ludwig Wittgenstein, *Tractatus Logico-Philosophicus* (trans. Charles Kay Ogden).

10.
Paul Celan, "Todesfuge."
Safed Spirituality: Rules of Mystical Piety, the Beginning of Wisdom (trans.
    Lawrence Fine).
The Zohar: The Book of Enlightenment (trans. Arthur Green and Daniel
    Chanan Matt).

Memory & Poppy
Marcel Proust, *Swann's Way* (trans. C. K. Scott Moncrieff, revised by Terence
    Kilmartin).

Homer, *The Odyssey* (Loeb Classical Library 104 and 105, trans. A. T. Murray, revised by George E. Dimock).
Alfred Lord Tennyson, "The Lotos-eaters."
Daniel Heller-Roazen, *Echolalias*.

Some Burial Rites
John Keats, *Selected Letters*.
John Keats, *Poems*.
Daisy Hay, *Young Romantics*.

Sibboleth
Jacques Derrida, "Shibboleth: For Paul Celan."
Paul Celan, *Selected Poems* (trans. Michael Hamburger).
Giorgio Agamben, *Remnants of Auschwitz: The Witness and the Archive*.

Gorgon Poetics
Paul Celan, *The Meridian* (trans. Pierre Joris).

ΟΥ ΤΙΣ
Bede, Caedmon's *Hymn*.
Dio Cassius, *Roman History* (Loeb Classical Library 32, trans. Earnest Cary).
Emily Dickinson, *Poems*.

18.
Plato, *Euthyphro. Apology. Crito. Phaedo.* (Loeb Classical Library 36, trans. Chris Emlyn-Jones).

Omens
Saint Augustine, *Confessions* (trans. R. S. Pine-Coffin).
Dio Cassius, *Roman History*, vols. 1–9 (Loeb Classical Library, trans. Earnest Cary).
Plutarch, *Lives*, vol. 3, "Fabius Maximus" (Loeb Classical Library 65, trans. Bernadotte Perrin).

Grave Work
Robert Pogue Harrison, *The Dominion of the Dead*.
Henry David Thoreau, *Walden*.
Paul Celan, *Selected Poems* (trans. Michael Hamburger).
Sophocles, *Antigone. The Women of Trachis. Philoctetes. Oedipus at Colonus.* (Loeb Classical Library 21, trans. Hugh Lloyd-Jones).
Virgil, *Aeneid* (trans. Robert Fagles).
Daniel Heller-Roazen, *Echolalias*.

23.
William Wordsworth, "Preface to the *Lyrical Ballads*."

24.
Plutarch, *Lives*, vol. 1, "Numa" (Loeb Classical Library 46, trans. Bernadotte Perrin).

26.
Plutarch, *Lives*, vol. 1, "Solon" (Loeb Classical Library 46, trans. Bernadotte Perrin).
Robert Pogue Harrison, *The Dominion of the Dead*.
Ralph Waldo Emerson, "Experience."
Robert D. Richardson, *Emerson: The Mind on Fire* (University of California Press, 1995).

Digestion
Robert Pogue Harrison, *The Dominion of the Dead*.
John Keats, *Poems*.

Monadisms
Gottfried Leibniz, *Monadology* (trans. Nicholas Rescher).
Jorge Luis Borges, "Pierre Menard, Author of the *Quixote*" (trans. Anthony Kerrigan).
Bede, Caedmon's *Hymn*.
Gertrude Stein, *Portraits and Repetition*.
7 Greeks, "Heraclitus" (trans. Guy Davenport).

Pythagorean Silence
Pythagoras, *Geometry*.
Diogenes Laertius, *Lives of the Eminent Philosophers*, vol. 2 (Loeb Classical Library 185, trans. R. D. Hicks).

Heraclitean Thirst
Heraclitus, *On the Universe*.
Diogenes Laertius, *Lives of the Eminent Philosophers*, vol. 2 (Loeb Classical Library 185, trans. R. D. Hicks).
Marcus Aurelius, *Meditations* (Loeb Classical Library 58, trans. C. R. Haines).

33.
Emerson, "The Poet."

Atlantis
Ludwig Wittgenstein, *Philosophic Investigation* (trans. G. E. M. Anscombe).
Plato, *Timaeus. Critias. Cleitophon. Menexenus. Epistles.* (Loeb Classical Library 234, trans. R. G. Bury).
Plutarch, *Lives*, vol. 1, "Solon" (Loeb Classical Library 46, trans. Bernadotte Perrin).
Strabo, *Geography*, vol. 1 (Loeb Classical Library 49, trans. Horace Leonard Jones).
Ignatius Donnelly, *Atlantis: The Antediluvian World*.

36.
Plato, *Republic*, vols. 1, 2 (Loeb Classical Library 237 and 276, trans. Chris Emlyn-Jones and William Preddy).
Euripides, *Suppliant Women. Electra. Heracles.* (Loeb Classical Library 9, trans. David Kovacs).

Circles
Emily Dickinson, *Selected Letters.*
Ralph Waldo Emerson, "Circles."
Sir Thomas Browne, *Urne-Buriall.*
The Greek Anthology, vol. 1 (Loeb Classical Library 67, trans. W. R. Paton, revised by Michael A. Tueller).
7 Greeks, "Heraclitus" (trans. Guy Davenport).
John Keats, *Poems.*

Waves
The Greek Anthology, vol. 2 (Loeb Classical Library 68, trans. W. R. Paton, revised by Michael A. Tueller).
Homeric Hymns. Homeric Apocrypha. Lives of Homer. (Loeb Classical Library 496, trans. Martin L. West).
Shakespeare, *Antony and Cleopatra.*
Catullus, *Poems* (trans. Peter Green).
Ralph Waldo Emerson, "Experience."
"Elements," *Radiolab* (podcast).
Emily Dickinson, *Poems.*
Sir Thomas Browne, *Religio Medici.*

40.
The Greek Anthology, vol. 2 (Loeb Classical Library 68, trans. W. R. Paton, revised by Michael A. Tueller).

, Even
John Keats, *Poems.*
Dante, *The Inferno* (trans. Henry Wadsworth Longfellow).
John Keats, *Letters.*
Marcel Duchamp, *The Writings of Marcel Duchamp* (trans. Michel Sanouillet).

43.
William Wordsworth, *The Prelude.*
Sir Thomas Browne, *Religio Medici.*
Herman Melville, *Moby-Dick.*

44.
Walt Whitman, *Leaves of Grass.*
John Berryman, *Dream Songs.*
Emily Dickinson, *Poems.*

45.
John Berryman, *Dream Songs.*

46.
William Wordsworth, *The Prelude* (lines not italicized from Book First).

47.
William Wordsworth, *Lyrical Ballads* (archive in Beinecke Library).

Signature
Henry David Thoreau, *Walden.*
Daniel Heller-Roazen, *Echolalias.*
Henry David Thoreau, *Journals.*
Simone Weil, *Gravity & Grace.*
Giorgio Agamben, *The Signature of All Things.*

49.
Henry David Thoreau, archival material, Beinecke Library, Yale University.

50.
Ezra Pound, archival material, Beinecke Library, Yale University.

51.
Sir Thomas Browne, *Religio Medici.*

Ψυχή
Jan Bremmer, *The Early Greek Concept of the Soul.*

Sirens
Homer, *The Odyssey* (Loeb Classical Library 104 and 105, trans. A. T. Murray, revised by George E. Dimock).
Maurice Blanchot, *The Book to Come* (trans. Charlotte Mandell).
Strabo, *Geography*, vol. 1 (Loeb Classical Library 49, trans. Horace Leonard Jones).

The Star Knot is the Chief Thing
Gerard Manley Hopkins, *Journals.*

58.
Sir Thomas Browne, *Religio Medici*.
Ralph Waldo Emerson, "Fate."
Gerard Manley Hopkins, *Journals*.

59.
Maurice Blanchot, *The Book to Come* (trans. Charlotte Mandell).

Whitenesses
Ralph Waldo Emerson, "Fate."
Marcus Aurelius, *Meditations* (Loeb Classical Library 58, trans. C. R. Haines).
Robert Frost, "The Oven Bird."
Herman Melville, *Moby-Dick*.

Confessions
Ludwig Wittgenstein, *Philosophic Investigation* (trans. G. E. M. Anscombe).
Martin Heidegger, *Basic Writings*, "Letter on Humanism" (ed. David Ferell Krell).

"Come and let us study the letters of the seers"
Safed Spirituality: Rules of Mystical Piety, the Beginning of Wisdom (trans. Lawrence Fine).
Midrash Rabbah, vol. 1, "Genesis" (trans. Rabbi Dr. H. Freedman and Maurice Simon).
The Zohar: The Book of Enlightenment (trans. Arthur Green and Daniel Chanan Matt).

Of Bees in Winter
Pindar, *Olympian Odes. Pythian Odes.* (Loeb Classical Library 56, trans. William H. Race).
John Keats, *Poems*.
The Greek Anthology, vol. 1 (Loeb Classical Library 67, trans. W. R. Paton, revised by Michael A. Tueller).
Greek: Learn to Read Ancient Greek, vols. 1, 2 (Yale University Press).

66.
Pindar, *Olympian Odes. Pythian Odes.* (Loeb Classical Library 56, trans. William H. Race).

The Tune of Many Heads
Homeric Hymns. Homeric Apocrypha. Lives of Homer. (Loeb Classical Library 496, trans. Martin L. West).
Pindar, *Olympian Odes. Pythian Odes.* (Loeb Classical Library 56, trans. William H. Race).

Homer, *The Iliad* (trans. Peter Green).
Midrash Rabbah, vol. 1, "Genesis" (trans. Rabbi Dr. H. Freedman and Maurice
    Simon).

Meditation on a Hut
Henry David Thoreau, *Walden*.
Martin Heidegger, *Basic Writings*, "Letter on Humanism" (ed. David Ferell Krell).

70.
Hesiod, *Theogony. Works and Days. Testimonia.* (Loeb Classical Library 57,
    trans. Glenn W. Most).

Shields
Hesiod, *Theogony. Works and Days. Testimonia.* (Loeb Classical Library 57,
    trans. Glenn W. Most).
Hippocrates, *Nature of Man. Regimen in Health. Humours. Aphorisms.
    Regimen 1–3. Dreams. Heracleitus: On the Universe.* vol. 4 (Loeb Classical
    Library 150, trans. W. H. S. Jones).
Ralph Waldo Emerson, "Circles."

72.
Homer, *The Iliad* (trans. Peter Green).

Titles of Forgotten Books
Diogenes Laertius, *Lives of the Eminent Philosophers*, vols. 1, 2 (Loeb Classical
    Library 184 and 185, trans. R. D. Hicks).

As the Wakeful Bird Sings Darkling
Homeric Hymns. Homeric Apocrypha. Lives of Homer. (Loeb Classical Library
    496, trans. Martin L. West).
John Milton, *Paradise Lost.*
John Milton, *Letter to Leonard Philarus.*
Sir Thomas Browne, *Religio Medici.*

Genitals / Asterisks
Walt Whitman, *Leaves of Grass.*
Plato, *Lysis. Symposium. Gorgias.* (Loeb Classical Library 166, trans. W. R. M.
    Lamb).
John Keats, *Letters.*

Epithalamium in the Archive
Marcel Duchamp, *The Writings of Marcel Duchamp* (trans. Michel Sanouillet).
Emily Dickinson, *Letters.*

Emily Dickinson, the Emily Dickinson Collection, Houghton Library, Harvard
University.
Emily Dickinson, *Poems.*

78.
John Keats, the Harvard Keats Collection, Houghton Library, Harvard
University.
Matthew Arnold, "Critical Introduction."

79.
Ralph Waldo Emerson, "The Poet."

80.
Branka Arsić, *Bird Relics: Mourning and Vitalism in Thoreau.*

Grief Substitute
Euripides, *Trojan Women. Iphigenia among the Taurians. Ion.* (Loeb Classical
Library 10, trans. David Kovacs).
Gregory Nagy, *The Ancient Greek Hero in 24 Hours.*
Homer, *The Iliad* (trans. Peter Green).

Art Credits

47: Siren-Com, from Campana Collection, 1861. [CC BY-SA 3.0 (https://creativecommons.org/licenses/by-sa/3.0) or GFDL (http://www.gnu.org/copyleft/fdl.html)], via Wikimedia Commons.

90: © Succession Marcel Duchamp / ADAGP, Paris / Artists Rights Society (ARS), New York 2017.

110: Rebecca Beachy, "Notes on an Indigo Bunting: in advance of making a study-skin for the Chicago Academy of Sciences," June 17, 2014.

120: © Google Earth, 2009. Map Data: Google, Data SIO, NOAA, US Navy, NGA, GEBCO.

139 (LEFT): Abake, via Wikimedia Commons.

139 (RIGHT): © cc-by-sa, accessed via Wikimedia Commons. By diverse contributors; mashup by User: ZykureOpenStreetMap contributors [ODbL (http://opendatacommons.org/licenses/odbl/1.0/), CC BY-SA 2.0 (https://creativecommons.org/licenses/by-sa/2.0) or CC BY-SA 2.0 (https://creativecommons.org/licenses/by-sa/2.0)], via Wikimedia Commons.

146: Image copyright © The Metropolitan Museum of Art. Image source: Art Resource, NY. © Man Ray Trust / Artist Rights Society (ARS), NY / ADAGP, Paris 2017.

147 & 149: © Succession Marcel Duchamp / ADAGP, Paris / Artists Rights Society (ARS), New York 2017.

166 & 169: William Wordsworth Collection. General Collection, Beinecke Rare Book and Manuscript Library. Photos 2017 by Dan Beachy-Quick.

180: Henry David Thoreau Collection. Yale Collection of American Literature, Beinecke Rare Book and Manuscript Library. Photo 2017 by Dan Beachy-Quick.

189: Stained glass window, Sterling Library, Yale University. Photo 2017 by Dan Beachy-Quick.

198: Receipt from Poudre River Public Library. November 14, 2012. Photo 2015 by Dan Beachy-Quick.

236 & 237: Ann Harvieux. August 11, 2017. Ink drawings.

294: Joseph Severn, circa 1829–1860. Houghton Library, Harvard University. Photo 2016 by Dan Beachy-Quick.

310: Iris Beachy-Quick. April 20, 2017. Pencil drawing. Photo 2017 by Dan Beachy-Quick.

310: Hana Beachy-Quick. April 20, 2017. Pencil drawing. Photo 2017 by Dan Beachy-Quick.

Acknowledgments

Thank you to Andy Fitch and everyone at Essay Press for publishing the first eighteen sections as a chapbook; most of those essays, some in slightly different form, appear here. Thank you to Cassie Donish and everyone at *The Spectacle* for publishing 31 and 33. Thank you to Andrew Milward at *Mississippi Review* for publishing the sections "Grave Work" through 25. Thank you to Ben Landers at *Fogged Clarity* for publishing "Heraclitean Thirst" and "Circles." Thank you to Evan Lavender-Smith at *Puerto Del Sol* for publishing "Ψυχή" and 53. Thank you to Sven Birkerts at *AGNI* for publishing "Sibboleth." Thank you to Valerie Duff and *Salamander* for publishing "Some Animal Poems for Children to Learn and Sing." Thank you to Wayne Miller and *Copper Nickel* for publishing 47, 49, and 50. Thank you to Kristen Case at the *Concord Saunterer* for publishing "Signature" in slightly different form. Thank you to Bruce Bond and all at the *American Literary Review* for publishing "Theseus's Ship." Thank you to Amy Wright and Susan Wallace at *Zone 3* for publishing ", Even," which won the 2017 *Zone 3* Prize in Nonfiction. Thank you to Laird Hunt at *Denver Quarterly* for publishing "Waves" and "Sirens." Thank you to Meagan Day at *Full Stop* for publishing "Whitenesses." Thank you to Abigail Rosewood at *EuropeNow* for publishing 24, 25, 36, 44, and 45 under the title "Sunlight and Arrows: Five for Tacita." Thank you to Mark Yakich at *New Orleans Review* for publishing "Atlantis." Thank you to Daniel Pritchard and Chloe Garcia Roberts at *The Critical Flame* for publishing "Shields."

I am in the debt of many whose kindnesses and generosities made this book possible. To find a press that is also a home is a gift I never expected to be given—thank you to Daniel Slager, Patrick Thomas, and all at Milkweed Editions. Thank you to Nancy Kuhl and Richard Deming, and the Beinecke Library, conversations and immersions. Thank you to Christina Davis and the Woodberry Poetry Room at Harvard University, for a Creative Fellowship that allowed me time to wonder, wander, and ponder; thank you, too, to the librarians at the

Houghton Library, for the patience, humor, and insight. Thank you to Kristen Case and Alex Manglis for including me in necessary conversations, and whose invitation to participate on a Thoreau panel led, in many ways, to beginning this book. Thank you to Ian Oliver for guidance in ancient Greek. I owe long doses of gratitude to Sasha Steensen who read through and made suggestions for edits for the book's first half, and for whose friendship—poetically and otherwise—has made this work better than otherwise it would be. Thank you to Sally Keith and Srikanth Reddy—as always, constantly—for reading particular essays with such superlative care. Louann Reid and Ann Gill have been inspirations and necessary supports in helping me find time to work—their vision has made Colorado State University a home. Thank you to Lyn Hejinian, Forrest Gander, Peter Gizzi, and Donald Revell, for all the years. For clear-eyed advice when most needed, thank you to Laynie Browne. Conversation and collaboration with Del Harrow guides me always back to the possibility of making. And to Kristy, who enlivens every word with her honesty and care. Lastly, my heartfelt thanks to the Guggenheim Foundation for the support that allowed this project to find what fruition it has managed.

Some specific dedications:

"Confessions" is for Lyn Hejinian.
"Ψυχή" is for Forrest Gander.
"Circles" is for Sasha Steensen and her daughter Phoebe.
"Shields" is for Srikanth Reddy.
"Meditation on a Hut" is for Mai Wagner.
"Atlantis" is for Sergio Vucci.
"Some Animal Poems for Children to Learn and Sing" is for Sally Keith.
68 is for Timothy Webmoor.
"Signature" is for Kristen Case.
"Epithalamium in the Archive" is for Christina Davis.
51 is for Nancy Kuhl.

Hana Beachy-Quick

Dan Beachy-Quick is the author of six collections of poems; two previous works of nonfiction; and a novel, among other projects. He is a contributing editor for the journals *A Public Space* and *West Branch*. His work has won the Colorado Book Award and has been a finalist for the William Carlos Williams Prize and the PEN/USA Literary Award in Poetry. He is currently a Guggenheim Fellow and a Creative Fellow of the Woodberry Poetry Room at Harvard University. He lives in Fort Collins, Colorado.

milkweed
editions

Founded as a nonprofit organization in 1980, Milkweed Editions
is an independent publisher. Our mission is to identify, nurture
and publish transformative literature, and build an engaged
community around it.

milkweed.org

Interior design by Mary Austin Speaker
Typeset in Sabon
by Mary Austin Speaker and Ann Harvieux

Sabon is a Garamond revival typeface designed by Jan Tschichold in 1964 for use at the Linotype, Monotype, and Stempel foundries. Sabon takes its name from Jakob Sabon, a student of the great punchcutter Claude Garamond, who brought Garamond's matrices to Frankfurt after Garamond's death in 1561. Sabon was famously used to print the 1979 edition of the Episcopal *Book of Common Prayer*, as well as the *Washburn College Bible*, in which biblical text was hand-set in a process called thought-unit typography.